Becoming A Catholic Christian

A Symposium on Christian Initiation

Becoming A Catholic Christian

A Symposium on Christian Initiation
Organized and directed by Christiane Brusselmans

General Editor
William J. Reedy

Sadlier
A Division of
William H. Sadlier, Inc.

New York
Chicago
Los Angeles

Acknowledgments

The publisher wishes to thank Mr. Edouard Haasl for his sensitive translation of the French papers in this collection. He worked tirelessly and enthusiastically both at Senanque and St. Siffret, editing and re-editing final manuscript copy. Mrs. Bea Dinger is likewise to be thanked for her skillful editing of the French translations. Rev. Kevin Hart typed and retyped the papers and worked on several of the translations. Rev. Ronald Amandolare co-ordinated the symposium and institutes during 1977-78. His invaluable skill in organization was basic to carrying out these important meetings. Dr. Tad Guzie is to be thanked for his work as facilitator of the symposium discussions. Deacon William J. Reedy was co-ordinator with Fr. Amandolare of the symposium and institutes. But above all, the publisher and participants of the symposium thank Dr. Christiane Brusselmans who conceived the idea of a symposium on Christian initiation and the catechumenate. She worked carefully and determinedly for more than a year preparing the meeting at Senanque and the work that followed at St. Siffret.

Becoming A Catholic Christian
A Symposium on Christian Initiation
Edited by William J. Reedy

Third printing, 1981.

International Standard Book Number: 0-8215-9326-9
456789/9876543

Published by
William H. Sadlier, Inc.
11 Park Place
New York, New York 10007

Printed and bound in the United States of America

Table of Contents

Publisher's Foreword

When in August, 1977, we decided to fund the symposium on Christian Initiation and the catechumenate, we were well aware that we were taking a step into the future. We were aware also that in taking this step there was risk as well as exhilarating adventure and the opportunity to serve. The history of William H. Sadlier, Inc., which has been publishing religious education materials and preparing programs for various aspects of Catholic education for over a century, is characterized by taking steps into the future.

In the mid-nineteenth century, Mrs. Sadlier, who taught catechism in the basement of old St. Peter's Church in New York, the oldest parish church in the city, invested what money she had in providing textbooks that reflected the aspirations and positions of Catholic minorities in an American educational milieu hostile to Catholics. It was Sadlier who published the early Baltimore Catechism, as well as a catechism for Polish-speaking people, and followed the development of Catholic religious education and catechetics through the years—always with an eye to the future.

In the early '50s the firm produced the first graded religion series of any note. Later in that decade, despite much dispute and misunderstanding in the catechetical community, Sadlier introduced the kerygmatic approach to teaching religion into a graded series of CCD and parochial school texts, as well as into high school programs.

The firm has always been, and is now, conscious of its apostolic commitment. Ours is an apostolate of the Word, reaching into every area of religious education from pre-school through adult including family, parish, sacramental, Marriage Encounter, and Respect Life programs.

It was evident to us, then, that the next step into the future encompassed Christian Initiation. We have taken that step at Senanque. And if this means going into the valley of frustrations, tensions, pain and sorrow as we work to develop whatever materials the catechumenal community eventually considers best suited to implementing the catechumenate, we will remember the hillside that winds slowly up from the Abbey of Senanque, sometimes torturously, to the top of a mountain wreathed in brilliant clouds set an azure sky. We look forward to the mountaintop where visions become clear, and hopes and dreams are realized.

We shall take other steps, but this we see as the future of religious education, liturgical growth, parish renewal, and evangelization. We welcome this opportunity to serve the Church in the exciting years that lie ahead.

Ralph J. Fletcher, President

Preface

The central task of the Church today is to give birth—or rebirth—to faith. Faith is becoming less and less self-evident and more and more difficult, particularly for the younger generation. The contemporary life of faith must be lived without the support of an all-embracing Christian culture and in the face of new forms of increasing religious indifference, materialism, and secularism.

Recent studies have shown that more then 80,000,000 Americans are unchurched. Among this number, there are many who have never been touched by the Gospel, never invited to join a church. This may seem astonishing, but it is being verified again and again among those who are flocking to the new sects. Others received baptism as infants, but their Christian initiation stopped there. Others received the sacraments of initiation as children but abandoned all religious practice in adolescence or young adulthood. And, finally, there is an increasing number who consider themselves alienated Catholics or Christians, who reject any form of membership in a Christian Church.

We are therefore obliged to analyze with honesty and very carefully the situation of so many of our parishes that are trying to survive in non-Christian milieux. There are those who would say that all that can be done is to hold the line, to be a "maintenance" Church. But if it is to be more than that—and to be true to the command of Christ it must be more than that—the Church must rediscover the vitality and the missionary dynamism it knew in apostolic times and in other privileged periods of its history.

The Church is and has to become more and more missionary. Two things have convinced me of this: first, reflection on the lives of the people, young and old, that I meet, and, second, my own experience of Christian community with groups that are surfacing throughout the world today. It is partly because the Church has too often forgotten its missionary character that a profound de-Christianization is abroad today.

The mission Christ gave to the Church demands that our efforts be focused in three interdependent sectors:

1. Evangelization: Each Christian community must evangelize those who have yet to hear the Good News of Jesus Christ.
2. Initiation: Each Christian community must initiate into the Christian mysteries those who desire and request the life of Christ. This initiation must be carried out via the successive stages of the catechumenal journey, culminating in the sacraments of Christian initiation.
3. Maturation: Each Christian community must bring its members to maturity in the life of Christ. For the Christian is never finished with conversion nor sated with the Word of God and the sacraments, just as the Christian is never finished with sharing Christ with those around him or her.

These three sectors are applied successively for the catechumens who commit themselves to this journey. But with regard to the men, women, and youth of our times, the Church must attempt to accomplish its mission in these three sectors simultaneously.

Because many Christian communities have lost sight of the importance of evangelization and Christian initiation, they are today moribund. Where evangelization ceases, there are no longer any catechumens and there is no longer any Christian initiation. And when the Church no longer gives birth to new members, the vitality, the youth, the very health of the community decays and senescence sets in. Evangelization, initiation, maturation—these three missions must be the motivating force behind all the ministries of the Church as well as of individual Christians.

For a number of years, and particularly since 1974 when the *Rite of Christian Initiation of Adults* was made available to English-speaking communities of Christians, I have cherished the dream of bringing together my African and European friends, with whom I worked in the catechumenate, and my American friends, who realized the urgency of reestablishing the catechumenate in the American Church, especially in the inner city parishes and in the black and hispanic communities with which I have worked since 1962. Last year that dream was realized at the Cistercian Abbey of Senanque in Southern France. Isolated, but still at the crossroads of so many lines of Christian history, Senanque presented us with the ideal setting to celebrate and reflect on the rites of the Christian initiation of adults. The purpose of the symposium was pastoral and pragmatic: to come to a clear understanding of what the Christian initiation of adults is, of where the catechumenal journey will lead and how that journey may be experienced. At Senanque, it seemed to me, we could draw on our diverse backgrounds and share those continents of experience that are often so alien as to be incomprehensible. And, I believe this aim was reached.

The Senanque Papers here published are only beginnings, only preliminaries. They are far from exhaustive. But they do pose a clear challenge to the Church.

What we shared at Senanque convinced me that the prodigious evolution that the Church has undergone since Vatican II is rooted in and reflects the evolution of the apostolic Church. The modern evolution is marked by the rediscovery of the place of conversion and faith in the Christian life, the respect for maturation and discernment in all stages of the journey of conversion, the importance of liturgical celebration of every stage of this journey, the originality of the accompanying catechesis, and the new conception of ministry and particularly of sponsorship associated with it.

All this is firmly rooted in the initial years of Christianity and is becoming more and more a reality in the Church of today.

Christiane Brusselmans
Louvain, Belgium
The Feast of the Epiphany, 1979

Introduction

Thirty-two people gathered at the Cistercian Abbey of Senanque near Gordes, France, in the third week of June, 1978. They came from Africa, France, and the United States to share their experiences on the *Rite of Christian Initiation of Adults* (RCIA). Some had pastoral experience in developing programs for the catechumenate, and others brought extensive theological reflection on the vision contained in the RCIA. This book presents the papers that were presented at the symposium and some of the results—those that could be committed to paper.

One important part of the week that is impossible to publish are the liturgical experiences. The liturgies were especially designed for this group to celebrate the progressive stages of Christian initiation. They were extremely important to us all, forming us as they did into a true community. The week would have meant much less to us personally if we had omitted this time of celebration and prayer. What is more, the conclusions sketched in the Epilogue would have lacked the depth of expression that only Liturgy can provide.

Dreams become realities when there are people willing and capable of fulfilling them. Dr. Christiane Brusselmans, lecturer at the Catholic University of Louvain, first proposed the idea for a symposium on the RCIA in the spring of 1977. Her proposal was enthusiastically received by William Reedy, Director of Catechetics for William H. Sadlier, Inc. and a permanent deacon in the Archdiocese of New York; and Ronald Amandolare, Director of Religious Education and a pastor in the Diocese of Paterson, New Jersey. They helped in planning and coordinating the symposium.

The symposium was endorsed by the National Catholic Education Association, the National Conference of Diocesan Directors of Religious Education—CCD, the National Organization of Continuing Education of Roman Catholic Clergy, and the Federation of Diocesan Liturgical Commissions.

The participants in the Symposium were:

Rev. Ronald Amandolare, former Diocesan Director of Religious Education, Diocese of Paterson, New Jersey; Pastor, St. Paul's Parish, Clifton, New Jersey, Representative of NCEA as Senanque

Mrs. Eileen Anderson, Vice-President, Assistant Publisher, W. H. Sadlier, Inc.

Rev. Blaine G. Barr, Pastor, Parish Community of St. Joseph, New Hope, Minnesota

Rev. William A. Bauman, Pastor, St. Charles Borromeo Parish, Kansas City, Missouri

Rev. Albert J. Benavides, Pastor, St. Timothy Church, San Antonio, Texas

Rev. Henri Bourgeois, Professor of Theology in Lyons, Director of the Center of the Catechumenate in Lyons, Member of the National Service of the Catechumenate

Rev. Jean Bouteiller, Assistant Director of the National Center for Religious Education in Paris

Rev. Edward K. Braxton, Theological Consultant, Archdiocese of Washington, D.C.

Rev. Dennis Brodeur, St. Ambrose College, Davenport, Iowa

Dr. Christiane Brusselmans, Lecturer at the Catholic University of Leuven, Belgium

Rev. John Costanzo, Pastor, Sacred Heart Church, Alamosa, Colorado

Most Rev. John S. Cummins, Bishop of Oakland, California

Most Rev. Maurice J. Dingman, Bishop of Des Moines, Iowa

Rev. Michel Dujarier, Pastor, Sacred Heart Parish, Cotonou, Benin, Secretary of the West African Bishops' Commission for Catechesis and Liturgy

Rev. James B. Dunning, Executive Director, National Organization for Continuing Education of Roman Catholic Clergy

Rev. Virgil Elizondo, President, Mexican American Cultural Center, San Antonio, Texas

Mr. Ralph J. Fletcher, President, W. H. Sadlier, Inc.

Rev. W. Thomas Faucher, Federation of Diocesan Liturgical Commissions

Rev. Joseph Gelineau, S.J., Professor at the *Institut Catholique* in Paris

Rev. Charles W. Gusmer, Professor of Liturgy and Sacramental Theology, Darlington Seminary, Mahwah, New Jersey

Mr. Tad Guzie, Faculty of Education, University of Calgary, Calgary, Canada

Rev. Kevin Hart, Vice-Chancellor, Archdiocese of Washington, D.C.

Rev. Thomas P. Ivory, Archdiocesan Director of Religious Education, Newark, New Jersey

Rev. Roger G. O'Brien Director Archdiocesan Office of Worship, Seattle, Washington

Rev. James V. Parker, Pastor, St. Paul's Church, Silverton, Oregon, Professor of Theology, Mt. Angel Seminary, St. Benedict, Oregon

Sr. Therese Randolph, RSM, Ministerial Formation Supervisor, Pastoral Center, Department of Theology, Catholic University of America

Ms. Jane C. Redmont, former Chaplain, The University Catholic Center, Madison, Wisconsin

Deacon William J. Reedy, Director of Catechetics, W. H. Sadlier, Inc.

Rev. Robert P. Stamschror, former Representative for Religious Education, United States Catholic Conference, Executive Secretary, National Conference of Diocesan Directors of Religious Education—CCD; College of St. Teresa, Winona, Missouri

Rev. Daniel B. Stevick, Professor of Liturgies and Homiletics, Episcopal Divinity School, Cambridge, Massachusetts

Rev. Théophile Villaça, Director of the Catechetical Center, Ouidah, Benin

Sr. Teresita Weind, SND, Co-ordinator for Black Religious Education, Archdiocese of Chicago, Illinois.

Rev. William B. Skudlarek, O.S.B., St. John's University, Collegeville, Minnesota.

Note:
Abbé Abel Pasquier and Rev. Alfred McBride, Director of the Forum for Religious Education for NCEA, were unable to attend the symposium.

Reflections

More Than A Meeting ...

Moved by a dream, we gathered at the 12th century Cistercian Abbey of Senanque for a conference to explore anew the vision of a renewed appreciation of Christian Initiation.

But what happened was more than a meeting. It was a taste of the best of what the Church is and can be. Nestled in the rugged hills of Provence, the Abbey is a timeless jewel in an enchanted valley. The aromas and colors of lavender, poppies, and scotch broom accompanied a cascade of flowers on the hillsides. The melody of the nightingale seemed to have been composed especially for us.

Even more awesome than the magnificent setting was the Abbey itself. Senanque is one of the best preserved of all the medieval French monasteries. And it was ours! We lived, worked, and prayed in the simple elegance of the pillared cloister among Gothic arches echoing the bells of the tower and the voices of monks long since gone.

The meeting turned into an event.

There was an African priest who possessed a regal dignity and genuine simplicity. As he spoke of the marvelous vitality of the African Church, his eyes danced and his hands sang. There was a young woman who had recently made the pilgrimage from Jerusalem to Christianity and was afire with the enthusiasm of new discovery. There was a gentle and persistent priest who spoke out of the profound depth of American Hispanic Catholicism.

There was a black woman from Chicago, a quiet and graceful woman, who sang for us and galvanized our attention on the depths of the sense of religion in many black Americans, who sang of the pain and estrangement that cripple the efforts of the children of former slaves and slave owners to form a community of faith.

There was a remarkable French priest who spoke from a lifetime of scholarly and pastoral reflection. A liturgist and musician, he was a Chagall come to life. His being overflowed and captivated us for he was a happy and holy man.

There were lay people, priests, bishops, a deacon, nuns, pastors and scholars. We worked long hours and the linguistic barriers dissolved as we found ways to communicate.

Rain clouds hung over the valley as we prepared to depart. Some suggested that these concealing shadows symbolized that Senanque, for us, was a kind of Tabor experience, a revelation of the Lord, that could never be fully shared. They were right, of course. But there was nothing gnostic, nothing esoteric or private there. We all knew that the hidden wholeness that we perceived was nurtured by the same flowing waters of baptism that are pouring forth all over the world the new and challenging visions of what we are as Church, and what we can become.

Michel Dujarier

A Survey of the History
of the Catechumenate

*Michel Dujarier is the pastor of Sacred Heart
parish in Cotonou, and the General Secretary of
the Commission de Catéchèse et de Liturgie for
French-speaking West Africa. He was involved in
the establishment of the first catechumenal
center in Paris in 1957. He has his doctorate in
theology from the University of Paris. His thesis
was on sponsorship in the early Church.*

It would be dangerous to consider the catechumenate as a
reality independent of the Church. There is no catechumenate
without the Church, for Christian initiation exists only in, by,
and for the Church. Likewise, there is no Church without catechumenal initiation, for the Church is a mother perpetually giving birth.

And, while the catechumenate necessarily involves some organization, it is not to be conceived as a means at the service of
the Christian community. It is not an instrument. It is a living
aspect of the Christian community, an indispensable facet of
the life of the Church. This is why we have to understand the
content and the exigencies of the maternal function of the
Church.

To orient our study, let us first consider what the Church is:
it is a mother ceaselessly engaged in the process of giving birth
and educating (Part I). Then, from this perspective, we shall
consider how the Church has tried to accomplish this by catechumenal education (Part II).

THE MATERNAL FUNCTION OF THE CHURCH

To begin, let us note some fundamental affirmations of the Second Vatican Council. On two occasions, the Dogmatic Constitution of the Church clearly speaks of the initiation of new members into the Church in terms of conception, gestation and maternity:

> Catechumens who, moved by the Holy Spirit, seek with explicit intention to be incorporated into the Church are by that very intention joined to her. With love and solicitude Mother Church already embraces them as her own (§14).
>
> The Church ... becomes a Mother by accepting God's word in faith. For by her preaching and by baptism she brings forth to a new and immortal life children who are conceived of the Holy Spirit and born of God (§64).

Such language cannot be dismissed as merely figurative. The maternal function of the Church is neither a metaphor nor an image, it is a reality of life. And if it is proper to speak of the mission of the Church with regard to Christian initiation, it is because Christian initiation springs from the very essence of the Church, which is maternal.[1]

This is what the Council forcefully affirms, following the Fathers of the Church,[2] in texts too numerous to cite here. The Church is called "our Mother" (*Lumen Gentium*, §6); she exercises her maternity not only when she gives birth but also when she educates, concerning herself with the totality of the life situation (*Gravissimum Educationis*, Introduction and §3); and moreover, her "maternal solicitude" must extend "to all men believers or not" (*Christus Dominus*, §13).

Thus, it is within the perspective of the Church as Mother that we must situate all pastoral activity,[3] and particularly the catechumenal dimension. Let us try to formulate this perspective in three propositions.

1. *The Church is essentially a Mother. It exercises its maternal function in three dimensions of the mission entrusted to it by Christ.*

a. When Christ, "the way, the truth, and the life" (Jn. 14:6) promised his disciples to be "always with them," he clearly showed that the Church would also have the mission to be the way, the truth, and the life (cf. Mt. 28:18-20):

- ◼ "Go and make disciples of all nations." The Church is Mother when it transmits the Word of Truth.

- ◼ "Baptize them in the name of the Father, and of the Son, and of the Holy Spirit." The Church is Mother when it communicates life through the sacraments.

- ◼ "Teach them to hold fast to all I have taught you." The Church is Mother when it leads its children along the way to the Father.

It is in these three aspects together that the Church fulfills its maternal function. These aspects merge for the Word already bears life, the sacraments do not give life apart from the Word, and the Way is nothing other than existence always animated by the Word and life. Each aspect, nonetheless, manifests in its own way the triple dimension of the mission of the Church as Mother: "She has the responsibility of announcing the way of salvation to all men, on communicating the life of Christ to those who believe, and of assisting them with ceaseless concern so that they may grow into the fullness of that same life" (*Gravissimum Educationis*, §3).

b. In order to be faithful to her nature and mission of Mother, the Church must purposely implement the totality of these three dimensions, both for individuals and for collectivities. And it must do this consecutively and concurrently:

- ◼ consecutively, because every community, as does every person, passes consecutively through the three periods of the proclamation of the Word, of entry into life, and of growth;

- ◼ concurrently, since every community and every individual, even if they have arrived at the stage of growth, always need to be converted to the Word and to enter more fully into the life of God.

It is because one or the other of these three dimensions has been forgotten that from time to time many of our Churches have lapsed into passivity and formalism. And it is in rediscovering the necessity of permanently accepting these three dimensions of its maternal mission that our Church will renew its youth and its dynamism.

2. *The catechumenate is one of the ways in which the Church fulfills its maternal role.*

The catechumenate does not exist autonomously. It springs from the life of the Church and can only be understood in terms of the Church. A survey of the history of the first centuries of the Church will help us to understand this.

a. The motherhood of the Church precedes the catechumenate. In fact, during the first century and a half of her existence, from 30 to 180, there was no catechumenal institution as such.[4] Nevertheless, the Church was exercising its maternal function seriously and effectively. The task that faced the early Church was simply that of initiating new members, the particular method was not of primary concern. Whatever may be the situation of our Church communities, and independent of what we may know or think about the catechumenate, we have the duty of bringing to birth authentic Christians and of fostering their growth, and, therefore, also to reflect on the way we take up this mission.

b. The catechumenate is what living communities create. No decree instituted the catechumenate. Born out of the life of the community, it was lived as an imperative of the mission of the Church. Gradually, forms and structures developed that were appropriate to the various circumstances the Church found itself in.

From the year 180 and during all of the third century, a more definite catechumenal practice emerged for better formation of converts. Faced with the many heresies, with the growing numbers of converts, and with the risks of persecution, the Church as Mother reacted spontaneously and adopted converging practices in the four corners of the Mediterranean world.

In the fourth and fifth centuries, the ease of the Constantinian regime led to a certain devitalization of the years of catechumenal formation. But the Christian communities succeeded in recovering their balance by developing the Lenten and Paschal seasons to maintain, albeit under a different form, the demands of serious initiation.

So it is not a matter of advocating one or another catechumenal formula! What is necessary is that we examine the pastoral situation closely and that we endeavor to respond to it creatively.

c. The word "catechumenate" is incapable of expressing, by itself, all of the vitality of Christian initiation. We must be suspicious of words, however rich their content, that risk limiting our conception of the realities involved. Especially when it concerns a vital reality, a single word cannot encompass the whole.

Remember that the word "catechumenate," in the sense of an institution, did not exist in the early Church. The liturgical, canonical, and patristic texts on which our knowledge of the catechumenal practice is based do not speak of an organization but of persons. It was not a question of a "catechumenate," but of catechumens.

Nor were these persons themselves designated by a single term. In addition to the word "catechumen," there were synonyms more suited to the stages of their journey, for example, "auditors," "elect," and "those who ask together." Note that most of these terms express an action: "those who are listening," "those who are being enlightened," and so on. In the second century, particularly in the Judeo-Christian milieu, we find the term "proselyte of Christ," i.e., one who is going towards Christ. And this expression was in turn reflected in such variations as "the one who is coming," "the one who is coming to the Church," "the one who is coming to faith."

Finally, a number of extremely rich images expressed catechumenal pedagogy.

■ The *biblical image of the "march"* was developed by Origen in particular. He compared the catechumenate to the exodus of the Hebrew people who, between the Red Sea

23

(entrance into the catechumenate) and the River Jordan (baptism), advanced together as a group, received the Word of God, and strove to live it.[5]

- The *concrete image of "gestation"* was dear to the Fathers of the fourth century. They saw the catechumen as an infant who was conceived and who developed in the womb of the Church until it was ready to enter the world at baptism.[6]

- The *military image of "novitiate"* was taken from the name for the training period young military recruits had to go through before taking their oath and going into battle.

There are also three other images that could be applied to the catechumenal journey:

- The *agricultural image of "plant"*: The catechumen, beginning from a seed, gradually grows, until he finally bears fruit.

- The *image of "apostle"*: The apostles, after having encountered Christ, answered his call, lived with him for three years, and then experienced his death and resurrection and the life of the Spirit.

- The *image of "covenant"*: In the sense of the commentaries on the Canticle of Canticles, the lover searches for his beloved; it is the engagement period before the wedding.

Far from being restrained or abstract, this catechumenal vocabulary abounds in terms and images, each bringing out a new facet. Let us draw upon them to widen our horizons and revitalize what only a misunderstanding of the origins of the Church could lead us to take as a fixed and rigid system.

3. *The maternal role of the Church is broader than the catechumenate. In addition to being a* mater in partu *by its catechumenal action, the Church must also be a* mater post partum *and a* mater semper in partu.

a. In order to be a true mother, the Church must continue to educate those to whom it has given birth. There is a great temptation to relax the catechumenal effort after baptism. For adult converts, we can mistakenly believe that a long period of catechumenal preparation is sufficient. For children, we think too readily that the family or parish climate is enough to sustain their Christian life.

The Church was aware of this and set out to fulfill its mission of educating *post partum*. Thus, for adults, it developed a kind of mystagogical catechesis during the paschal season. For children, it gradually evolved a catechesis to give them what they were incapable of receiving before baptism. This effort, more or less successful at different periods of the Church's history, remains a fundamental need that we shall never completely satisfy. Catechesis will continue to be an integral part of the maternal mission of the Church.

b. Ever a young mother, the Church must always be giving birth through the actions of all its members. It is, perhaps, here that some of the most nagging questions occur. Is not our pastoral activity often reduced to maintenance rather than growth? What concern have we to bring the Word to the ever-increasing number of people who are strangers to it? How attentive are we in helping along the way those whom the Lord continues to call? What care do we take to bring to birth in the Life of the Spirit those who unknowingly seek it? We, collectively and individually, must ask ourselves these questions—and we must insist on them. For it is we who are the Mother-Church.

The Church is not just a mother *for* its children, it is and must always continue to be a mother *through* its children. Each Christian is both child and mother, for it is by means of its children that the Church becomes a *mater semper in partu*.

This mission of the Church must be carried out simultaneously in three sectors:

■ the sector of the first evangelization where the Good News is announced to non-Christians;

- the sector of the catechumenate where the converts are initiated into the Christian mystery and into the evangelical life;

- the sector of the eucharistic community where the members must ceaselessly grow and expand.

The Church will not be fully a mother unless it acts in all three of these sectors.

In the light of this fundamental principle, which was so strongly emphasized by the Fathers of the Church and affirmed by the Council, we now turn to the evolution of the catechumenate. We shall see how, despite human limitations, the Holy Spirit has never ceased to renew, under various forms, catechumenal pedagogy.

THE CHANGING FORTUNES OF THE CATECHUMENATE THROUGHOUT THE HISTORY OF THE CHURCH

It is not my intention here to trace in detail the history of the catechumenate. I shall only present some historical milestones that serve to shed some light on the pastoral situation that confronts us today in the last quarter of the twentieth century.

Schematically, we can distinguish four major periods in the evolution of catechumenal perspectives:

- The Beginnings: This period from the first to the fifth century encompasses both the high point and the decline of the catechumenate.[7]

- The Eclipse: For a thousand years, from the sixth to the fifteenth century, the catechumenate seems to have existed only as a relic of the past or as an ideal that was never realized.

- The Modern Missionary Period, from the sixteenth to the twentieth century, saw the progressive but halting rediscovery of catechumenal pedagogy.[9]

- The Conciliar Period, beginning in the 1950's, marks the renewal of catechumenal initiation.

A. The Beginnings

Without going into all the details of this rather well-known period, let us consider three principal periods that are rich in pastoral education.

1. *During the first two centuries*, the preparation of converts for the sacraments of initiation was very flexible. Atlhough there was no fixed organization of the catechumenate in the strict sense, we can discern three essential elements:

a. *Admission to the sacraments* was contingent on two specific requirements: faith in Christ and conversion of life. The leaders of the community confirmed whether or not the candidates did in fact meet these requirements, basing their decision on the testimony of witnesses and other guarantees.

b. *The formation of the converts was the task of the laity.* Far from being a sign of carelessness, the non-existence of a defined catechumenal structure shows that this task was assumed spontaneously by individual Christians—who took upon themselves the responsibility of announcing the Word to their relatives and friends, and of helping them to change their lives—and by the community, which frequently gathered to pray and meditate on the Word.

c. *Sacramental initiation took place over a period of time and in celebrations* in which the participation of the community was essential.

It is precisely the seriousness with which these three fundamental elements were taken that enabled the catechumenate to evolve into the form that we know from the *Apostolic Tradition* of Hippolytus.

2. *The third century* was certainly the period when catechumenal instruction was carried out with the greatest degree of seriousness and intensity. This was due in large measure to the important role played by the stages and by the quality of the formation.

a. The preparation for baptism was a journey marked by two thresholds, which one did not cross unthinkingly. The first threshold consisted of admission to the catechumenate. It presupposed a general though real conversion accompanied by a willingness to conform to the Christian way of life. And no one was admitted unless witnesses could be furnished. The second threshold was that of admission to baptism and this was crossed only after close examination of the candidate's behavior. It also relied on the testimony of witnesses.

b. The second factor responsible for the high quality of Christian initiation at this time was the importance placed on the periods of formation that prepared the candidate.

Before being admitted to the catechumenate, the candidate had already received a basic formation covering the central aspects of the faith and had already had some experience in living the Christian life. The catechumenate stage lasted for a rather long time (three years on the average) and included community catechesis practically every day. Finally, the baptism of the candidate was a liturgical celebration spread out over the course of a full week and experienced by the entire community in a particularly intense fashion.

Thus, throughout the third century, we find the same three fundamental elements of initiation that were present at the very beginning, only now they are reinforced in order to be lived more authentically during a longer and more communal journey.

3. The *fourth and fifth centuries* saw first a tolerance of and then privileged freedom for the Church. This new situation brought with it both a deterioration of the catechumenate as well as a certain renewal of baptismal preparation.

a. Historians generally agree that the catechumenate, properly speaking, deteriorated during this period. Why? Part of the reason was that the catechumenate began to admit people whose conversion had not been verified. To gain certain social advantages, many sought to obtain the title of "Christian," which was conferred at the ceremony of entrance into the catechumenate, but in their hearts they had not decided to follow Christ.

Thus, catechumens put off their baptism indefinitely, and ceased to come to the assembly for the required instructions. It was this lack of authenticity at the crossing of the first threshold that unleashed the decline of the catechumenate.

b. Well aware of what was happening, the Church reacted by proposing a kind of renewal in the formation process that consisted of the creation of a catechumenate during the season of Lent.

Since for many converts the necessary conversion had been bypassed and since no formation was being provided, the bishops instituted a new catechumenate corresponding to the forty days before Easter. The examination of the candidates and the ceremony of inscribing their names that opened the season of Lent were, in fact, revivals of the entrance rite into the catechumenate. Lent thus became a time of catechumenal formation that, though brief, was intense and serious and that culminated in the crossing of the second threshold, that of admission to the sacraments, at the beginning of Holy Week. Yet, for all its seriousness and intensity, the preparation was still insufficient. So there developed the practice of continuing the formation by means of a mysagogical catechesis during Easter Week.

Nevertheless, it is difficult to remedy something that is structurally flawed. Despite its value, the Lenten catechumenate always suffered from a double weakness. First, the entrance ceremony had value only if the conversion was authentic, and second the length (about seven weeks, which was soon reduced in practice to four or even three weeks) was insufficient for serious formation since there was not enough time for real moral conversion.

Inevitably, from the fifth century onwards, the Lenten catechumenate lapsed into the formalism that foretold its own eventual demise.

B. The Eclipse of the Catechumenate

Historians often explain the disappearance of the catechumenate as a result of the general adoption of the practice of infant baptism. While this did have an effect, we must also have the honesty to consider all the aspects of the situation. There were, in fact, many mission areas, especially from the sixth to the ninth century, where adult baptism was still more common than infant baptism. Let us look at some facts that will oblige us to perform a salutary examination of conscience.

1. *First, we must stress that there was a kind of "catechumenate" for infants.* It is interesting to note that, even for babies, the celebration baptism was not limited to one single liturgical ceremony. The practice of the seven scrutinies on the weekdays of Lent developed when there were many infants among the candidates. The testimony of Caesar of Arles in the sixth century is irrefutable: addressing himself to mothers bringing their babies to the scrutinies, he urged them not to miss these celebrations. This custom was undoubtedly a vestige of the tradition of baptizing infants at the same time as adults. It shows that the normative rite of Christian initiation was baptism by stages, since the sacrament supposes faith and therefore progress in the faith.

This custom also had the great advantage of having the parents of these infants participate in the preparation for baptism. Since the parents "answered" for their children, it was normal that they make the catechetical and liturgical journey leading to baptism.

2. *With the phenomenon of the increasing number and rapidity of adult baptisms in the mission areas, there were always voices raised demanding at least a minimum of serious preparation.* Unfortunately, these appeals had little effect.

Following Pope Siricius (385) and Pope Leo the Great (447) the Council of Agde (506) and Pope Gregory II (at the beginning of the eighth century) insisted that baptisms be celebrated only on the feasts of Easter and Pentecost. By thus reducing the number of celebrations, it was hoped that serious preparation could be more easily provided. Unfortunately, there were those who pleaded that it was urgent to convert the pagans and that there were far too few priests to limit the celebration of baptism to just two days a year.

In any case, what was most important was the provision of all least a minimal period of preparation. Among those who struggled for this reform were:

- Martin of Braga, the Apostle of Sueves, succeeded in having the Council of Braga (572) adopt a law requiring three weeks of preparation so that the catechumens would have the time to be instructed in the Creed.

- Boniface, the famous apostle of Germany at the beginning of the eighth century, instructed his catechumens for at least two months, and even longer.

- Alcuin, faced with the mass baptisms Charlemagne was imposing by force, succeeded in launching a certain catechumenal reform. Drawing upon Augustine's *De Catechizandis Rudibus*, Alcuin pressed for serious catechesis. In practical terms, he demanded a preparation of between seven days and forty days.

Timid reforms, certainly, but in their context, they did signify real progress. Unfortunately, these attempts were quickly forgotten; even though they sometimes carried the weight of written Church law, they had little effect in the following centuries. But the attempt to reestablish catechumenal practice centuries later drew its inspiration from Martin of Braga before turning directly to the customs of the early Church.

C. Modern Missionary Efforts

Between the sixteenth and the twentieth centuries, an authentic movement to recover the catechumenate developed. Everywhere that the Gospel was preached by the missionaries, a very strong spirit of reform attempted to restore catechumenal preparation. There was much enthusiasm, but it encountered strong resistance. To succeed, almost five centuries of constant effort were necessary. These efforts, like successive waves, washed over Latin America, then Asia, and then Africa before finally returning to old Europe. Let us briefly consider how three successive reforms culminated in the renewal of the catechumenate.

1. *Sixteenth Century*

a. Latin America. From the 1500's onwards, the Franciscans, under pressure from the civil authorities, directed their attention primarily to mass conversion. Indians were baptized by the tens of thousands without much preparation. The Dominican and Augustinian missionaries began to counteract this situation upon their arrival in Latin America in 1526. In 1534, the Augustinians requested that baptisms be celebrated only four times a year: at Easter, Pentecost, the Feast of St. Augustine, and the Epiphany. In 1538, an episcopal conference urged pastors to return to the missionary principles of Alcuin and required a catechumenate of forty days that included fasting, catechesis, exorcisms, and scrutinies. But these proposals never found their way into general practice. Provincial synods found it necessary to repeat these demands in 1585.

b. Asia and Africa. The same tendency of quick and easy baptism existed in Central Africa and in the first missions of Asia. St. Francis Xavier, at the beginning of his apostolate, baptized great numbers of people very quickly. But it was impossible to ignore the fact that many of the neophytes just as rapidly abandoned the Christian faith.

In reaction, St. Ignatius Loyola, in 1552, successfully urged the establishment in India of catechumenal houses where the converts gathered for three months of baptismal preparation. It was also at this time that the first catechisms appeared. There were those, to be sure, who opposed Ignatius in this matter, but the bishops succeeded in establishing this discipline.

2. *The Seventeenth and Eighteenth Centuries*
Though the victory had yet to be won, the battle had been

joined. Many liturgists and missionaries tried to solidify the base of the renewal and to extend its practice.

a. Some Notable Proponents of the Renewal.[10] Cardinal Julius Anthony Sanctorious, a close aide of Pius V and later of Gregory XIII and Clement VIII, did extensive research on ancient liturgies. After twenty-five years of study, he published in 1602 a book entitled, *Restored Roman Ritual Based on the Practice of the Ancient Church*. In it, the baptismal liturgy was extended throughout the duration of the catechumenate. This ritual of 712 pages was never promulgated, though it was distributed to the members of the commission responsible for drawing up a ritual.

It was a Carmelite by the name of Thomas of Jesus who, sensitive to the needs of the apostolate, brought Sanctorius's work to wider attention. In 1613 he published a weighty tome of 926 pages entitled *On the Manner of Procuring Salvation for All Pagans* that took up the project of Sanctorius and added practical suggestions for the catechesis of catechumens and even neophytes.

b. The efforts to establish a catechumenal pedagogy in Asia were particularly significant, but they lacked a liturgical dimension. The Congregation for the Propagation of the Faith, founded in 1622, distributed the work of Thomas of Jesus to the missionaries leaving for Asia. At that time, the *Missions Etrangères* of Paris began to issue their "Instructions," which gave very practical advice for the realization of an authentic catechumenal initiation.

These developments formed the basis for the young Asian Churches to establish a progressive journey through the stages of initiating the catechumens into the faith. Unfortunately, the liturgical renewal did not include any stages. True, certain signs were used to mark ceremonially the passage along the journey to baptism, but they were not liturgical rites properly speaking. And finally, this progressive pedagogy gradually faded

33

away in the 19th century, faithful as it was to the tradition of the Church and to the needs of the pastoral situation.

3. *The Nineteenth and Twentieth Centuries*

a. New Attempts at Renewal in Africa. It was in Africa that the century-old effort for the renewal of the catechumenate was relaunched. It was a renewal whose results have now been realized throughout the Universal Church, thanks to the perseverance of generations of missionaries in the four corners of the world.

From the eighteenth century on, the Capuchins and the Holy Ghost missionaries strove to restore baptismal preparation. But Cardinal Lavigerie deserves the credit for re-establishing a vigorous and traditional catechumenal discipline.[11] His pedagogy rested on two key elements: (1) Preparation for baptism must be carried out in stages, each step marking a progression in catechesis and in conversion. (2) The preparation for baptism presupposes a certain length of time in order to assure an initiation that will lead to perseverance in the Christian life.

Practically speaking, these two principles led to the establishment of a period of postulancy (two years), followed by a period of the catechumenate (two years), and finally to a major baptismal retreat.

Unfortunately, these developments still lacked a proper liturgical dimension. The giving of medals, rosaries, or crucifixes was an attempt to signify the progress of the catechumens, but there were no liturgical stages signifying the progressive gift of divine grace. The restoration of the liturgical dimension would be the contribution of the old European continent, only lately awakened to catechumenal pedagogy.

b. It was the example of the African catechumenate that roused the Churches of Europe.[12] Its most unique characteristic is the restoration, *ad experimentum*, of liturgical steps accompanying the journey of the catechumen.

D. The Conciliar Renewal

The Church today is at a crucial turning point. The restoration of the catechumenate is something already accomplished and something yet to be done. Fundamental decisions have been taken and the plans have been made, but the real work remains.

1. *Fundamental decisions were taken on two occasions.*

a. First, the Sacred Congregation of Rites, without waiting for the imminent opening of the Second Vatican Council, published on 16 April 1962 a decree restoring the rite of baptism in stages.[13] The ritual was divided into distinct stages that, in keeping with the ancient tradition of the Church, would sustain the catechumen throughout the course of his formation and his journey toward baptism. This revised ritual was authorized for use where the bishops deemed it necessary.

But the text was still that of the old ritual for the baptism of adults. The revised ordo simply divided the rite into seven parts, but did nothing to modify the rites and prayers, many of which were repetitive and not in their authentic order. Therefore, the decree of 1962, though significant insofar as it opened the door to renewal, made the need for reform of the ritual all the more obvious.

b. The Second Vatican Council affirmed and specified this fundamental decision. The Constitution on the Sacred Liturgy promulgated the restoration of the "catechumenate of adults comprising several distinct steps" (§64). The Decree on the Church's Missionary Activity presented the nature and the meaning of the different moments of the journey of Christian initiation (§§13 and 14). Other texts added further specifications:

- on the responsibility of the bishops to restore the catechumenate (Decree on the Bishops' Pastoral Office in the Church, (§14);

- on the maternal role of the Church in catechumenal action (Dogmatic Constitution on the Church, §14);
- on the role of the community in the initiation of catechumens (Decree on the Ministry and Life of Priests, §6);
- on the reform of the ritual of Christian initiation (Constitution on the Sacred Liturgy, §§65 and 66).

2. *The outlines of the work to be undertaken were proposed by the Commissions after consultation with the Churches.* In 1966, the Commission on the Liturgy drew up a provisional ritual and distributed it for experimentation to the different Churches throughout the world. After an examination of the responses, the second draft was formulated and distributed in 1969 to elicit still more remarks and suggestions. The responses to this second draft formed the basis for the new *Rite of Christian Initiation of Adults*, which was promulgated on 6 January 1972.[14]

3. *Let's Get to Work!*

The appearance of this new ritual does not put an end to the research into, and the development of, the catechumenate Quite the contrary, it is an invitation to adaptation and creativity.

a. A Guide, Not a Recipe. Before using the new rite, it is necessary to plumb its spirit and to understand the theology it affirms and the pedagogical orientations it proposes. This is to say that it is a guide that permits different ways of application that are to be determined both by the culture of the people and by the concrete circumstances of their lives.

b. Not a Ritual to Be Translated but an Instrument for Creating a Ritual. When it comes to liturgy and ritual, a valid "translation" demands adaptation, and true adaptation is, in reality, a new creation, for liturgy must spring from the hearts and the lives of those who celebrate it. This is why the introduction of the Ritual leaves a great deal to the initiative of the regional episcopal conferences, as well for the style of the prayers as for the choice of the most expressive rites.

As indicated at the outset, my purpose here has been to help situate ourselves with respect to:

- the Church whose maternal role both includes and transcends the catechumenate;

- the history of the Church, which confirms how, throughout the ages, catechumenal action was an essential dimension of the Church's life and that the Church must continually be rediscovering its dynamism in new forms.

NOTES

1. M. Dujarier, "Le catéchuménat et la maternité de l'Eglise" in *La Maison-Dieu* 71, pp. 78-93.

2. J. Plumpe, *Mater Ecclesia, Studies in Christian Antiquity* 5, Washington, 1943.

3. K. Delhaye, *Ecclesia Mater chez les Pères des trois premiers siècles. Pour un renouvellement de la pastorale d'aujourd'hui (Unam Sanctum* 46), Paris, 1964.

4. M. Dujarier, *La parrainage des adults aux trois premiers siècles de l'Eglise, (Parole et Mission* 4), Paris 1962.

5. A. Laurentin and M. Dujarier, *Catéchuménat. Données de l'histoire et perspectives nouvelles (Vivante Liturgie* 83), Paris, 1969. pp. 52-54.

6. M. Dujarier, "Le catéchuménat et la maternité de l'Eglise."

7. Ibid., pp. 25-82.

8. L. Kilger, "Zur Entwicklung der Katechumenatspraxis vom 5. bis 18. Jahrhundert," in *Zeitschrift für Missionswissenschaft* 15 (1925), pp. 166-182.

9. J. Beckmann, "L'initiation et la célébration baptismale dans les missions, du XVI siècleà nos jours" in *La Maison-Dieu* 58, pp. 48-70.

10. J. Christiaens, "L'organisation d'un catéchuménat au XVIe siécle" in *La Maison-Dieu* 58, pp. 71-82.

11. J. Perraudin, "Le catéchuménat d'après le Cardinal Lavigerie" in *Parole et Mission* 14, pp. 386-395.

12. On the history of the renewal in France, see "Vers un catéchuménat d'adultes" in *Documentation catéchistique* 37 (July 1957) which was revised and expanded in "Problèmes du catéchuménat," supplement of *Catéchèse*, Paris, 1961. See also J. Vernette and H. Bourgeois, *Serait-ils chrétiens?* Paris, Châlet, 1975.

13. For more on this decree, see *La Maison-Dieu* 71.

14. *Ordo initiationis christiane adultorum*, Vatican, 1972. In order to appreciate the full significance and the dimensions of the new ritual it is imperative that one be well acquainted with these preliminary studies.

15. Among the many studies dealing with the new rite, see R. Beraudy, "Le nouveau rituel de baptême des adults" in *La Maison-Dieu* 121, pp. 122-142 and M. Dujarier, "Le nouveau rituel de l'initiation chrétienne des adults" in *Le Calao* 21.

Henri Bourgeois

The Catechumenate
in France Today

Henri Bourgeois is a professor of theology at the Lyons Faculty of Theology in France. He holds a doctorate in theology from the University of Lyons. He is also Director of the Centre du catéchuménat *in Lyons and a member of the* Service national du catéchuménat. *He has published extensively.*

The Catholic Churches and communities of Europe are today in the process of discovering the catechumenate or what they call the catechumenal ministry. They are not attempting to reconstruct the catechumenate that existed in the early days of the Western Church but to build something that will meet their own current needs and goals. For them, the catechumenate represents more a creation than a restoration; it constitutes in Europe less a return to the first centuries of Christianity than an effort to organize for the future. In reviving an ancient name, the catechumenate, and an ancient institution, Christian initiation, European Catholics are less concerned about reviving a tradition than about responding to contemporary exigencies.

I should like to analyze the various significant phases that the catechumenal idea has gone through in France in the last forty years. This analysis will confirm how this restoration is, in fact, a reinvention and also how the tradition, recovered and revived, can respond to the responsibilities of today.

NEW BEGINNINGS OF THE CATECHUMENATE
IN FRANCE (1940-1953)

The World War of 1940-1945 was, for France, a dark and trying time. The Nazi occupation, the sufferings caused by the deportations and arrests, the underground struggles and the hope of the Resistance—all this not only brought with it the darkness and the mist, but it also gave rise to an effort to rediscover identity in the Liberation. In the midst of the flames of the bombardment and the ruins of the demolition, a courageous springtime was born. In Christianity, this period was one of very important initiatives—missionary (worker-priests), spiritual, and theological (the biblical renewal, the collection *Théologie*). The famous book by Godin and Daniel, *France, Pays de Mission?*, came out in 1943 and symbolized rather well this situation (it was translated and published in New York in 1950 with the evocative title: *France Pagan?*).

A. Missionary Orientation

It is in this context that, I believe, a kind of "pre-history" of the catechumenate in France must be placed. No one spoke of the catechumenate before 1945, but, little by little, certain insights developed that had to lead to a reviving of the spirit and the practice of the old catechumenate. Nor did anyone, at this time, refer to the "missionary" practices in black Africa, and certainly not to the catechumenate that existed there at that time. The French, though feeling that Christianity could no longer be presumed in their country, rarely considered the African experience. In France, they thought, everybody was baptized. Their problem was different: they gradually discovered that many of their countrymen were "poorly baptized," or, in any case, "defective believers," far from the faith and the Church.

In other words, during World War II awareness of the state of the Church revived in France, but that awareness was not focused on the catechumenate. Evangelization was spoken of, and efforts were made to discover where people were, in order to announce there the Word of God. But those the French missionaries encountered in their own country were already baptized. The problem was seen to be one of leading them to rediscover their baptism in the discovery of the Gospel. This was not, the missionaries thought, a true catechumenal situation.

B. Requests for Baptism

Is this to say that there were no requests for baptism by adults at this time? No. This did happen from time to time; generally the requests came from young non-baptized people who wanted to marry someone who was baptized. But they were looked on as exceptions. In a country where everybody, in principle, was considered to be Christian, the non-baptized were forgotten, almost abnormal figures. For these people, it was necessary to envisage a sort of "recapturing." And this recapturing, episodic as it was, had very little structure. The few adults who wanted to be baptized contacted either a priest, who gave them a more or less brief course of instructions, or a religious (Helpers of the Holy Souls, Little Sisters of the Assumption, Religious of the Cenacle, Dames of Sion), who tried to provide catechesis and to put the candidate in contact with a priest.

This was the situation from around 1945 to 1950, when France was emerging from the War. This situation, therefore, had two significant features: on the one hand, there was rapid development of missionary efforts, directed particularly towards the working class world, although this apostolic effort had nothing to do with the catechumenate; on the other hand, there was some pastoral care provided for adult baptismal candidates. But this pastoral care was poorly defined and seems particularly to have been addressed to the forgotten ones of Christianity for whom it was a question of regularizing or normalizing their situation in order to integrate them into the Church according to the socially recognized norms of Christianity. This perspective was not directly apostolic, and this for many reasons: first, because the baptismal candidates "came" of themselves, while the missionaries (worker-priests, members of Catholic Action) "went" to the world of unbelief; second, because the request for baptism was doctrinal and liturgical and hardly affected the daily lives of those requesting baptism; and finally, because the priests and religious who received them were, as a whole, at the service of believers and practicing Catholics and had little to do with the mission as it was then being presented and lived by the worker-priests and the Catholic Action militants.

C. How to Respond Better to the Requests for Baptism?

Nevertheless, there was development in 1950, and this for an apparently minimal reason that had significant consequences. At Lyons, some religious who were not satisfied with the catechesis they were providing baptismal candidates wanted their work to be better organized, more coherent. They thus requested the assistance of a priest. A student priest answered their appeal, which, though it did not facilitate relations with the local clergy, did assure the enterprise of a certain amount of theological and historical guidance. So one began to speak again of the catechumenate.

Documents in the Lyons archives preserve something of this germinal catechumenal discussion. These documents insist on the bond of the catechumenate with the whole of the Church:

> There is a danger, of which we are well aware and which we are doing our best to avoid, of replacing the parish, of forming a sort of parish alongside the parishes. . . . It is necessary that we accomplish our task of catechumenal instruction while maintaining close liaison with the parishes. We think . . . that a center for the catechumenate must strive to be at the service of the parishes and not constitute a group apart. . . . We are very much on our guard against forming something that would be like a little group among others, closed in on itself. Such a group, as warm and attractive as it might appear, would destroy the Church instead of building it up.[1]

The various catechumenal functions also emerge:

> The preparation of adults for baptism cannot be made properly if it is restricted to teaching. It is necessary that teaching be accompanied by insertion into the life of the Church and by participation in a liturgy.[2]

This catechumenate was the first humble European attempt since the disappearance of the ancient catechumenate. It received official recognition in the Diocese of Lyons in November 1953. The implications of this "restoration" were remarkable. It seemed that adult candidates for baptism constituted a new problem for the Church that makeshift efforts could not cope with; it was therefore necessary to create something new. And this new thing had already existed. So one set out to restore it because the practices of long ago seemed to be the answer for the urgent necessities of the moment: a liturgy adapted to the successive phases of the catechumenal progression; a catechumenal community where the laity would have their place and could ensure sponsorship; openness of the catechumenal groups to the rest of the Church and particularly to the parishes and other Christian groups; the importance of the message and the mentality of the baptismal candidates for a Church wanting to be missionary. Obviously, there is no antiquarianism in any of this. It is simply a Church that discovered the absence of Christianity in, or the de-Christianization of, the world in which it lived. It just rediscovered and put into practice its catechumenal responsibility.

THE PERIOD OF MATURATION (1954-1965)

The ten years that followed these new beginnings constituted a period in which the catechumenate was established in most of the dioceses in France. Its identity was enriched by its being applied in practice.

A. Catechumenate Centers

The format adopted was that of "centers," that is, definite places, often on the premises of religious communities or parishes, where the catechumens of the same area and Christians—catechists, associates or sponsors—would meet, generally once a month. It was not a question of "withdrawing" the catechumens from the parish or from other Christian groups. However, noting that the parishes were often poorly suited to welcome the new arrivals to the faith and that the Catholic Action groups were not necessarily capable of providing assistance of a catechumenal type—i.e., assistance that would be progressive and permit the expression of the faith as it was being discovered—those responsible for the catechumenate centers tried to create a form of the Church that would permit true Christian initiation. Still, orientation towards the parishes and the various Christian groups continued to be no less a concern. Parishioners were "sensitized" to catechumenal concerns by meeting with the catechumens and by preparing with them the celebration of baptism, which took place, in principle within the parish framework. As far as the Catholic Action groups were concerned, their role was no less important. Some Christians involved in these groups also participated in a catechumenal group. And some of the catechumens were led to discover, little by little, how to live their new faith with a commitment similar to that made by the Christians who were active in the various movements.

B. In Service of Conversion

The years between 1954 and 1965 saw an expansion of the catechumenate. From 1950 on, there was an increase in the requests for baptism—and for confirmation and the eucharist. A study done in 1957 revealed that more than 4000 adult baptisms were celebrated that year in France. The great majority of these requests stemmed directly from marriages between baptized and non-baptized people. Because such motivation could be ambiguous, there was an insistence on conversion, that is, on personal commitment to Jesus and the Gospel via the witness of the Church. If a catechumen can, in the strict sense of the term, be called a convert, one can speak here of a pre-catechumenate. The pre-catechumenate is thus the process by which the initial request is purified and in which conversion begins to happen. The catechumenate prolongs this preliminary stage of evangelization in order to develop the new faith formed by catechesis, liturgy, and ecclesial experience. Finally, and this was typical, the French pastoral orientation recommended the dissociation of preparation for baptism from preparation for marriage: "that marriage with a dispensation be accepted more readily and that its celebration in the church without mass be authorized if the non-Catholic party is admitted to the catechumenate."[3]

During this same period, the catechumenate clarified and refined the functions it performed. Three were usually distinguished: ecclesial community and evangelization, catechetical, and liturgical.

C. Community and Evangelization

The function of ecclesial community and evangelization denotes, basically, the establishment of an ecclesial community assembled around the Gospel and thus because of Jesus Christ and his Spirit. In this sense, the catechumenate is a form of the Church. Or, better, it is the Church taking on the form of beginning and progressing towards the profession of baptismal faith. The catechumenate is the welcoming Church and, thanks to the new arrivals, it is the Church renewing itself. Thus the importance given to community. The "centers" were meeting places of communities assembled around one or two catechumens, of Christians called to witness to the Church and also to rejuvenate their own faith through the intervention and witness of the catechumens. Spouse, fiancé, friend, Christian sponsor—each entered into the ecclesial experience. And this took place in the cordiality and simplicity of a sharing in which one dared to speak of oneself because of the Gospel and where one tried to listen to what was being said because of the faith.

A place for community, the catechumenate from then on refused to be a simple school of Christianity. The Christian faith was proposed within the framework of a living Church, it being understood that the situations and the sensibilities in the Church are diverse and that this diversity is to be given maximum respect. In the group, everyone was at home, known and recognized, called by name. And each reflected what he lived outside the group, at work, at home, in this or that organization. Thus an evangelical way of experiencing events and reacting to what they mean gradually took shape.

I have used two terms to specify this first catechumenal function—ecclesial communion and evangelization. This combination is not arbitrary, for it seems to be that they express rather well the catechumenal effort of the years between 1955 and 1960. If evangelization, of which there was much talk in France at this time, is realized (or can be realized) in the whole of life and thus outside of an ecclesial grouping, it still remains that the catechumenate brings about evangelization, that is, announces the Gospel in a community come together "for that." And it is indeed a matter of evangelization: one tries to listen to the words and the message of the Gospel in function of the gestures and events of daily life. And the community context provides this exchange with possibilities and a style not often available in the normal course of life.

D. Catechesis

The second function exercised by the catechumenate is catechesis, that is, comprehending and expressing the faith in a way that is coherent but still adapted to each individual. Catechesis, in the French catechumenate, has always had a "tailor made" character. It could, of course, be collective, that is, addressed to several catechumens who share socio-cultural affinities or simply circumstances. But, even in this case, care was given to the "journey" of each individual. From its beginnings, the catechumenate in France, as well as that in many other places, was aware of the time factor. Christian initiation, though capable of being organized, cannot be programmed like a course of studies. The catechetical itinerary cannot be strictly mapped out in advance, though there are, of course, reference points. But all catechumens or all members of the same catechumenal group do not necessarily advance at the same pace. The concern of Christians that assures the discovery of the faith and its "presentation" consists, in fact, of not adding a layer of cut and dried knowledge, dogmatically exact but spiritually unattractive, upon that which the candidate for baptism is living, hoping, and searching for. Without fading into vagueness, and recognizing that evangelical faith is not reducible to subjective impressions, catechumenal catechesis tries to enkindle faith in the catechumens and, simultaneously, in the Christians accompanying them in order that Jesus might be confessed in the unity and diversity of mentalities and cultures.

E. Celebrations and Liturgy

Finally, the third catechumenal function is the liturgical function. Today, after Vatican II and the liturgical progress of these last few years, this aspect seems self-evident. Between 1950 and 1960, however, the efforts of the French catechumenate in this regard seemed very original. Profiting from the post-war liturgical renewal and also from the rediscovery of the ancient rituals of catechumenal celebrations, the groups and centers of the catechumenate developed during that time a liturgy in the vernacular, rediscovering the meaning of the symbols and of the participation of the assembly. This liturgy played a role beyond catechumenal circles. Many French priests found, in the catechumenate, an occasion to renew their way of presiding over a celebration, and many lay people discovered in the catechumenal liturgies the possibility of taking an active part and the chance to pray in a manner suited to them.

F. Theological Reflection

These diverse catechumenal functions obviously required reflection and formation. Neither was lacking. Like the other renewals of this period, the development of the catechumenate in France between 1950 and 1965 made heavy demands on theology. Here again, these demands were not for the restoration of a prestigious past. Through the patristic homilies and the ritual stages leading to the baptismal font, an ecclesiology became apparent. Urged on by the requests of adults for baptism, the thinking of those responsible for the catechumenate centers sought to create a Church capable of truly welcoming these requests and bringing them to maturity. Thus, baptism presented itself as a Christian reality that must urgently be renewed. The sign of infant baptism, often in a pastoral context of wavering and hesitant faith, was hardly sufficient to maintain in Christians the meaning of the baptism they had long ago received. Catechumens and neophytes could be more effective witnesses to that which baptism is by manifesting the conversion and commitment that now marked their lives. On this was based the theological, ecclesiological, and sacramental research that was carried out then in the catechumenates. The laity, those in charge of catechesis and group leaders, found in this thinking nourishment for the catechesis they were doing and inspiration to orient their efforts toward renewal of the Church.

G. The Catechumenate and Catholic Action

I should like to emphasize another contribution of this period. This was the concern for collaboration with the Catholic Action movement, distinguishing the latter from the catechumenate. Many shared perspectives united Catholic Action and the catechumenate: concern for non-belief, focus of attention on daily life, group sharing, and so on. Nevertheless, the two realities were not identical. The catechumenate insisted on presenting to the baptismal candidates a global vision of the Church prior to the specialization that, for some of them, would occur.

A choice was made here that has not always been well understood but which, once made, seems to have been fortunate. While diversity is essential to the Church, while false unities are to be rejected in the name of truth, the unity of the communion of believers must also be manifested. And this perhaps particularly on the level where the Church is being born and where it appears more clearly as a gift of God than as a human organization. On the other hand, by trying to open the catechumens to a real apostolic sense (which led many neophytes to join the movements), the catechumenate quickly realized that not everyone had the charism to be militant in the strict sense. The catechumenate could not be simply assimilated into Catholic Action. Though finding themselves to be interdependent, the two institutions succeeded in remaining distinct.[4]

H. Official Organization

The considerable amount of catechumenal research done in France between 1954 and 1965 came to a head in 1964 and 1965. In 1964, a national office of the catechumenate was created in Paris. Its objectives were to guarantee communication between the French catechumenates, to encourage research, and to provide contact with catechumenates abroad. Its journal, *Catéchuménat-Réflexion*, was begun in 1966 to promote this program (in 1970, it became *Croissance de l'Eglise*). In 1965, the Second Vatican Council, which had already mentioned catechumens the preceding year in No. 14 of *Lumen Gentium*, published a substantial text on the catechumenate *(Ad Gentes*, No. 14). I do not intend to discuss this document here. I simply want to note that it takes up many characteristics of the African as well as the European catechumenal experience. All at once, the French catechumenates had to recognize the bonds they had with the many other analogous initiatives throughout the world and particularly those in the so-called mission countries. The European catechumenates are certainly different from the catechumenates of the young Churches—there are fewer catechumens and also the ecclesial situations and pastoral traditions are hardly comparable. Nevertheless, Vatican II gave the catechumenate, wherever it was and under whatever forms, a world status. Again, the ecclesiological aspect of the catechumenal project was emphasized.

NEW AND SERIOUS CHALLENGES (1965-1973)

The third phase of the French catechumenate began. From this time on, it was rather well "implanted." It could rely on solid theological attention and official ecclesiastical recognition. It could also enter into dialogue with catechumenal experiences in other countries.

Was everything now to develop with the momentum the catechumenate had acquired? To assume this would certainly be naive with regard to our times and certainly imprudent as far as the Holy Spirit is concerned! Indeed, difficulties did not hesitate to thrust themselves forward.

A. The Catechumens and the Church

The first of these difficulties, evident since 1965, was the problem of the relationship between the catechumenate and the Church—not theologically or theoretically, but in fact. Many of the newly baptized were not able to assume a real place in the Church. Their "perseverance," considered according to the criteria of Sunday practice and participation in the movements, was feeble, hardly better than that of Christians baptized at birth: between 10% and 20%. Why? One could ask, of course, if the catechumenate had given enough attention to introducing those it led to baptism into the Church at large. Perhaps, too, the preliminary conversion and the duration of the pre-catechumenate were not adequately secured. But there is also a complementary question: Were the parishes and the Catholic Action groups really capable of welcoming the new arrivals?

These two kinds of questions arose together between 1965 and 1970. They were posed somewhat guiltily but also with a certain realism. Why did the newly baptized not enter into the established Church? Probably because they were called to "make" the Church, to construct it with what they were, their culture and their new faith, without having to join themselves to forms of the Church established before them and without them. Thus, in 1969, the first National Convention of the Catechumenates of France courageously confronted the theme of new communities. The episode—or disturbance—of 1968, so decisive for France at the time, was not without importance for this new question. But, even before this date and notably in terms of the perspectives opened up by Catholic Action in the working class world, the fact of community had occasionally been emphasized. Was it therefore necessary to try to realize the initial vision of the catechumenate and orient the catechumens and newly baptized to the local Church? Or was it necessary to "give birth" to the Church around them and with them?

The 350 delegates to the National Convention chose the second:

> During these last years, those responsible for the catechumenate in France (priests, laity, religious) have prepared adults for the sacraments of Christian initiation. They have tried to integrate the newly baptized into the existing communities.
>
> Even though they would guard against denying the accomplishments of these Christian communities, they are obliged to note that:
>
> 1. Many people cannot pose the question of the faith for themselves because they have not encountered Christian communities that challenge their life of faith at the core of their human existence.
>
> 2. Some men and women, adolescents and adults, when searching for the faith, cannot ask their questions or are put off by the image that is too often presented by the Christian communities, including the catechumenate in its institutional form.
>
> 3. Many baptized adults, especially the poorest, the most demanding, the most involved in temporal affairs, do not succeed in finding a place in the Christian communities. They are not received. They do not feel at home. They can hardly have their voices heard, nor the voices of the non-believing environment of which they are a part.
>
> 4. Christians—priests, religious, laity—who wish to live, to announce, to celebrate their faith in the current historical setting are led to search for new forms of Christian community because they do not feel capable of achieving it in the traditional communities, which often have little vitality.
>
> Many people do live with others in true Christian community, sharing the same fundamental aspirations. Some of these unique communities fashion an explicit relation to the Word of God and celebrate the Eucharist.
>
> That is why we think, in profound agreement with other similar efforts being made elsewhere in the Church, that it is necessary today to accept and to promote the birth of *new communities* of catechumens, newly baptized, searchers, and those accompanying them.[5]

It is clear that this position constitutes a break with previous orientations, though concern for communities was certainly not a novelty of the catechumenate. Previously, however, these communities were provisional groups that prepared, in a way, for the Church of the parishes and the movements. But from then on, it was accepted that these communities would endure possibly and even often beyond the baptism of the neophytes. Is this a desire to create a mini-Church and to yield to the current demon of dispersion? I don't think so, because the communities do not want to be autonomous, to be closed in on themselves. And also because, though twenty years ago the well-established forms of the Church seemed to be the only ones for making the Church, ecclesiology has changed: the parochial forms and the movements were no longer considered as having a monopoly. Other expressions of the mystery of the Church were seen to be possible and desirable. Thus, the French catechumenate turned toward "small groups."

Consequently, doubt was cast on the "centers" that, up till that time, provided a visible form to the catechumenate and served as places for large meetings, gathering together several catechumenal groups. In many places, these institutions faded away, but not everywhere. And it may be that today some catechumenates are rediscovering the importance of a certain visibility, without which the groups and communities cannot maintain perceptible bonds with each other.

B. Unbelief and the Catechumenate

Another question was posed in France around 1970. This had to do with what was called secularization, unbelief, or the crisis in the Church. While analyses of these terms have become as banal as they are numerous, one can say that the catechumenate, sensitive to the world of unbelief since its beginnings, was not long in discovering, on its own "terrain," the effects of unbelief or of indifference to religious values.

First of all, since before 1968, there has been in France a perceptible decrease in the number of requests for baptism. Was this because the Christian faith and the sacrament of baptism were being offered less often to the non-baptized by priests and Christian laity, particularly during preparation for marriage? Perhaps. It is clear, in fact, that requests for baptism on the occasion of marriage no longer hold the preponderant place in the catechumenate that they did around 1960. More probably, however, the decrease in the number of catechumens after 1968 seems to reflect an increasing religious indifference that was becoming apparent everywhere. Between 1955 and 1960, most of the non-baptized that came into contact with the Church already knew of the existence of baptism and had formed a certain "idea" of Christianity. In a few years, these cultural presuppositions were no longer valid. Combining this with the fact that the Church today gives to those "the farthest away" an impression of hesitation and opportunism that hardly attracts them, one will no doubt understand why the French catechumenates experienced a rather significant decline in the number of requests for baptism between 1968 and 1973. I would also add that the number of baptisms actually celebrated was also less. Certain candidates were sometimes engaged in hesitant religious search and thus lost sight of the sacrament.

The situation is currently changing. But it seems to me that the French catechumenate is still being affected by this sort of crisis. After the enthusiasms and the "successes" of the beginning, the crossing of the desert cannot be avoided.

The impact of unbelief on the catechumenate after 1968 can be gauged by examining the cultural or spiritual identity of many of the catechumens. Among them, many are only marginally integrated into society: dropouts, foreigners, youth, and so on. It was as though most of the people well situated in the consumer society of the 1970's had very little desire to be baptized if they were not so already. As for those who were socially disadvantaged or were suppressed, they were no longer drawn to the Church, which appeared to them as hardly inviting for people of their kind as it seemed too monopolized by members of the dominant social categories. Among the catechumens of this period, there were certainly people belonging to the middle classes, to the working class world, to some levels of the bourgeoisie, and to rural society. Not all catechumens came from the fringes of society. But those who did possess a definite social status were often rather "classic" in their religious questions. A report of the Paris catechumenate is rather severe on this point:

Who are the catechumens? We wonder if those whom we know are not very often "products of Christianity."

That is to say, they stress, even before belonging to it, a Church that is much more "cultural" than "confessing." They resemble more the Christians of yesterday than those of tomorrow. They seem to be old before being born. If the catechumenate is a "result," it seems to be only the result of an encounter of the old Church with those who are only too ready to love it as such. Of course, there is no question of rejecting those who are there, but of asking ourselves if we are not responsible for the fact that the greatest number are from the same category.[6]

Two observations: On the one hand, the number of catechumens decreased. On the other hand, the catechumens no longer represented unbelief and its sensitivities as much as before. And yet, as everyone knows, the Church cannot live in this century without staying very much oriented toward those who live the new cultures and new sensibilities of which most Christians remain unaware.

C. Moving Out

In 1973, the second national convention of the French catechumenate sought to develop a perspective and a method adapted to the situation. Instead of confining the catechumenate to the reception of baptismal candidates and their pastoral care, the delegates considered an institutional shift. While maintaining their proper mission of welcoming those requesting Christian initiation of the Church, they committed themselves to a "change in direction" in order to rejoin people where they were groping and questioning.

Instead of simply waiting on the threshold, they saw that it would be necessary to go out and encounter the "searchers for God." Instead of being content with communities of faith in the usual style they realized that they would have to dare to create free "spaces," room for dialogue, and to promote "informal" encounters or to join in them. The following are the policy changes adopted in 1973:

1. The places of conversion today being very diverse, it is necessary to recognize the very diversified routes being taken by some in an open-ended search and not simply for the reception of a sacrament.

2. The catechumenate will thus be at the service of conversion to Jesus Christ in the places and the groups where this occurs today.

> From a wider perspective, rejecting the policy of "all or nothing," is is a point of reference for those who request the sacraments as well as for those who are simply "searching." It becomes a "space of welcome and of liberty"—if it is a place where people as they are can speak for themselves and decide their journey for themselves without a destination determined in advance, if it reflects ("prophetically") the fundamental confidence that the Church has in the liberty and the liberation that Jesus has brought to all.

3. And the "new" communities of the Church are then born. Groups discover the faith on different levels of ecclesial experience but their experience always centers on the Gospel.

> Many see themselves better reflected in this form of the Church, a Church less characterized by institutional problems, less enclosed in definitions, but closer to the real lives of men and groups, more in harmony with the words of Jesus on the Kingdom.[7]

These orientations were not totally new when they were adopted. They translated experiences that several catechumenates had been having for some time. And they signified that the French catechumenate was not afraid to redefine its purposes to correspond better to the needs of the times and the call of the Spirit.

THE CATECHUMENAL TREND AND THE CATECHUMENAL MINISTRY (1973-1978)

The second national convention of the French catechumenate, the orientations of which I have just noted, was held in

April of 1973. In October of the same year, a typical event occurred that should show how analogous intuitions and experiences were developing elsewhere. A certain number of French scholastic chaplaincies (parent committees, lay leaders, religious, priests) published a manifesto called "The Catechumenal Ministry."

A. Ministry in the Schools

The text stated that, for many young people, most often baptized and catechized, unbelief was more or less characteristic: indifference, saturation, rejection of the faith, allergy to the Church, and so on. Still these young people frequent the premises and participate in the groups of the scholastic ministry and they even invite their non-baptized friends. Why? Maybe out of habit. But perhaps because some chaplaincies have become "spaces of liberty," the need for which is vividly felt by young people in a hyper-organized, controlled, and intellectualized world like ours. Today, even if one does not believe, even if one does not belong to a Church, it is still possible to look to Christianity for the possibility of dialogue and free searching—on the condition that the Churches not be "recouping" and that they demonstrate respect and disinterest.

"New ways are being sought," noted the authors of the Manifesto, and added, "Via them, we link up in many places with the goals of the adult catechumenate."[8]

Such a situation and such an analysis lead to certain pastoral emphases. The Manifesto stressed the importance of duration, or what is commonly called in France, the "journey." "If time is not respected, all will be destroyed."[9]

In addition, the text insists on liberty:
We know, of course, that this liberty is to be aroused, that is does not grow of itself, that youth need to be challenged, stimulated.

But liberty also needs to be personal. Without this, education is a deception and group sharing is illusory.

Now in Christianity as in our hyper-organized society, there is found the same imbalance between what is imposed by the adult system and what is left to the liberty of youth.[10]

Such perspectives constitute a challenge to the catechetical and sacramental pastoral care of children:

We hope that the sacraments will no longer be given mechanically to young children.
   We agree with those who favor a parental decision before the baptism of their child. Certainly, infant baptism is legitimate. But we want other possibilities; we want baptism to be able to be delayed and we want an institution, like the catechumenate, to aid the journey of young people toward an adult baptism.[11]

The catechumenal orientation is clear: "In a catechumenal situation, one has to discover the faith before celebrating the sacrament."[12]

This text caused some disquiet in 1974, notably on the part of Christians disturbed by the audacity of the "new ministry." Clarification came out of the resulting debate. There was no question of discounting catechesis or the sacraments. The idea was rather to offer to those young people who desired it the means of undertaking their journeys in a manner adapted to their own situations.

B. Catechumenal Ministry

Spontaneously, other ecclesial forms and institutions gave rise to similar analyses. Many young people preparing for marriage were "in a catechumenal situation." Rather than lead them come what may to a hasty sacramental celebration, would it not be better to involve them in a spiritual program in the catechumenal style, that would permit them to rediscover the faith? Here and there in France in the last few years, there has been discussion of a "catechumenate of marriage," or rather "marriage by stages." This discussion, linking pastoral studies with canonical, historical, and theological aspects, is now going on. Similarly, in the Catholic Action movement, concerns surfaced in 1975 and 1976 that were catechumenal in nature. Already in 1973, the Catholic Action movement among the workers published a booklet with the significant title of "Chercheurs de Dieu" ("Searchers of God"). It seemed that what was received from Christianity or from the established faith, and which many militant Christians had lived up until 1968, could no longer be considered sufficient. It is necessary not only to live the faith in the world and in socio-political commitment but also to provide oneself with the practical means to organize and to renew continuously Christian membership. And, in certain cases, it is even necessary to "learn again how to believe" by returning to the fundamentals of the Christian faith.

This more or less convergent collection of insights and studies brought into fashion the use of the adjective "catechumenal" in France in 1974-1975. One spoke of catechumenal ministry, of catechumenal liturgy, and even of the catechumenal Church. The significance of this went beyond just a change in vocabulary. It indicated an awareness and an orientation. Still, it was necessary to avoid misunderstanding and ambiguity. Catechumenal concern is not enough to create a catechumenate, that is, the effective proposal of means for spiritual advancement. And also, the need for freedom and hospitality is not equivalent to pastoral care that is really catechumenal— this, of necessity, also involves other components.

C. The Catechumenate Reaffirms Its Identity

In addition, the catechumenate in France tried to redefine its own orientation in this context. It did this in two ways.

First, it turned to the signs or the reference points of conversion. In a rather "destabilized" period, this seemed to be important. What is it to be converted? This does not necessarily imply, it is true, conversion to Jesus Christ. Our times know of many forms of conversion. But one cannot for all of that use the term arbitrarily. To be converted is to make a discovery or, in other words, to experience a spiritual transformation that creates a difference between what one was and what one tries to be. This presumes that this discovery—and particularly the discovery of Jesus Christ—involves a significant investment for oneself and for others. The result is fellowship: conversion opens oneself to those other than oneself; it makes communication possible. Finally, it manifests an activity the modes of which can vary but which constitutes one of the criteria of the change that has been experienced: he who is converted becomes an active agent of change around him.[13]

Second, French catechumenal attention turned to the redefinition of the "components" or the major axes of the catechumenate and consequently to catechumenal ministry. The national journal "Croissance de l'Eglise" often took up this point. Four components were referred to. First, the catechumenate needs to respect the necessary time factor and thus the concrete liberty of each individual and each group. Second, it stressed the importance of an explicit announcement of the Word of God. Not everything is catechumenal. Having room for dialogue is catechumenal only to the extent that one agrees to see in it what the fact of being Christian means, no matter what may be the way of living or of manifesting this reference. The third element of the catechumenate is the community dimension. There is no advance toward Jesus Christ in isolation. Finally, the fourth component is that the catechumenate tries to be fundamentally attentive to the cultures of those who request baptism and those who are searching for faith. This focus provides for the recognition of diverse forms of unbelief, or of nonbelief, in which the members of the catechumenal teams have lived.

D. Catechumenal Trend

It is rather interesting to note that this redefinition of what the catechumenate fundamentally is clarifies the perspectives of catechumenal ministry and particularly the kinds of groups and study that can be useful for those who are already baptized and who are, in fact, like catechumens. Around 1976-1977, one began to speak in France of the "catechumenal trend." This perspective consists of joining the search of the catechumens, in the strict sense, with that of the baptized who actually need initiation or re-initiation into the faith. These latter are found in the school chaplaincies, in the pre-marital conferences, in meetings of parents whose children are in catechetical groups, and so on. They are not unbelievers, but their faith is uncertain and obscure. They often have only sporadic contact with the

Church. They are on the threshold. And what the Church offers them is most often not appropriate for they are not on the level of the sacraments or of the activities of committed Christians.

I would add that the apostolic concern thus expressed in the catechumenal trend is in no way a "recovery" operation. The intention is not to regather into the fold the brothers and sisters who have wandered away. It is to respond to the needs of our times. There are many people today in a state of spiritual suspension, and the sects or religious groups imported from the East are sometimes, for them, an answer to their needs. Perhaps it is necessary that the Church, without any sense of rivalry or annexation but in the spirit of service, offer a way of access to the mysteries of the faith that would be other than the classic childhood initiation. Henceforth, the Church is not going to form itself solely through children. It will address the Word to the masses of adults, baptized or non-baptized, who have in fact never been evangelized.

The catechumenal trend in France is still a modest one, because the greater part of the Church in France is still essentially very much occupied with internal administration or internal quarrels. But, here and there, there are definite signs of a progressive shifting of interests and preoccupations. To be "missionary," as many Christians who are taken with this point from Vatican II like to say, means to offer to all those who desire it effective and appropriate ways of discovering what Christian faith really is.

E. An International Observation

In any event, these orientations seem to be appearing more and more on the international level. European catechumenate meetings verify this generalization and this set of concerns. The most recent, which was held in Lyons in 1977, definitely did this. From bold and ardent Holland to Spain seething with initiatives, the message was practically the same: the catechumenate and the catechumenal ministry correspond to a need of these times. The participants from the Anglican Church were of the same opinion. And, starting in Spain and Italy, "neo-catechumenal" communities are being formed here and there. They were mentioned at the world Synod of Bishops in 1977. Perhaps they are particularly concerned with a catechetical deepening of Christians already very much involved in the Church, whereas, the French or European catechumenal trend would give priority to "non-practicing" or "non-militant" Christians. But in their own way, they too represent the pastoral orientation I have just analyzed.

F. The Catechumenate, a Future for the Church?

These orientations of the catechumenate in France were expressed recently by the third National Convention, which was held in November 1977. The theme was significant, even if it might seem a bit ambitious: "The Catechumenate, a Future for the Church?" Across the diverse tendencies, whose variety reflected well the variety of attitudes in current French society, two basic things came out in the discussions. The first is expressed in a metaphor: "to restore the ecclesial fabric." In other words, the French catechumenates want to create, as far as they are able, Church models where sharing and communication occur, without letting themselves be hindered by nostalgia or caught up in the problems of the past. The second theme indicated a priority without which there could not be a Church: "to reexpress the faith," to restate it in a new language based on the words and formulas that the Spirit has placed on the lips of the "searchers of God," based on those who, in liberty, are today engaged in the quest for Jesus and his sacraments without renouncing the cultural and spiritual solidarity that binds them to unbelievers and people far from the Churches.

There are two striking qualities of the propositions that this Convention defined. The first is the concern for the culture of those who accept the faith:

The particular experience of the Catechumenate shows that adults of diverse cultures, of diverse languages, can accept the faith and be respected in their cultures. This is, moreover, its mission. By inviting the communities of the Church to implant the faith in the diverse cultures, the Catechumenate is forced to reject the ever present temptation to "deculturate" those who are searching.[14]

Second, concern for the Church is vigorously stressed, that is, for the bond between the catechumenal experience and other forms of the Church. The accent is placed on the future. If one particular Church dies, another is born:

> Thanks to the "catechumenal spirit," the real dynamisms of the established Church, as it exists, that are exploring the ways of the future can be challenged by non-belief and can envisage new births of the Church in new places.[15]

Abstract formulae, certainly! But what these catechumenal groups are concretely experiencing is a humble and tenacious hope. The catechumenate does not see itself as more than what it is. It realizes its limits and its fragility. But it thinks it can, in France, witness to what the Spirit accomplishes in the hearts of those of our contemporaries involved in conversion and liberation. Is this not a sign for the entire Church?

CONCLUSION AND OVERTURE

This rapid historical survey of the catechumenate in France illustrates rather well the position I took in the introduction: the restoration of the catechumenate in 1953 and its conciliar reestablishment by Vatican II were not the work of antiquarians or of those nostalgic for a bygone era. It evolved from the real tradition, if it is true that the tradition consists of gathering support from what was in order to welcome what is and to go towards what will be.

Through the historical stages outlined here, perhaps some constants can be observed. The first is, no doubt, an apostolic concern. The French catechumenate has always taken great care not to be imprisoned by intramural preoccupations. It defines itself not only by catechesis, but also by presentation of the faith and by the "growth of the Church." It has also always been attentive to the shifts in requirements and needs. The concern now being given to the "catechumenal trend" for the baptized who are like catechumens seems to illustrate well this mobility and capacity for renewal. The second constant complements the first. It can be defined as an ecclesial concern, but in a restricted way. It is not a concern for a Church that often is burdened by its past and intoxicated with the abuse of words and formulae. Rather, it is a preoccupation with a Church of men and women wanting to live the Gospel with the real feelings and commitments that constitute their lives.

Two constants, two lines of force that are mutually supportive. In practice, nothing is easy. In France, 1978 is the year in which we shall see the death of certain illusions born in 1968 and in which we shall search for hopes for a more realistic society and Church, that is, a society and Church more courageously oriented towards tomorrow. The situation of the catechumenate in France is, in this sense, a sort of symptom of the current social and ecclesial situation. It is probably good that it is so!

NOTES

1. "Vers un catéchuménat d'adultes," *Documentation catéchistique* (later named *Catéchèse*) 37 (July 1967): 130.

2. Ibid., p. 130.

3. Ibid., p. 19.

4. J. Vernette and H. Bourgeois, *Seront-ils chrétiens?* (Châlet, 1975), p. 42. This work deals with the French catechumenal situation in 1975.

5. Ibid., p. 96.

6. Ibid., p. 57.

7. Ibid., p. 134.

8. Ibid., p. 151.

9. Ibid., p. 151.

10. Ibid., p. 152.

11. Ibid., p. 152.

12. Ibid., p. 152.

13. In Vernette and Bourgeois, *Seront-ils chrétiens?*, a certain amount of theological data is given not only on conversion (pp. 122-131) but also on the catechumenal ministry (pp. 177-196), the ecclesial experience (pp. 204-208), and the liturgy of the catechumenate (pp. 209-218).

14. *Croissance de l'Eglise* (4 Avenue Vavin, F-75006, Paris) 45 (January 1978): 21.

15. Ibid., p. 18.

Jean Bouteiller

Threshold Christians: A Challenge for the Church

Jean Bouteiller, a parish priest involved in the establishment of a catechumenate in Paris, is Assistant Director of the National Center for Religious Education in that city. His apostolate is to those who either "cross parish lines" or seek a community in which to affirm or reaffirm their Catholic commitment.

THE BACKGROUND

France is known as a country with a long Catholic tradition, and even today, more than 90% of the French are baptized.[1] The title, "Eldest Daughter of the Church," is still sometimes bestowed on it by some newspapers and in some official speeches. But such figures and titles have not prevented the Church from taking note of a sad fact when Fathers Godin and Daniel published in 1946 their famous book, *France, Pays de Mission.*[2] This book too readily gave the impression that France had been dechristianized and that it had lost the ground gained down through the centuries. Immediately, forces were marshaled for a sort of reconquest. "We will make our brothers Christian again!" This was the theme often proclaimed by the Catholic Action movements, which formed the spearhead of the missionary effort. The French were to become Christians again.

65

The problem was cast in terms of mission and of apostolate and not in terms of re-initiation. The catechumenal themes came later.

Today, the missionary effort is suspended, and one can more realistically see the limits of yesterday's Christianization. Historians go so far as to say that in certain areas and on certain social levels, Catholicism has never been more than a varnish, which casts doubt on the idea of total Christianization.[3] At the same time, it has been discovered how much the Church has been politically and culturally present, how much some of its influences are enduring, and how these influences have affected—perhaps partially, but still profoundly—the great majority of the French. Indeed, in the last twenty years or so, many sociological studies have been bringing to light the complexity of the relations between the French and the Church—its message, its institutions, its activity. Faced with these facts, the Church has thus been brought to change its modes of presence and activity in order to establish contact with an increasingly large number of people who, though they are no longer unconditional members of the faithful, show interest, discrete and occasional, and who acknowledge that they are more or less of this family.

THRESHOLD CHRISTIANS

When Church leaders (pastors, theologians, etc.) want to describe Christians who only go to Church occasionally and whose behavior does not correspond to the norms usually laid down, they like to use the term "defective believers." Does this mean that one recognizes in these people the quality of believers but that one denies that they are good ones? I cannot but think that this term "defective believers" partially reflects a projection of the discomfort of the leaders of the ecclesiastical institution who cannot bear to admit the lack of correspondence between their propositions and the people to whom they are speaking. In their minds, these "defective believers" are people

66

who do not use, or make poor use, of the services the Church offers and who call themselves Christian. In a word, they are lukewarm. The same label is also applied to those who are not satisfied with the language, practices, and institutions offered or required by the Church and who demand something else in the service of the Gospel. Defective believers are therefore people who more or less deviate from the normal program of the institution. In the cases, the Church's leaders seem to be saying that these believers are not all that they should be. They are too frivolous or too demanding; in short, they are not comfortable enough with the ecclesial project they are presented. However, these people describe themselves as Christians and only rarely as "defective believers."

Rather than use this label, I prefer to call them "threshold Christians." But we must agree on what this means. When one speaks of threshold Christians, one pictures the Church as a building or as an open space, places arranged more or less for entering or leaving, coming and going. These are the building's entrances, the doors. One can easily imagine the many activities that can take place on these thresholds: meetings, movement, mixing of people, waiting, initiation, revelation, discussion, ceremonies, and so on. Moreover, the threshold is an integral part of the building; it is neither an accessory nor an appendix. In our former Church, we were more accustomed to the antechamber and to the vestibule than to the thresholds. Baptized very soon, the child was placed directly in the Church; it was born human being and Christian, Catholic and French, almost without distinction. It was spared the threshold.

The image of a Church that has opened its windows in the hope of a sort of osmosis between it and the world is readily used with regard to the last Vatican Council. The windows must have been opened because now a number of Christians are complaining about the drafts! And indeed, since Vatican II, some breaches have developed in the walls of the Church. I know that too often statistical studies tempt us to interpret the resulting movement in terms of a hemorrhage, of a loss of influence. One could also interpret the migration that followed upon Vatican II more positively as a somewhat better manifestation of the vocation of a Church that is a transitory sign among the nations.

In its present fluidity, the Church can be seen as a *caravanserai* where many tribes are meeting. It has, perhaps, gained in flexibility what it has lost in stability, and in diversity what it has lost in uniformity. An intense and confusing life has developed along its edges that yearns for or rejects yesterday's generations that were used to another style. Many men and women are encamped at its doors and maintain extremely diverse links with it. The Church is therefore much more exposed than it was previously. It is still visited, frequented, questioned, explored, loved, criticized by a crowd of people who call themselves more or less Christians. These threshold Christians do not all have the same traits or the same expectations, but they all do have in common the need to establish a new relation to the institution. This relation is probably to be seen more in terms of participation than in terms of inclusion. Thus many encamped at the Church's doors are willing to be recognized as being of the Church and to be linked to it, but they are very hesitant about being recognized as being integrally *within* the Church. No doubt, operative here is a very strong collective unconsciousness that fears that the institution would acquire for its own advantage or absorb into its own program the aspirations of many who feel challenged by the Gospel or inspired by another ideal. It is well known that the number of priestly and religious vocations, like the number of declared activists under ecclesiastical auspices, are extremely low. This seems to me to be a significant symptom of this refusal to be entirely moved by the ecclesiastical program and totally engaged under its flag. This said, I quite agree that there are still totally dedicated Christians—men and women completely loyal to the program of the institution. I would also agree that unbelief exists and that a number of our contemporaries are not at all interested in the Church and locate their ethical references and the inspiration for their lives elsewhere.[4]

JUNCTIONS—FRONTIERS

The sole purpose of these remarks is to show the threshold areas, those points of meeting and contact on the frontiers of the Church. Today it is these junctions that are perhaps the most interesting areas for ministry. On these thresholds are sometimes found real catechumens seeking entry into the Church, which will, of course, be shown in the course of some discussion. As for myself, I should like to draw your attention to the considerable number of Christians who have been baptized from birth, catechized during their childhood, sometimes educated in Catholic schools and in Christian youth movements and who, today, belong to this category of threshold Christians. It is not enough to say that they have been baptized but not catechized. The present situation is not to be imputed to the failure of the catechetical system alone. Other factors are also involved. What is at issue here is the total attitude and pastoral disposition of the Church.

I shall limit myself to pointing out a few typical situations where one can find threshold Christians.

These situations are often called catechumenal situations. There are ambiguities in this description, as it implies an extension of the word "catechumenate" that is sometimes unwarranted. Certainly these situations include features that are found in any catechumenal approach: slowness of the journey, mutual explanations of positions, gradual approach to the passing on of the Christian faith, phases of instruction, witness, prayer, and so on. But the activities carried out there are not directly oriented toward a profession of the Christian faith and for entry into the Church. The immediate objective is to procure and maintain a "contact area" between the Church and a geographically extremely mobile population that is culturally diverse and more or less ideologically uncommitted. One expression, which is having much success in ecclesiastical circles, well expresses this willingness to establish another area for work and communication. One speaks of remaking the "ecclesial fabric," which means weaving another material, setting up a new communications network, and reestablishing contact with the many who are excluded by the traditional activities of the parish.

The key words of these groups working on the frontiers are most often communication, exchange, sharing, and offering. They are not instruction, imposition, and integration. There is more than just an attitude involved here. It is almost a strategy.

Three poles seem to me to be particularly favorable for this sort of contact: the educational, the dramatic, and the religious. I shall treat each of these areas in turn and try to indicate what the Church is doing there.

I. EDUCATION

The Church has long been linked with education. One cannot deny the role of cultural matrix that it has played down through the centuries in our country. Instruction of both the elite and the masses has rested on its shoulders for a long time. And even today, many people, without necessarily submitting to it, acknowledge that the Church has some kind of authority over consciences and a moral function in the society. The Church is considered to be the bearer of a certain ethic, of a certain vision of the world, of society, of man. The ambiguities and compromises, which can appear, are sometimes vigorously denounced. But this area of activity is acknowledged as legitimately belonging to the Church. When the Church calls itself "Mater et Magistra," it indeed intends to occupy this place and perform this educative function. The importance it has attached both to catechism and to confessional schools as well as to vigilance on the part of the Magisterium on ethical and social questions has given concrete form to its intentions in this field.

All things considered, it will not be surprising, therefore, to see education as a meeting place for a number of our contemporaries and the Church.

(a) First, we have the catechetical institution in all its dimensions. Today, one can see various changes in catechesis, the traditional method for dissemination of the Christian message and integration into the Church. While the level of attendance at catechism classes has dropped significantly—families and children are less diligent—the most important changes are qualitative.

Catechesis of children now proceeds much more by exchange, dialogue, and witness than by stereotyped instruction. Within groups of children, ideas from various sources confront each other, and Christian revelation then finds itself debated.

Today one finds upbaptized children in catechetical groups. They are enrolled by their parents or have come by themselves at the instigation of their friends. Their curiosity is often very great and their criticism can be very fruitful. Some of them ask to be baptized and this offers an opportunity for the community to progress. In 1977, a ritual was published with the approval of the French-speaking episcopacies for the baptism of school age children.[5]

For more than fifteen years, a considerable effort has been made to promote the participation of parents in the religious education of their children. On the basis of this education, the Church has been able to renew contact with adults who scarcely ever went to church. With varying degrees of boldness and skill, it thus helps many parents in their educative task, for example, by teaching them to maintain good relations with their children and to examine their environment together. At the same time it encourages religious reflection on the part of the parents by inviting them to take stock of their own religious situation and the vitality of their faith. It is not uncommon to hear parents say that they have regained interest in the faith after having thus accompanied one of their children. All the same, a rather large scale participation of parents in the religious awakening and catechesis of their children does have its negative aspects. When there is not enough support from the clergy or from a competent catechetical staff, it can easily provoke a sort of regression and impoverishment, especially if the child is entrusted too long and too exclusively to its own parents, thus depriving it of a necessary openness to a wider community than the family.

How does the Church reach these adults? Often it is through meetings in which choices and programs intended for the children are presented and discussed. There are also numerous periodical publications to keep them up to date. And sometimes it is by way of liturgical celebrations or festivals to which the parents are invited.[6]

(b) Another ecclesial institution that also is concerned with education and catechesis must be mentioned here. This is the secondary school chaplaincy. Even more than the catechumenate for children, these chaplaincies are in tune with the catechumenal perspective to the point that there is, among these chaplaincies, a current called the "catechumenal chaplaincy" that wants to radicalize certain options inspired by the catechumenate and deliberately to make chaplaincies catechumenal *loci*.[7]

(c) Finally, there are two institutions that, though they are not part of the Church's organizational structure, do constitute important contact areas for many people. These are the Catholic schools and the educationally oriented Catholic press.

Catholic schools today do not restrict themselves to Catholics for their teaching staffs or for their pupils. For a long time, the headmaster or principal acted as the priest's right hand man, but this is rare today. Catholic schools are increasingly more separated from the local parish, and they themselves plan catechetical, liturgical, spiritual, and missionary activities for their pupils. As for the educationally oriented Catholic press, attempts are being made to situate the problem of the Christian faith among contemporary problems through articles directed to children or young people as well as to their parents.[8]

Bringing together the strong points of the pedagogies developed in these educational centers, one could outline them as follows: It seems that there is an attempt to educate a free, responsible subject, capable of standing upright in the present fluidity and in the flood of information that flows over him. Apprenticeship in discernment, appreciation of situations and what is at stake, work on relations and the life of groups—all this leads to a kind of Christian appreciably different from the Christians who came before us who were above all people of duty and obedience.

II. THE DRAMATIC

I do not know whether the category of the "dramatic" is adequate to cover what will follow. By it, I should like to indicate situations in which one becomes more sharply aware of the destiny that possesses him and evaluates what is involved in this condition. These may be the very questions of existence: birth and death, love, the use of one's life, and so on. In several of these areas, the Church has been involved for centuries. Indeed, what is more traditional than to link the question of God to that of origins and ends, to link salvation to "works" or to social evolution? Today many still turn to the Church to solemnize certain stages of life, to organize certain events that touch profoundly the heart of man.[9]

A. Birth and Baptism

Birth and baptism, so closely linked up till now, are tending to become separated. Infant baptism is still common, but more and more parents are not having their children baptized or are delaying baptism out of respect for their freedom.[10] Whether it be before infant baptism or a delayed baptism, the Church tries to encourage reflection on the part of the parents by using the occasion to suggest meetings at which parents can share their experiences and work out the meaning of the sacrament they are requesting. The favored themes are no longer those of purification from original sin but much more those of the fatherhood of God, of the gift and the reception of life. Baptisms are often celebrated collectively and this can provide an opportunity for meeting the parish community as well as other families in similar circumstances.

B. Marriage

With regard to marriage, the catechumenal tradition is more anchored in habit. There was a time when the catechumenate centers would receive young engaged couples who, unbelievers or unbaptized or not having made their first communion would begin or re-begin to move toward the Church and seek the faith's sacraments to seal a Christian marriage. Because Canon Law has since relaxed, many engaged couples are content to request a religious celebration of their marriage without taking up Christian initiation. Thus, there are young people who, while admitting they are non-believers, still accede, out of respect, to their partner's desire for a Church wedding. Being aware of this situation, the Church now asks the couples to declare their marriage plans at least three months in advance so as to be able to work out with them a series of meetings either with Christian couples or with a priest. The primary objectives here are to allow the engaged couples to specify their plans, to see more clearly what life together involves, to pursue their dialogue with the help of a third party, and to incorporate the religious dimension into this dialogue. Often the engaged couples are asked to give a personal touch to the religious celebration of their marriage. They respond gladly. The canonical investigation is secondary to these meetings. In fairly large parishes or towns, these meetings on the occasion of marriage are sometimes taken up again one or two years later on at the preparation for a child's baptism or on the invitation of the priests or of those in charge of this portion of the Church's ministry.

The ministry of marriage preparation is rapidly evolving in France. A recent survey revealed that there are approximately 9,000 lay people staffing and directing marriage preparation centers.[11]

C. Death

When death strikes a family, the Church is often called in. This is an old reflex, but a few changes in it should be noted.

Formerly, the Church in the person of the priest would help the individual to die in a Christian manner by administering the sacraments of passage: confession, extreme unction, and viaticum. The Church dealt with death as it was happening, and its activity consisted mainly of allowing the individual brought to the gates of death to be reconciled with his life and to draw hope from the Christian faith. The Church presided over the passage. Having baptized this child, it now administered the last baptism and completed the initiation. After having given him to the world at birth in the name of Jesus, it would now give him to Heaven under the same patronage.

In the past few decades, there has been a shift in the practice of the Church. Nowadays the Church intervenes much more *post mortem* than *in mortem*. People turn to the Church for the funeral, and not so much for the dying itself. There are many reasons for this, and they are related not only to the decrease in the number of priests but also to the dedramatization of death and its now more private character. Urbanization and generalized hospitalization of the sick are certainly reasons why many die alone and away from home. In the best cases, they are surrounded by a few relatives and friends. Dying is no longer a social act. In view of this, the Church now has to speak more to the families and friends of the deceased rather than to the dying persons themselves. It finds itself, especially at funerals, before a diversified congregation that is more or less touched by the drama that has brought it together. The kind of language it uses in these circumstances is felt to be rather neutral. If it chooses to be dramatic about it, it appears anachronistic; the time has passed for brandishing the fires of hell or the bliss of paradise and for preaching to the sinner to change his ways while there is still time. It is also difficult for it to adopt a personal tone because the priest who is speaking is not even in a position to witness to the life of the deceased who often is a stranger to the priest. Moreover, Catholics do not like panegyrics. In many cases, all that is available is rather dogmatic language about resurrection. Here, as with baptism, the themes of sin, purification, and forgiveness take second place to other more optimistic themes. Nevertheless, the Church is reproached for no longer knowing how to treat death as before and for making funerals slightly naive protestations of hope by prematurely proclaiming resurrection without having gone through the experience of death. Yet this is the place for last words. Here the Church reveals itself more than anywhere else. The person whom it claims to have initiated, educated, and accompanied must here be vindicated. For those who are still on the way, what the Church says here and the way in which it acts reveals more than anything else it does. Here it shows how it perceives the end of the journey. The paradox explodes. The Church speaks of life, resurrection, and eternity while everyone looks on death and the end of a man's life. Will our contemporaries be concerned by the way in which the Church acts and deals with death?

D. Man and the World

Another aspect of the dramatic that touches on death is the feeling of failure that one may experience in the task of constructing the world. All men today have enough information to know that the world is incomplete and to suffer the profound defects that mark its development. What sensitive man today is not affected by the price of justice? The Gospel does have something to say about the liberation of oppressed peoples of all kinds. Can the Church offer anything to this struggle? The time no longer seems opportune for a social doctrine and even less for a Church stranglehold on politics. But where is the Church going in this field? Of course, the ethic it is offering has been deliberately separated from a too individualistic perspective predominated by a concern for accomplishing the duty of one's state in life. The problem arises on another scale. In addition, many Christians are finding themselves involved at the heart of these struggles and sometimes on opposing sides. Can the Church intervene to support life styles that are not inspired by progress and profit? Here is where some people are waiting for the Church.

III. RELIGION

The religious question is once again open. The imposing number of atheists is forcing the Church to explain what it means by the possibility of God's existence and the qualities it can attribute to him. The faith does not seem so self-evident as it used to, and the believer has to be able to account for his choice. Another new fact in France is the presence of non-Christian religious streams. The Moslem religion is now numerically in second place, given the number of immigrant workers coming from the Maghreb and the Middle East. In this proximity, the uniqueness of the Christian God must be demonstrated. At the moment, there are few adult communities involved in these inter-religion problems, but it should be noted that the question is often discussed at the catechism level where the children bring up the questions asked by their Jewish or Moslem friends. From the very beginning, the question of God today calls for a broad, ecumenical treatment. To promote this openness, catechists can now have at their disposal comparative notes on the different religious traditions.[12]

Within the Catholic tradition, the liturgy today is clearly an extremely sensitive point where the Catholic representation of God is at stake. It seems to me that a large number of Catholics have trouble abandoning certain religious practices largely inspired by deism.[13] The quarrels about rites actually mask deep divergences about the countenance we intend to give to God. While the liturgical reforms of Vatican II do challenge many deeply entrenched habits of the Christian people, the basis of the debate is theological, turning on the place of Christ and his paschal mystery. Too often, with regard to the liturgy, objections are made to the liberties taken by communities or groups of the faithful and particular attention is given to denouncing ritual blunders or tendentious textual innovations. Even if unfortunate things have occurred, they should not prevent us from appreciating the quality of the efforts that have attempted, on the basis of liturgy and prayer, to establish a new relationship to God that is more in harmony with the Gospel. A clear sign of this renewal is the impressive number of books published since 1968 offering prayers for personal or collective use. Moreover, a number of groups, especially of the young, are themselves composing collections of prayers for their own use. These are undeniably elements of initiation into another kind of relation with God.

CONCLUSION

Here I want to discuss some of the sensitive points on which the Church is being challenged by our contemporaries. It is partially on the explanations it offers and the discussions it enters into in these frontier zones that the existence of the Church will depend. Will it, by awakening a taste for the faith, be able to attract the conversion of those who challenge it and play a catalytic role in the world?

For this dialogue and pre-initiation, it has limited forces, often novices, at its disposal. As we know, the clergy and the parish communities see their influence diminishing, and those who bear the burden of the debate on the faith and of its witness to the frontiers of the world are often lay people, sometimes organized, sometimes isolated. They are fathers and mothers who have had little specialized training to be spokesmen for the Church and active artisans of its construction. These lay people—along with a large number of nuns—often accept the investment of a considerable amount of time in the study of the Christian tradition and the Scriptures, in meetings with other Christians. For many it is a long and arduous undertaking that takes them beyond the Christian language that had been theirs to a new integration and interpretation of the data of the faith. This can be like a second Christian initiation for adults preoccupied with related questions or involved in similar activities. It is these new "initiators"—catechists, school chaplains, those who work with engaged couples, leaders of Catholic Action groups or prayer groups—who will make up tomorrow's Church. Their strength is fragile. They, too, are on the journey, but they are not exactly in the same position as the ordained clergy and ministers who were the initiators of yesterday's Church. Must we speak of them as ministers? On their level they lead, often gropingly, a small group of Christians in the knowledge of the Scriptures, in prayer, in the adventure of changing the world. They bear a part of the burden of a Church that is dispersed, and their isolation is sometimes painful. They often appeal to the eucharist as the symbol of faith and unity of individuals who are increasingly ever more dispersed. They incarnate a Church that still resonates to the sound of the Gospel of Jesus Christ but that is no longer able to translate into organization, structures, and institutions its awareness of its mission and the urgency of spreading the Good News upon which it is founded.

A diffuse system, a more fluid structure, a house open to all winds, the Church today evokes the confusion, the upheaval, and the improvisation of a Pentecost rather than a powerful fortress with well-marked entryways and well-guarded faithful. It still offers the sign of communion to those who recognize themselves linked by baptism in Jesus Christ, but it is difficult for it to find concrete forms of community, so strong is the hold of the parish model that has dominated for centuries. I find it impossible to say at the present time what sorts of communities threshold Christians need in order to come to the faith and to make it fruitful in them. The Church is, in my opinion, in the prefatory phase of the great debate officially opened at Vatican II. It will take several decades to give form to this historical phase and to organize it institutionally. After fifteen years of turmoil, it seems that the initiators and artisans of the Council are themselves tired and would like a respite, if not normalization, on many issues. Let us, however, guard against the temptation to withdraw or form a coterie. And let us guard against locking the catechumenate and all that is associated with it into such a perspective.

NOTES

1. Here are a few figures from a survey by the *Sofres-Nouvel Observateur* published on 20 January 1978: of 1000 people interviewed, 96% stated they had been baptized, 82% were Catholics, 3% Protestants, and 2% were of other religions.

2. Published in English under the title *France, Pagan?*, 1950.

3. Cf. Jean Delumeau, *Le christianisme peut-il mourir?*, Hachette, 1977.

4. Cf. Marie Heraud, *Croyances et incroyants en France, aujord'hui*, Le Centurion, 1977.

5. "Rituel du baptême des enfants enáge de scolarité. L'initiation chrétienne des enfants non baptisés en scolarité dans l'enseignement primaire," Paris AELF—Chalet-Terdy, 1977, p. 64.

6. Cf. "Les familles, l'Eglise, la foi," CNER dossier under the direction of G. Duperray, Centurion, 1973, p. 200.

7. Cf. "Manifeste de l'aumônerie catéchuménale," September 1973, and the booklet, "Nomades et Fidèles," 1977.

8. Cf. a periodical such as "Pomme d'Api" for children from three to six, and the Bavard-Presse series of periodicals.

9. Cf. J.-M. Domenach, "Le retour de tragique," Seuil, 197.

10. In too few parishes there is a ritual for the presentation of a child to the Church with the inscription of its name in a special register, baptism being deferred until later when the child will be able to choose for itself.

11. Cf. "Accueil-Rencontre No. 73-74. Préparation au Marriage," Rencontre Nationale, 1977.

12. "A l'écoute du Judïsme," CNER, Chalet, 1977; "Un seul Dieu, Tous Frères. Pour un dialogue chrétiens-musulmans," CNER, Chalet, 1975.

13. Cf. E. Germain, "L'héritage du déisme," in *Catéchèse*, no. 69, October 1977.

Therese Randolph, RSM

Preliminary Survey on the Catechumenate in America Today

Sister Therese Randolph, RSM, was a supervisor for Ministerial Formation in the Department of Theology of the Catholic University of America and was the project director for a study on the development of the catechumenate in the United States sponsored by the Bishops' Committee on Liturgy.

In August of 1977 the Bishops' Committee on the Liturgy began a study of the implementation of the *Rite of Christian Initiation of Adults* in dioceses in the United States. The project has two goals:

1. To gain an overall picture of the pastoral work in the process of adult initiation throughout the dioceses of the United States.

2. To develop and share various models of faith formation (Christian initiation) based on existing geographic, cultural and ethnic pluralities within the American Church.

Each diocesan liturgical office was invited by mail to participate in the study. Over 80 dioceses responded to the initial questionnaire with 35 indicating there was some work in adult initiation developing in their dioceses. Of these, 18 indicated an interest in participating in the study. Previous experience in developing the adult initiation process; the need for cultural, geographic and ethnic representation; and the financial resources available, led to the choice of the following dioceses for more intensive study: Pueblo, CO, Denver, CO, Kansas City-St. Joseph, MO, Chicago, IL, Richmond, VA, and Washington, DC.

A notice about the project in the USCC Department of Education Newsletter, NEXUS, in December of 1977 brought letters of interest from additional (40) diocesan education offices. Follow-up on this will add 3 or 4 dioceses to the study process.

The study was conducted through an initial visit to the dioceses by the project director, a questionnaire seeking extensive information about each parish program, and a follow-up spring visit to collect the data. Parishes were asked to share all materials used in their catechumenate work. The following observations come from the experience of the first visit and a preliminary questionnaire response.

The following elements seem to be "prerequisites" for the development of a catechumenate in a parish. They existed in some form in all of the parishes involved.

1. Group Effort. Perhaps inherent in the communitarian vision of the document, it takes the shared vision of at least two or three people to work adequately with the catechumenate process. Minimally, this is pastor/religious educator, often it is these plus lay leadership from the parish who form the nucleus of staff for the program.

2. Commitment to Process. The RCIA presents a challenging vision of a complex process by which an adult would be initiated into the Church. It demands relinquishment of the priest/convert, one-to-one instruction and the inquiry class model. Where the RCIA is successfully developed, there is a serious willingness to work at the growth of all its elements—prayer, catechesis, community involvement, individual direction, etc.

In addition to these dispositions, common elements emerged in the programs of adult formation as they were developed in the participating parishes.

1. Sponsor Role. Individual, couple, family, or group sponsors are the primary key to the integration of the candidate into the parish community. As participants in the formation process, their relationship to the candidate facilitates mutual sharing as a Christian life style is embraced. This ministry is one of several developing as the RCIA is being implemented. Others include: the welcome and witness of the community itself, god-parents, prayer leaders and groups, witnesses to personal faith, catechists, and the ministry of the catechumens themselves.

2. Time of Formation. Most programs are operating on a schedule that begins with pre-catechumenate experience in the early fall (August/September). In this schema, entrance into the catechumenate comes in early Advent, the Rite of Election on the first Sunday of Lent, the Sacraments of Initiation at the Easter Vigil and concludes the mystagogic period with Pentecost. This school-year model enables the formation to be integrated with other catechetical programs and focuses on the most active period of parish life. This is not to say it is without problems, but it is very common.

3. Background of Candidates. Initial evidence indicates that candidates come from a variety of religious backgrounds: non-baptized, baptized but not catechised, baptized and active in non-Catholic faith community, baptized as a non-Catholic but active in the local parish through family ties. No matter what their background, the candidates generally take part in the same formation programs with individual conferences meeting their specifically different needs. Rituals are generally adapted to fit the variety of backgrounds. Most professions of faith presently take place at the Easter Vigil due to the community experience the candidates have shared through the formation process.

□ □ □

Given these noticeably similar characteristics, it is now helpful to look at areas of clear divergence among the participating parishes. The following seems important for future development.

1. *Different Time Frames.* Some programs are being developed which utilize an 18-month period and some a six-month process. The latter exists in highly mobile communities such as a military base.

2. *Dismissal of Catechumens.* Perhaps no issue has such emotional support, both pro and con, as this directive from the RCIA. Those parishes who choose not to do this cite ecumenical concerns and the sense of isolation that may result as their main reasons. Those who do express the value it has for the rest of the community and the need to do catechetical work with the candidate after the dismissal.

3. *Confirmation.* There is some diversity about the practice of confirming the newly baptized adult. A number of parishes choose to wait for the Bishop to do this. They desire the new members to have an experience of the wider church. Others provide this opportunity for a sense of diocesan church by some step in the preparation process. They then confirm as an integral part of the initiation rite.

4. *Cultural Differences.* The following general directions are found:

a. In the Black parishes there seems to be greater efforts at evangelization and seeking new membership. There is often work with non-Catholic families using the parish school. The catechumenate is characterized by its strong sense of community, its freedom to adapt to individual needs, and its struggle to separate cultural and faith values in the catechetical process.

b. In suburban parishes the catechumenate is noted for its well-planned program, its emphasis on catechesis, its efforts to integrate this work with other parish programs, and its candidates who have often been "in the parish" for years.

c. In Hispanic parishes the true catechumens are often of non-Spanish origins. The use of the catechumenate for those baptized, but not catechised in the faith is developing rapidly in many Hispanic communities.

The foregoing remarks illustrate the present state of the implementation of the RCIA in the U.S. As the full data for the study will not be available until late summer, 1978, they are based on the initial visit to each diocese and a small amount of written information about the situations. Based on the experience so far, the following issues emerge as important for the future direction of the development of the initiation process.

1. *Criteria for Membership.* Each staff person representing the Church community in the process of formation uses some criteria, often not verbalized, to discern with the candidate, his or her readiness for the sacraments of initiation. There is a tension in practice as well as theory between minimalist criteria for being Christian and the maximalist criteria. In a strongly plural church this question is heightened.

2. *Person vs. Program.* Related to the above issue is the tension between the need to program and structure a process of formation and the need to respect the individuality of the faith journey each person is engaged in. The growing use of individual conferences for a kind of "spiritual direction" helps in this issue. It is important to a vision of what the initiation process entails and a commitment to the principles of the RCIA. It is equally important to have the flexibility that respects each person's differing rate of development.

3. *Liturgical Adaptation.* There is a need for more extensive work in adapting the rites of the RCIA. It may be necessary to develop parallel rites for those already baptized who participate in the formation process.

4. *Parish Renewal Focus.* There is a tension also between the clear focus of the use of the RCIA in the initiation of adult converts and the focus on it as it relates to general parish renewal or to other sacramental experiences. The choice of direction will be important for the future of the Church. The former focus will lead, in time, to the latter. A parish renewal/child-sacramentality orientation may be so broad as to lose the intense experience the initiation process is meant to provide.

5. *Charismatic Community.* Some study will be necessary of the relationship between the RCIA and the growth of the pentecostal/charismatic communities in the Church. As the latter use their own initiation process in various ways, an interchange between the two movements will be valuable.

These and many other issues will provoke crises of development as the rather small catechetical experiment grows. The ability of people to share their experience and reflective dialogue about it are essential elements of further development. The model of initiation with its theological foundations provided in the RCIA clearly contributes a framework for an adult-centered response to the gift of faith.

Virgil Elizondo

The Catechumen in the Hispanic Community of the United States

Virgil Elizondo is President of the Mexican American Cultural Center in San Antonio, Texas. He has a master's degree in religious sciences from the University of Manila and his doctorate in theology from the Institut Catholique in Paris. He has published extensively on the theme of Christianity and culture.

Since the greater number of the Hispanic Catholics in the United States are baptized, we will limit our remarks to the baptized catechumen who is one of the *fideles* who has not yet fully heard or responded to the mystery of Christ. (Cf. *Rite of Christian Initiation of Adults*, 295). There seems to be general agreement among the writers on the catechumenate that the ongoing conversion of the catechumen will take place in, through and towards the ecclesial community. The process is to be carried out by the whole church and the objective is to initiate and assist the catechumen into a deeper and more personal relationship with the local church and, in particular, the parish church.

In the RCIA and in other writings on this subject, it is presupposed that the local church and especially the parish church is the visible and tangible sign of the living mystery of Christ. It is too quickly presupposed that regular church going and contributing persons ARE the community of faith, hope and charity who are living out the Christian life in the midst of today's world. This should indeed be the case, but in many instances it is not. Due to various historical and cultural reasons, in relation to the Hispanic people, the typical U.S. Catholic parish, rather than being the sign of the mystery of Christ, has been its antithesis—it has been more an obstacle to faith than an invitation of Christ.

A. The Hispanic in the U.S.

It is estimated that there are sixteen million Hispanics living in the U.S. and it is evident from the demographic and immigration data that this is the fastest growing minority in the U.S. By the mid-1980's it is projected, there will be thirty million Hispanics in the country. Spanish is rapidly becoming the second language of the U.S. Approximately 25% of all U.S. Catholics are Hispanics. The group is composed of various subgroupings; the two largest are the Mexican American and the Puerto Rican. These two groups did not *migrate* into the United States, but rather became a part of the new cultural-political orbit when the United States, expanded its boundaries to include Puerto Rico and half of the Republic of Mexico.

The Catholics of these two regions likewise found themselves subjected to a new expression of the Catholic faith. Because of various historical reasons, the tradition of Catholic faith of Latin America has been quite different from the tradition of Catholic faith which has been developing in the U.S. with its emphasis on institutional belonging, Sunday church attendance, clerical control and Americanization. This faith tradition similarly has been different from that of Europe in the last century when rationalization, secularization and laicization have prevailed. The emphasis in the Latin American tradition had been on a religion of the heart through personal devotions, home religious practices—"religion casera" ("home religion")—and massive celebration of the key moments of Paschal Mystery. The symbolic has always played a key role in the religious traditions of the Latin American. The absence of presence of clergy appears to have made little noticeable difference in the Catholic faith of the Latin American people. While North Americans have experienced "church belonging" by identifying with a specific parish, the Latin American has experienced "church belonging" simply by being a Latin American.

To understand the Hispanic peoples in the United States, it is important to emphasize that the colonization process of Latin America proceeded in a way radically different from that of North America. In the United States, any type of race mixture between the European newcomers and the native inhabitants of this land, and later on with the Blacks, was strictly forbidden by law. The legal term for the offspring of any such union was. *bastard*; there is no polite or proper way of speaking of a child who was born of Indian and European parents. The evangelization of the natives was never the primary motive in the formation of the U.S. The U.S., furthermore, has been fundamentally a Protestant, Anglo-Saxon, White purist and English speaking country. The colonization of Latin America, conversely, proceeded in a totally different way so as to give rise to a totally different collective personality. From the very beginning, the biological and cultural mixture of the two races started and was encouraged. Even though there has been and continues to be much racial preference in Latin America, the reality of race-mixture continues to produce new mestizo groups.

Furthermore, the evangelization of the native inhabitants was undertaken as one of the two primary goals of the crown. The colonizers did not come to form a biblical kingdom for themselves, with an attitude of "to hell with the Indians," as had been the case in North America, but they came to form a biblical kingdom precisely among the natives and often the missionaries tried, without much success, to keep the Spaniards out so as not to contaminate the native inhabitants. The Spaniards took their own salvation for granted and it was the salvation of others which pre-occupied them. This process gave rise to a new and very rich human group—the Latin American of today who is a mestizo in every sense of the word: biologically, culturally, religiously, linguistically.

Even though the general language of Latin America is Spanish (or Portugese for Brazil), the mindsets are not those of

Spain. Many of the traits and the world vision of the indigenous have become part of the Latin American *personalité de base* of today. The Latin American who is the catechumen is the biological and cultural mixture of Europeans, Native inhabitants, and the Africans who came in the early stages of the colonization. The offspring of this race mixture proudly see themselves as La Raza but, they are often looked down upon in the U.S. as a mongrel race. The famous Mexican writer, Octavio Paz, has called the meeting between the two Americans as the frontier between absolute otherness. The basic personality of the Latin American tends to be the exact opposite of that of the U.S.: *Catholic* in a rich *mestizaje* of the Spanish Catholicism of the sixteenth century and the indigeous religions of this land; *mestizo* in a blending of European, native and African; *Brown* and *Spanish speaking*.

The Hispanic in the United States, furthermore, suffers much the same lot as do the masses of the people in Latin America: poverty, illiteracy and exploitation. From the very first contacts with the United States, the racially conscious U.S. immigrants into Mexican territory looked down upon the Mexicans because they were mestizos and Catholic, inheritors of two bad races, the Spanish and the Indian. With the elimination of slavery in the United States, a new institution had to be set up to guarantee the presence of cheap labor which could easily be exploited by the farmers and ranchers. Thus, the Mexican peon took the place of the Black slave. Illiteracy was instituted into the school systems of the South and the Southwest of the United States to insure a permanent presence of semi-illiterate workers who could continue the work of the slaves without making trouble. Even Catholic seminaries did not allow Mexicans to enter and religious congregations allowed them only to become working brothers and lay sisters.

The stereotypes which the white dominant group has set up, perpetuated and transmitted in relation to the Mexican have always been bad—"Mexicans are lazy, dumb, irresponsible, drunk, dirty . . ," while in reality the Mexican has been willing to do the hard, back-breaking work that no Anglo would undertake. The intelligence of the people has been verified by the achievements of the various members of the group; their responsibility has been proven in numerous ways, especially during World War II when the Hispanics, according to percentage, were the most highly decorated group in the U.S. armed services. In spite of the subhuman conditions to which the people, especially the migrant workers, are condemned to live, they are usually very clean. Yet the stereotypes continue to be perpetuated in multiple ways because they serve to hide the real causes of poverty and illiteracy: the greed and racism of those in control of the power establishment.

In discussing the situation of the catechumen vis-a-vis the Church, it is necessary to say that the Church itself has contributed to this ongoing and downgrading segregation by not making the effort to understand and welcome these people as they enter into its ranks. The institution has even told the Mexican Catholic directly, "Go away! This is not *your* Church!" It has often demanded that Mexicans become Anglo Americans before they can be allowed into regular practice. Brown faces have not appeared in religious visuals. Hispanic religious practices have often been scorned by uninformed clergy who tend to see them as superstitious. Our most sacred devotion, devotion to Our Lady of Guadalupe, was often omitted from religious texts as "that Mexican devotion"; only the "true" devotions, such as those of Fatima, Lourdes, and others, were spoken about. "The White madonnas are OK, but the Brown madonna is that backward Mexican stuff!" The institutional Church has not radiated the image of Christ who welcomes all, especially the most rejected of society. This is the historical and socio-human situation of the catechumen who is the subject of discussion today.

B. Evangelized? Sacramentalized? Catechized? Ecclesialized?

It has been frequently stated that the people of Latin America have been sacramentalized, but not evangelized. Contrary to the opinion of many, I do not believe this is the case. The people have been evangelized, but they have not been sacramentalized. They have been merely ritualized. Neither have they been catechized, for, at best, they have been indoctrinated with meaningless formulas and they have not been ecclesialized—merely institutionalized.

The evangelization of Latin America is one of the greatest moments in the missionary history of the Church. In spite of the great geographical distances and the great diversity of languages and countless other obstacles, the missioners were able to implant the Gospel into a great portion of what is today the Americas: from the Southwest of the United States to the tip of South America. The great Christian symbols of God, Christ, Mary, the Saints, and the key moments of the Paschal Mystery are functional symbols in much of Latin America and certainly in Mexico and among the Hispanics of the United States. The full implications of the meaning of these symbols (the explaining mythology) might not always be too clear or even known explicitly, but the symbols are really symobls in the lives of the people.

The people and the cultures were so effectively evangelized by the early missioners who first brought the faith to the peoples of this part of the world that the cultural expressions themselves have been the most effective transmitters of the personal knowledge and appreciation of Jesus Christ as "the Lord of My Life." Through the cultural celebrations of the principal moments of the Paschal Mystery, the people have entered in a vicarious way way into the foundational experience of the first Christian group. Through these celebrations, the people have experienced a Christian sense of belonging because they have shared a common experience. The principal moments of the Mystery of Christ have become living symbols for the people. They have not just heard about the various moments of the Mystery of Christ, but they have personally lived them with the other members of the community though the collective reenactments of these moments—Posadas, Noche Buena, Semana Santa, Pentecostes, Dia de los Muertos, y Cristo Rey. Thus, the Christian creed has not been transferred in a merely cerebral way, but in a total living way which involves the collective experience of the believing group. The positive aspect of this evangelizing process through the cultural expressions—which themselves were developed by the missioners so as to evangelize—is that the most important aspects of the Mystery of Christ become living symbols in the lives of the persons and the group. They are transmitted to the newcomer by the whole group. This is the context of the potential catechumenate for the Mexican American.

The difficulties or deficiencies with the Latin American tradition of faith is not at the level of evangelization, but at the other three levels of the process. The first of these is initiation into the sacraments. Except for the period of the original catechumenate, the sacraments and the sacramentals have been dispensed in a mechanical and commercial way. Often, the people have not gone to the sacraments because they were convinced that they could not afford them and when they did receive them, it was in a very mechanized, magic-like and commercial manner. The sacraments have thus not been the dynamic moments when the believing person, through the medium of a visible and tangible reality, enters into direct experience of the invisible and the ultimate. The people have often found more sacramental meaning in their sacramentals than in the official sacraments of the official church because the official sacraments have been reduced to a mere clerical ritual, rather than experienced as the dynamic moments of encounter with the Lord which celebrate the various moments of the ongoing process of evangelization. The people have hardly ever participated in the proper ecclesial celebration of the sacraments and have taken part only in the rituals of the clerical institution. In such a system, the sacraments appear to have little or nothing to do with the process of evangelization. "If they work *ex opere operato*, then why worry about evangelization?"

Catechized? Catechesis as the ongoing penetration into the meaning and implications of the Christian mystery has not really taken place. The people have been given a few formulas of superficial indoctrination, but they have not been helped to enter into an adult and mature reflection on the meaning of their faith. True catechesis will be the continuing task of the theological reflection of the Christian community—faith seeking understanding. Without this ongoing theological reflection which is, in effect, catechesis, religious education or catechetical programs may give much knowledge, but they will not effect the growth in faith which catechesis intends to accomplish.

Finally, we may say that the people have been institutionalized, but never really ecclesialized because the structures of the Church and the hierarchy of the Church have remained totally foreign to the people. Native vocations have not been encouraged and many times have been forbidden and discouraged. The truly local and particular churches, thus, have not been allowed to emerge—churches which holistically incorporate the art, music, wisdom, philosophy, customs, traditions and language of the people. Until this emergence takes place, the people will be *institutionalized* in various ways, but they will not be *ecclesialized* because the local assembly of believers will never come together as a truly local assembly. If there is no local assembly of believers, the Church will continue to appear as something foreign, rather than the incarnated presence of Christ who has truly become one of us so that as our Brother, he might invite us to the kingdom of our Father.

Father Alfonso Nebreda, Director of the East Asian Pastoral Institute and an expert on the process of faith and the catechumenate, on his frequent visits to the United States has often stated that by every rational standard, the Mexican and the Hispanic people in the United States should not only not be in the Church, but they should be very bitter against the Church, yet the mystery of faith is that even though many are leaving the Church, many more still want to be an active part of the Church, if only the Church is willing to accept them and make them feel welcome in terms understandable to them. In spite of all the external obstacles, it is the profoundly personal and personalizing nature of the faith of the Hispanic which has maintained him in the church in spite of the multiple obstacles. This dynamic and deeply personal belief in the various aspects of the Christian mystery is not just a type of implicit cultural faith, but a living force which continues to animate not only the poets, artists and singers, but likewise the lives of the ordinary persons. The conviction that "I live in the presence of the living God with whom I can easily converse" runs very deep in the lives of the Hispanic Christians in the U.S.

Even though the faith symbols of the Hispanic of the U.S. are similar to those of the Latin American Catholics, they do not function in the same way for the simple reason that in Latin America they are the popular faith symbols of the majority of the people, while in the U.S. they are the faith symbols of a small minority group which is struggling to survive as a people—with its religion and its culture—while a strong dominant group is trying to destroy in multiple ways through ethnocide and conversion from our Latin American Catholicism to the U.S. Catholicism—as did those who tried to make the Greek Christians become Jewish Christians so that they could become fully Christian. It is in and through the collective celebration of these faith symbols that the people experience their deepest identity, unity and sense of belonging. They are not understood, and often ridiculed, even by clergy, yet they are the final language of resistance of a conquered and oppressed people who continue to refuse to be religiously or culturally dominated by the majority group.

Because of the failures of the U.S. Catholics to welcome, appreciate and minister in a truly catholic way to Hispanic Catholics, many are moving to active and dynamic ecclesial life in other Christian denominations. Ten years ago we were saying comfortably that 85% of the Hispanic in the U.S. were Catholics. Today, we can at best say that 75% of them are Catholics. The Hispanic is not leaving the Catholic Church freely, he/she is still being chased out by pastors and parishes who do not want them around. Many are being de-churched by the church herself. There are certainly marvelous exceptions to this accusation, but the tragedy is that they are the exceptions and not the ordinary case. Many of the Hispanic Catholics are discovering warmth, dynamic prayer life, knowledge of the Scriptures and a sense of belonging in the growing number of Hispanic Protestant churches. In the case of the Hispanic, it is often the Protestants who are providing the personal catechumenate programs, while the Catholic church is still chasing them out by refusing to pray, sing, teach and celebrate in the culture and language of the people. In many instances, the U.S. Catholic church is still insisting more on conversion from the Hispanic Culture into the U.S. Anglo-Saxon-Protestant based culture than in conversion to Christ within the Hispanic culture itself.

The Hispanic Catholic, like every Christian, is certainly in need of ongoing evangelization and catechesis, and that he is sometimes not receiving this ministry is not the fault of the Catholic Church in the U.S. alone. In the best of parishes, there are many who will not respond. Yet, in parishes where there is a healthy parish life animated by good organizations and a dynamic liturgical life, the active participation of the Hispanic people is phenomenal. Wherever the Church is going out to the people and ministering to them in ways that are familiar to them, the people are responding in great numbers. At this moment of history, our people will want to be good Christian Catholics and will respond well to programs that do not force them to go through a type of cultural ethnocide in order to take part in the activities of the Church.

In the light of this brief description of the experience of Catholicity in the Mexican American community, one can see some of the particularisms an effective catechumante would exhibit. Catechesis must come through the popular faith expressions present in this community; it is here that the interpenetration of the divine and the human is experienced by this faith group. Surely the Mexican American will be led to the experience of the post-Vatican institutional Church with its openness, its recognition of the dignity of the individual, its reverence for the truth of each culture. But these very qualities should enable the institutional Church to allow itself to be enriched by the people's Church of the Mexican American.

The Church will include in its search for new symbols of contemporary Catholic faith those symbols, however vaguely understood, which have sustained the faith of the Mexican American. In its diversified whole, it will affirm the vibrant, centuries-old faith expressions with the same welcome as it has for the newly Christianized nations. It will, in creative and liberating ways, indigenize this mestizized Church and rejoice in its growth as the power of the Spirit brings it to the full stature God intends for it, trusting that the new and the old will be a part of the treasure of a contemporary catechumenate.

Suggestions for a Catechumenate Program for the Whole Church by the Whole Church

1. The U.S. Church, especially the local parish, must make a radical conversion so as to truly become servant and be the dynamic image of the living Christ who did not hesitate to begin by converting totally to the local people among whom he was to begin his mission: Jesus the Galilean from Nazareth. Jesus became one of the "little ones" of his society, one of the marginated, despised and rejected, so that along with the "little ones" of his society he might counter the culture, values and status of the dominant and established groups. By becoming one in every way with the "little ones" of today's U.S. society, by enjoying their foods and their festivals, by appreciating their values and customs, by speaking their language and valuing their religious practices, by taking part in their struggle for justice, the U.S. Catholic Church will be welcoming those who for too long have been rejected by the Church, for in rejecting them, the Church has rejected Christ. (Cf. Mt. 25:31-46.)

2. There is a need to revitalize the parish so as to make it the center of life for the people of the neighborhood—with senior citizen programs, pre-school programs, political meetings which concern the people of the area, religious education at various levels, groups to help the undocumented people and others who are having troubles with the law. The parish must be seen and experienced by the people, not just as the place where sacraments and Mass are dispensed, but truly as the center of their life. Only then will the liturgies become fully alive and attractive to the people.

3. The parish needs to develop an ongoing program of evangelization which will be directed:

a. To everyone—the masses of the people—through the full, festive and dramatized celebrations of the key moments of the liturgical cycle.

b. To the ordinary church-going group. On Sundays and special events it will be important to bring out the cultural implications of the liturgical events and scripture readings and to celebrate liturgically the cultural events of the community—there is an ongoing need to culturalize the liturgy and to liturgize the culture—to bring out the human meaning of the divine and the divine meaning of the human.

c. To those who show special interest and need. The Church must invite and encourage as many as possible to take part in such programs as Cursillo, CEB, MFC, Jornadas de Juventud, Bible study groups, prayer groups.

d. To lay leadership. The Church must especially invite those who exhibit leadership abilities to take part in programs which prepare for Christian ministry.

e. To clerical and religious leadership. The Church must encourage vocations and help seminaries and seminary faculties to also convert, for they have too often been and continue to be the greatest obstacle to the building up of a truly local church—they force out any one who is not exactly like them.

f. To priestly leadership. The Church must ordain more bishops from among the people. If there are not enough qualified priests, then some qualified laity should be called to the episcopacy. This will not be anything new since in our Latin American Christian tradition, some of our best bishops were laymen at the time they were named bishops (e.g., Vasco de Quiroga). Only when there are "Fathers" from among the people—Bishops—will local church truly flourish.

Teresita Weind, SND

The Black Catechumen

Sister Teresita Weind, SND, has her master's degree in theology from Mundelein College, Chicago, and is currently Adult Religious Education Coordinator/Black Parishes for the Archdiocese of Chicago.

In the face of the opposition, rejection, oppression, and well-meaning ignorance that often marks the Roman Catholic community in certain instances as a racist institution, the American Black, particularly the Northern Urban Black, has sustained a real hope for the future of redemption and liberation for both the oppressed and the oppressor. Today's catechumens, the aspirants and candidates for full, active, participating membership in the Catholic Church, can effectively influence the beginnings of new relationships for the future.

The American Black has been the victim of discrimination and hatred and has been forced for the most part to include the Catholic clergy, religious, and laity among his enemies. Bound and imprisoned by mistrust and fear, too many of us have learned how to hate and have been caught up for decades in the vicious cycle of returning evil for evil, wrong for wrong, and sin for sin. None of this is a part of the morality of the Gospel nor of the values of those who dare to follow the Way of the Man who constructed a new covenant of love. Jesus' steady and firm demand of those who desire to join his family is conversion, change of heart. Concretely and sociologically speaking, this is an invitation for the American Black to break the cycle of hatred and revenge and to turn to the building of relationships based on respect and reverence for difference, equality, and human dignity. Our sin-sick oppression has blinded us to the good within ourselves and that of our own race. We are burdened with self-hatred, not always conscious, but still expressive of much of our behavior. When we can't strike directly at the oppressor, we work out our anger on each other, warping our personalities, our culture, our souls. This is precisely what happened when Dr. Martin Luther King, Jr., our prophet, our speaker-for-God, was assassinated. We burned our own neighborhoods.

Hatred destroys whatever it touches, and particularly the one who hates.

The Blacks have no monopoly, we must remember, on being exploited and oppressed. Perhaps, our color is an advantage for we do not blend so easily into the anonymous background as does the Appalachian white, the brown migrant worker, or even the middle class dropout and reject. Black can be seen, and therefore can give more effective witness.

The very first step we have to take—and this is not a new idea, but it needs to be repeated again and again—in our effort to destroy hatred, is to change our attitudes about ourselves. We must affirm our worth and sing over and over again about where our soul is anchored. Our soul is anchored in the Lord, the Lord of life and of love, of feeling and emotion, of rhythm and movement, of passion, yearning and desire, of birth and death, of the pregnant life-forces vibrating in the universe and ourselves. Our soul is anchored in the Lord who, in the words of James Weldon Johnson, "scooped up a lump of clay in His hands, and like a black mammy bending over her baby, breathed life (His own life) into its nostrils, and said, 'That's good!' "

The Black American catechumen must begin the steps of initiation with the resounding acclamation, "It is good to be black, beautiful, different, ecstatic, soulful, and anchored in the Lord!" Every stage thereafter, every rhythm and cycle made public by liturgical celebration will be another opportunity to testify to the deepening and the growth of this process of conversion, this expulsion of self-hatred.

It can be neither the goal nor the intention of the American Black to be integrated into a white, racist Church community. That community must be redeemed. Difficult though it will be, the Black catechumen is called to usher in a new society where love operates as the unifying force, where the sense of family and the conscious feeling of belonging supports cooperative effort against economic and social injustice, where evangelical faith remains "the assurance of things hoped for, and the conviction of things not yet seen"in overcoming hatred and evil (Heb. 11:1).

Not without tension and tears, then, will the American Black catechumen continue the struggle "to pluck up and break down, to destroy and to overthrow" (Jer 1:10) the middle class values of competition, aggression, rugged individualism, and economic exploitation. With the purifying and transforming fire of biblical prophecy, it will become clearer and clearer that what has often created racism in the Catholic community is the malignancy of blind egoism ultimately refusing to accept the other as other or even to note his or her existence.

The presence of Black Catholics and Black catechumens, growing continuously in this liberating and affirmative self-image, is a redemptive gift to the Roman Catholic Church in America. She must decide whether to accept or reject this opportunity to be freed from her crippled past.

Conversion shatters the syndrome of hate and revenge. It will become increasingly difficult for anyone to oppress us once we learn how to love. Every victory of love over hatred is a victory of life over death, of justice over injustice, of equality over inequality. With this love, justice, and equality, the Catholic Church in America will begin to look and act differently. This new posture and presence will be something to sing about, laugh about, cry about, shout about. And it can be preached in that rousing and rhythmic poetic form that is Black preaching. And the people will answer "Amen!" For the Catholic Church with its Black members will be proclaiming the Good News of saving love that embraces and unconditionally accepts every human being regardless of race, color, social or economic status. It forgives the sins they have committed and the sins committed against them.

The task is arduous and the journey is long, but this is the only authentic Gospel reason for the American Black to become a catechumen in the Catholic Church. The Church, too, must be redeemed.

Throughout its history, the American Black community has worked out nearly every aspect of its social, cultural, political, and economic situation within a church community. If this tradition can be applied to and envelop the Catholic Church, then the Catholic community, with her Black members and leaders, could well become the agent for change in those areas of life where the scars of history and the perversions of society still warp Black—and white—families.

Abused children, miseducated and mistreated, emasculated men, exploited and dehumanized, battered women, insulted and raped, will finally be able to discover new images of themselves and, indeed, new selves that are blessed and made holy in the eyes of the Lord and in their own eyes. The Catholic Church will then be able to stand proud in a world of injustice, of war, of exploitation for she will have earned the credibility the Lord promised her. She will be recognized as the teacher, the prophet, the healer of the sin-sick, hate-filled soul. With her own racism healed and atoned for—but not forgotten—she will become the "wounded healer," the "suffering servant," and will move again with the power to make whole.

Songs will be written and sung about her, dances will be created and danced for her, and souls will overflow with joy and happiness at the presence of the Incarnate God.

We will be able to sing with Delores Kendrick:

> What glory is yours, O Lord,
> For you have brought me out of Egypt
> Into the quiet land.
> The night is ended.
> All the demons have fled,
> Though they have rubbed their backs

Against the bed of my dreams.

I awake singing
Though they have left their footstains
On the edge of my night's memory.

I have come back from the death of sleep
    to the light of life
    borne in you
    born in you
    back from the dead I come
Resurrected in the God of Promise
    the Lord of Endurance
    and the Christ of Joy.
And in the thinness of my dreams
In the powerlessness of myself
I am given you again.

William A. Bauman

An Experience of an
Urban Parish In the Midwest

*William A. Bauman, a priest of the Diocese of
Kansas City, Missouri, is the Director of the
Center for Pastoral Ministry in Kansas City. He is
the author of* Lent and the New Holy Week, To-
gether at Confirmation, *and* The Ministry of
Music.

INTRODUCTION

St. Stephen's Parish is a small urban parish established 70
years ago in the northeast section of Kansas City. Originally
founded by the Irish, it is now multi-ethnic with a predomi-
nance of Mexican, Polish, and Italian nationalities. Within these
groups there is the strong practice of infant baptism so they
tend not to be interested in the catechumenate. Instead, the
catechumens tend to be a universal sampling of lower and middle income families from the area, from the poorer area near
downtown Kansas City, and from the nearby rural Ozarks
population.

The catechumenate developed in St. Stephen's Parish as part
of a three-parish team ministry in 1972. The religious education
component was developed in the 1970-72 school year under
the direction of Sr. Therese Randolph and served four parishes
in the area. Previous convert work had been sporadic and need-
responsive. From the first session prepared for the Easter Vigil
1972 on through and including the Easter Vigil 1978, the pro-

gram continued to develop and in these seven years prepared 113 catechumens for entry into the church at the Easter Vigil, 51 of whom are from St. Stephen's and personally known to me as pastor. These are the sample that will be the basis of the paper.

Having given up the pastorate at St. Stephen's in January, 1978, in favor of establishing a Diocesan Center for Pastoral Ministry, I cannot but observe that the most significant cause of real and lasting renewal in my eight years at St. Stephen's was in fact built around the sacraments of initiation. In this grouping the catechumenate was the model and the leader. To be able to stand in the midst of an overflowing church at the Easter Vigil (1977) and after nine baptisms and eleven confirmations turn to the people and say, "Now it is our turn ..."and know that they were with us in their understanding of church and salvation—was indeed a significant experience in my own faith life.

AN ANALYSIS OF ST. STEPHEN'S CATECHUMENS

I will first try to give some hard data on these individuals for our reflection; then, in a later section, share some of my own reflections and conclusions.

Over these seven years a remarkably high percentage of our catechumens have truly been catechumens—the unbaptized numbered 54%. On the other hand, 44% came to our program already baptized in a Protestant community. Less than one-fourth of these latter had any significant uncertainties about their baptism which would cause serious consideration of conditional baptism. Catholics from birth numbered 2% but were never raised in the faith or confirmed. With the exception of three individuals who came with very strong Protestant active membership, I never had any misgivings about mixing the baptized with the unbaptized in the program. The degree of being "churched" was identical regardless of baptism or non-baptism.

Often the baptized had only experienced a Protestant church for a few weeks while the unbaptized might have had three years of education and participation. Over 90% of the total had a knowledge of the Scriptures equal to that of our average Catholic members. When it was clearly called for we never baptized conditionally in public; this was done privately earlier in the day. At the Easter Vigil all professed their faith, were clothed in white, and were confirmed, and, of course, the unbaptized were baptized. To further distinguish the groups would have been offensive to the baptized, making them feel somewhat "left out." First, the summary of facts is this:

54%—never experienced Baptism
    44%—significant protestant experiences
    10%—totally unchurched

44%—previously baptized protestant
    6%—strongly active in protestant church
  28%—significant protestant experience
  10%—totally unchurched except for baptism.

Secondly, we can break down the catechumens by age. The total age range was 7 to 85 years old. I have chosen the following categories on the presumption that a child under 16 is entering as part of a family; that prior to age 25, a wide variety of family and marriage facts, conformity, revolt, idealism, etc. are at work making the results a bit uncertain and independent of the program; that ages 25-40 is a period of serious choices and significant changes of direction in life; that 40-60 is a very solid and self-determined era; that over 60 may well be finally taking time to do what one felt called to long ago. It may be presumptuous, but the people in the categories tend to confirm these observations. In our situation the age groups in the catechumenate broke down as follows:

21%—under age 16
38%—age 16-25
19%—age 25-40
10%—age 40-60
12%—over age 60.

My third subdivision is based on marital status. The first fact is the hardest on pastors: 32% of all catechumens need marriage cases—and one person required four cases (two for her two previous marriages and two for her Catholic spouse's two previous marriages). Here are the general categories:

22%—preparing to marry a Catholic
16%—married a Catholic in the last two years
16%—married to an active Catholic for more than two years
12%—married to an inactive Catholic for more than two years
20%—pre-marriage, too young
6%—post marriage (widow, divorced)
8%—couple enters Church together

A few comments on the above statistics. The premarriage problem is one with which a catechumenate must deal. We tried first to clearly separate the two actions (marrying a spouse and entering a church) and generally with good results. The non-Catholic was grateful for the clear choice and did not want to rush his/her entrance into the church or feel that there was pressure. The results were about the same whether the couple then chose to prepare (from September to April) to enter the Church before a summer wedding, or chose to marry and then return in the second or third year of marriage. The problem arises where the Catholic spouse is a nominal Catholic and insists on hurrying the other into the Church with no intention of then practicing the faith. Without a strong legalism and rigidity, I know of no way to stop this, but the results are disastrous in most cases.

On the other hand some of our strongest converts are the spouses of non-practicing Catholics. They want to do something for their family. They struggle to learn a new religion. The spouse remains non-practicing for several years or forever, but the convert becomes a parish leader and makes theirs a Christian home. Somehow, the Catholic spouse brings too much "baggage" along to be able to join in the spouse's new enthusiasm on the journey of faith.

In case you are interested in the division of such cases by sex, it is remarkably even. In our group it has been 54% female who wish to enter the Church and 46% male. In 1977 and 1978 the group has been 75% male which is something of a problem, since our sponsors who took training for this ministry are 90% female.

Finally, we can analyze our now baptized catechumens in terms of their present involvement in the church community:

44%—Highly active in worship, ministry, leadership;

40%—Practicing sacramental catholics, with varying degrees of re-occurrence of the nominalism so prevalent in the neighborhood;

16%—Have left the church and the sacraments.

Such statistics are both encouraging (many are the life of the parish, while before the catechumenate few if any rose to this level) and discouraging. I suppose some would judge our treatment of a few cases "lax" and yet in pastoral practice it seems so important not to set qualitative standards so high they exclude any person whom the Lord might be calling to His Church. There are questions of life style, of alcohol and drug problems, of mental health, that are disconcerting but real. And of course if entrance is only for the sake of marriage, exit is just as easy when the marriage fails.

SPECIAL NEEDS OF THE CATECHUMEN

If one were to look for the "marks" of the Church as they exist in the minds of the catechumens seeking entrance into the community, I would judge them to be *openness* and *completeness*. In our lower and middle class neighborhoods there is a constant procession of avid promoters of the more fundamentalist Protestant sects who continue a campaign of condemnation against the Roman Catholic Church and some of the main line Protestant groups.

On the east side of Kansas City nearly everyone who comes to us has experienced this both in propaganda and in preaching. They are attracted to a Church that is open, to a Church that never condemns another Church, to a Church that never condemns them. In our catechumenates we can carefully sort out all traces of elitism and relate well to our catechumens. They want to know why we believe in our Church but they hear an answer in terms of completeness ("I am a Catholic for in this religion I find a fullness of all the Scriptures and Jesus' teachings"). We do not want to judge the completeness of other denominations. This is often easier for staff and leaders but harder for sponsors who get so enthused about making this person a Catholic forever.

We have had good success in beginning with strong *affirmation*, letting the Scriptures, especially Isaiah, do the work for us. Our pre-evangelization starts with simply letting the catechumens-to-be hear the Lord say, "I love you." Self image is a big problem in our society and the person who comes to us searching will often have strong symptoms of worthlessness. These are not generally leaders of people; they are the *anawim* of today. Hearing that they count personally is the best thing that ever happened to them, like the preaching of Jesus in his time.

There is a certain body of *information* that is also needed. There has often been some mis-information conveyed which has been put aside and not corrected. Creating an atmosphere where they can seek correct information is important. There are certain common misconceptions about confession, about Mary and saints, that continue to endure (among Catholics and non-Catholics as well). There is little if any knowledge of the history of religious denominations. Before choosing to be a catechumen some information is certainly necessary.

The background of almost all our converts is fundamentalist. Therefore, we need a gentle but thorough easing into a deeper understanding of the *Scriptures*. Our catechumens love to use the Bible and two-thirds of them can find their way around in it. But they expect the single passage approach and need to be coaxed into accepting the message of God as it comes through the whole of Scripture. Different literary genres need to be explained and carefully presented form criticism as well. The need seems to be for a reverent introduction to the best of modern understandings of the Scriptures.

Our catechumens have a deep need for *community*. The catechumenate model is so well suited to the Church today in that it brings the growth process into a community model. Beyond the parish staff there are lay leaders sharing in the pro-

110

cess. There are as well, committed sponsors, public ceremonies of welcome and small communities of ministering Christians to which the newcomer will finally belong.

At first the converts were a close community, relating well with the team staff—often a better community than the parish. But with subsequent growth of ministry in the parish it becomes even more powerful to have converts explore the active ministries, choose one for themselves, and be ready when they are baptized to begin working with established parishioners among the poor, the elderly, the youth, families, the liturgy, etc.

Formation for liturgy is one of the catechumen's greatest needs. In many people's background, prayer is words of intercession. The use of sign and symbol is apt to become for them a tolerable ritual or even an act of magic unless there is prayer formation. We try in the spring semester to move strongly and clearly from information to formation and prayer is primary in the process. We begin to pray with simple objects and signs like a candle or water. By the time we come to Ash Wednesday we have prayed with burning palms and are ready to pray in action and in sign. By the time the Easter Vigil is celebrated every sign and symbol is familiar by actual use. This seems more significant than a theology of the sacraments which presumes an experience and may be more appropriate in post-baptismal catechesis. To gather in reverence and awe before the goodness of God and pray in sign and gesture is essential to a catechumen's formation.

A not uncommon need of the catechumen is the need for *privacy*, the need to be unnoticed in the crowd. I was alerted to the importance of this need when a couple of my converts quietly went elsewhere for private instructions. I knew how much they were missing, how much richer their life would be if they were integrated into our community. But they were afraid to read aloud, to share, to stand in front of an assembly. Maybe the decision to go elsewhere is the right one. Yet a certain sensitivity might accommodate them.

One girl was so shy we had to baptize her privately earlier on Holy Saturday. She was in the fourth pew that night (as far forward as she felt comfortable). Her mother put her white robe on

111

her at the baptism time so she could be identified at her first communion that evening.

For the main group courage grows through the year. When enrolled as catechumens, I place the group in the front pews (December). On the first Sunday of Lent at their Rite of Election they step forward. By the Easter Vigil they sit in special places, walk to the front, etc.

Finally, catechumens of today have a great need for new marriage policies and procedures in the Church. We simply cannot do significant evangelization if those invited are later to be judged unworthy for something they cannot now change. The presumptions about sacramental marriage must be shifted to put the burden of proof on us that a marriage that is gone is nevertheless a sacrament. We can't require our catechumens to provide many witnesses as if they were lying. This area is, of course, beyond our scope of endeavor but it is a real need for fully one-third of our catechumens.

In conclusion, I would like to suggest that we as local and simple church community—me especially and the people I have worked with in the parish—have a great need for a *simple terminology* that eliminates words like catechumenate, pre-evangelization, catechesis, mystagogia, etc. If our conference is to be pastoral let us help create a simple but uniform terminology that will allow many more to understand and appreciate the great tool we have in this community sharing of the Lord.

Albert J. Benavides

An Experience of a Large Urban Mexican-American Parish

A priest of the Archdiocese of San Antonio, Texas, Albert Benavides is pastor of St. Timothy parish in San Antonio. He has his master's degree in theology from St. Mary's University.

For the past eight years, I have served as a parish priest of the Archdiocese of San Antonio, Texas. During that time I have worked in two distinct parishes. One, St. John's which has a people mix of 70% Mexican-American, 29% Anglo-American, and 1% Black American. The other parish is St. Timothy which is 100% Mexican American.

I speak to you from that base and I speak to you about a very concrete experience. It is my intention to convey to you my reflections on the faith experience of which I have been part, an experience that has had as its nucleus reaching out to people in order to share with them the Christ of peace, the Christ of love, the Christ of freedom. This reaching has taken place in the only way I know and that is through the Christ of Community, the parish-church.

I refer to the parish as the Christ of Community because that is what it is and because that is what it must always endeavor to become. In San Antonio, as in most of South Texas (wherever—in fact—there are Spanish speaking peoples), the Mexican American Catholic relies on his/her Church not only to help fulfill that spiritual dimension that is part of all of us, but also to help fulfill that material and social dimension as well. The Mexican American Catholic comes to the Church not only on Sunday to worship with the faith community but also on Monday to seek help for an imprisoned friend or relative or assistance for a sick child.

On Tuesday they come to meet with a Church-Society; on Wednesday when there is no money to pay for utilities; on Thursday in order to settle a neighborhood or family dispute; on Friday when the food runs out, and on Saturday just to talk, celebrate, or perhaps even dance.

The Church, for the people I serve, is a worshiping Church, a teaching Church, a consoling Church, and a social church. This, to me, is important to understand. It becomes the arms through which the local Church reaches out and touches the lives of its people and becomes the way that people are catechized and evangelized.

The tragedy is that many times the Church refuses or denies its own role; many times the Church judges certain functions as being irrelevant or impertinent. Many times the Church sarcastically replies "I am not a social agency," "I am not a political body," "I am not a community organization"; and people are turned away. At other times alienation prevails instead of acceptance, resentment instead of affection. The basis for catechizing and evangelizing which is *acceptance* is obliterated and people walk away empty in heart, head, and hand. No wonder some never return, no wonder others take the symbols of their faith and culture to develop underground or backyard rituals.

I have often wondered why this happens and I have yet to come up with a complete or satisfying answer. But I will tell you this. Most of the people who come to our churches are what I would call catechumens; most of them are people who have not fully heard or responded to the mystery of Christ. They are people still very much in the process of conversion. But if our people are still in the process of conversion, that fact makes of us a catechumenate Church, itself very much in the process of conversion. While that fact might seem obvious to some and impossible to others, to me it is an essential fact because recognizing it begins to establish that acceptance necessary for catechizing and evangelizing.

When the parish church—the ecclesial community—recognizes and admits that it is also and always groping towards a fuller response to the mystery of Christ, then will we accept all people (as Jesus did) and all ways of reaching out to them (as Jesus did). Only then will the people who are the ecclesial community feel enough at home to share who they are and what they have. Only then will there be a basis for true evangelizing.

When I left St. John's Parish and arrived at St. Timothy's as its new pastor, I encountered a truly diverse situation. This parish is 100% Mexican American. Approximately 60% of its members fall below the United States poverty index. The other 40% are low to middle class civil service and maintenance workers. A full third of the parish lives in Government subsidized housing projects. There are also a plethora of social agencies serving the parish, agencies for the most part subsidized by the Federal Government.

The parish encompasses two independent school districts—one of which is the poorest in the nation. There are within the parish itself five primary, middle and secondary schools. As I became aware of all these facts and of all the facilities available I began to envision an alert, alive community coming together to care for its own needs.

I found in time that this was not so. The schools and all the agencies in the parish had little to do with the people of the area who felt little loyalty to any of them. The school taught their children, the agencies served those in need. And there the relationship ended! There was no involvement in the life of the people beyond giving the service expected.

It became clear to me that of all the institutions in the neighborhood, the only one to whom the people still felt bonds of loyalty was the Catholic Church. St. Timothy's was truly a neighborhood Center. But as I became aware of this fact I also became aware of certain feelings on the part of the people. A small nucleus of leaders—about 20 in all—felt dissatisfied with

115

their role in the Church. They wanted more of a say in running the church with fewer things imposed by either episcopal or clerical fiat. They wanted to help formulate policy—not just consent to it.

Another and larger group of people felt alienated and disenchanted. They wondered if the Church no longer cared about them, their culture, or their traditions. They came because they cared; but it was no longer a joyful experience.

The largest group of people did not come to church at all. They in fact took part in nothing! As I talked with them, I noticed a hint of desperation in their voices. They felt as if no one cared for them or their opinions. Daily they would see their children walk through mud to school. Each time it rained, they would helplessly watch as the water cascaded into their homes. Utility costs would increase and many people had to make the choice of either heating their home or eating. All of this over a long enough period of time had plunged many people into a kind of apathetic desperation.

As I became aware of all this, as I heard what the people would say or wouldn't say, as I watched what the people would do or wouldn't do, it occurred to me that all of them in one way or another were saying the same thing. They were saying that they were tired of having no say in their church or in their lives; they were tired of not having any control over their own destiny; they were tired of not having any options. I knew right away that if I were to have any success in reaching out to all of them, if I were to have any success in helping bring about a community of faith, hope, and love, the first reality that I would have to confront would be the people's powerlessness and the first place that I would have to begin would be the Church.

About two months after I arrived at St. Timothy an interesting thing happened that I believe truly opened the way for better understanding and the formation of a deeper faith-community based on acceptance. In 1972 a new church was built *over* the protests of the people. It was a modern building that excluded many of the things the people felt comfortable with. One of the things excluded was a large crucifix that the people especially loved. They had worked for it, paid for it, and installed it. The crucifix was to the people a symbol of their faith-community. But in the new church, it had been replaced with an ultra-modern wrought iron crucifix. They resented this immensely and so took the old crucifix into their own homes for safekeeping.

When I arrived, I began to receive hundreds of requests. Would I install the old crucifix in the new church? The architects and builders objected strenuously. The crucifix, they said, would destroy the architectural lines of the church.

As I reflected more and more over the request and the controversy it had spawned, I became aware that the controversy had actually become a symbolic conflict. It was no longer merely a question of the crucifix. It was now a question of who the church belonged to. What the people were asking for was a church in which they could feel comfortable, in which they would be accepted as they are with their foils and imperfections.

Since I felt the people were more important than architectural lines, I met with the leadership and we made plans for a large festival celebrating the return of the people's crucifix to their church. The crucifix was unveiled by the original donor during a Mass celebrated by our bishop. Nearly a thousand people attended. Seeing their smiles, their tears, and their exuberant joy was for me a tremendously moving experience.

It was the beginning point of my ministry there, for that event established the groundwork necessary for moving ahead. That event established the mutual acceptance so necessary for catechizing and evangelizing. It also indicated to me that one of the principal catechetical experiences of the community would have to be the liturgy. Virgil Elizondo describes the Spanish-speaking as being sacramentalized but not catechized. I feel that this is true. There is a very intimate affinity between culture and sacramentalization. The challenge to all of us is to begin with sacramentalization and let it become an effective catechetical tool. This I wanted to do with the liturgy.

In all the years I attended the seminary, I was never taught an effective liturgy course. At that time, liturgy was very much in process and my principal learning-tool was observing and studying the Vatican II discussions on liturgy. From that document and from the many liturgies I have presided at—many beautiful, many fair, some terrible—I have come to recognize two principal dimensions. There is first of all the relationship between the worshipers and God who is their Father; and there is the relationship between the people who come who are brothers and sisters. As the fellowship becomes more and more real, the community becomes more and more Christ.

There is also, within the liturgy, both the elements of celebration and of commitment. There is celebration of life, of what is. Life is the most precious gift we receive from our Father. It is what binds us to him as sons and daughters. And so we celebrate the fact by praising him. But there is also present the element of commitment. We commit ourselves to bettering the life that God has given us and that makes us all brothers and sisters.

However, in order for life to be celebrated in a satisfying way, the liturgy must also reflect life as it is. This I believe is what orients the liturgy and makes it relevant to a particular people in a particular time. While the liturgies at St. Timothy were more than adequate, I felt that one element missing was that the liturgies did not reflect life as the people lived it. There was very little relationship between what happened inside the Church and what happened outside. I wanted very much to do something about this, and I wanted to do it in as natural a way as possible. It seemed to me that the liturgy could very much be enhanced as a catechetical tool if it would deal somewhat with the main issues of the people's lives and deal with them both culturally and carefully.

As I discussed this at length with the leadership of the parish and with the pastoral team (myself and one other priest at the time), we agreed that we would develop blocks of catechetical themes that would be celebrated within the liturgy and in conjunction with prominent cultural feasts or events. We felt that this would bring together people, culture, and liturgy in such a way that people could reflect on the totality of their lives. We also felt that this could be most valuable catechetically. The decision to go ahead was made and we began work on the first block of themes.

It was by this time the month of September. On September 16, Mexican Independence Day is celebrated. This is a big day not only for Mexico but also for Texas because at the time Mexico declared its Independence from Spain, Texas was still a part of Mexico. We felt that Mexican Independence gave a logical place to begin and provided us with a forum to speak of powerlessness and its effect on people. The first block of Themes was therefore on Jesus Christ, the Liberator who frees us from sin, which is the utlimate root of all injustice and oppression.

The first week was spent reflecting on Jesus as a free man. We developed the theme of liberation and liberty which is the nucleus of His message. We also developed the theme of oppression and people's response to it and in developing this theme we utilized the Exodus event as exemplifying the process of a people's going from oppression to freedom. This particular theme ended with the celebration of Dia de la Raza in which confluence and community are celebrated.

In Advent, we celebrated the theme that all of us are in pilgrimage, in the process of conversion and liberation. We celebrated the Posadas which are a reenactment of the pilgrimage of Mary and Joseph to Bethlehem. Likewise we celebrated the Virgen de Guadalupe who is to us a symbol of both culture and freedom.

Ash Wednesday began the theme of Reconciliation. We stressed that in order to be reconciled, people must be free— free enough to make a choice, free enough to make a decision. Holy Week closed this block. The year ended with a celebration of both cultural and religious personages who have meaning for our people.

We stressed in this final theme that at the basis of salvation and redemption, lies the truth that man must be master of his destiny. If he is not, then he cannot make a free response, he cannot make a total commitment. We talked about Jesus (Sacred Heart) as master of his destiny. We talked of John the Baptist, Sts. Peter and Paul. We discussed Pancho Villa, Padre Miguel Hidalgo, Emiliano Zapata, and Fray Antonio de Margil.

At the same time that we were developing our liturgical-cultural themes, we also gave our attention to other elements of the liturgy. In any Spanish-speaking community there is always a great love for good music and song. This was true of my growing parish community but unfortunately music and song did not spill over into the liturgy. I felt that to be truly effective liturgy, the selection of music would have to reflect not only life as it is but also incorporate the music and song of the people as it is sung. We decided to bring together musicians from the parish to form a choir.

I was told at the beginning that there were no musicians, and that I was wasting my time. I felt that every community has its artists just like every community has its leaders. The trick is to find them. I spent one month visiting and talking with people until I had found seven musicians who were willing to play.

When the call for voices went out, approximately forty people volunteered. The choir took off from the very beginning and sang at our major Sunday Mass and at other important occasions. The result was incredible. People responded to the music in a total, exuberant way and our liturgies were immensely improved. People appreciated hearing and singing songs that carried good messages and sounded good as well. In four years' time the choir has grown to 15 musicians and almost a hundred voices. It has won numerous contests and is an essential part of our reaching out to people through song and in liturgy.

Along with emphasis on music, we also included other elements in our liturgy. Borrowing an idea from Bishop Patrick Flores of El Paso, we began to introduce out-of-town guests who had come to our church to celebrate. This provided something of a host-community atmosphere for the parish and gave our people a chance to introduce their friends and relatives to our community.

We also introduced the monthly custom of asking all couples who had celebrated their wedding anniversary during a given month to stand and let us know the number of years they were celebrating. People enjoyed standing and the rest of the community enjoyed hearing. Every month we have couples celebrating from 4 years to 60 years of married life. It points out not only the vitality of our community but the seriousness of marriage. These spontaneous additions have meant a lot to all of us at St. Timothy.

At the end of this first year of what we can call our liturgical-cultural calender, we took time to reflect and evaluate. The response of the people was overwhelming. What we had talked about and celebrated in our liturgies had had an impact. People understood. They felt accepted. Particularly did they enjoy the heroes we put before them. Never before had all of this been brought together. Never before had it been put together in this particular way, and it made sense. It was as if what we reflected on and celebrated reached into the souls of the people and touched them. In the discussions and evaluations, it was suggested that this same approach be incorporated into our doctrinal-catechetical program. This set the stage for our next step.

Throughout the week many people come through St. Timothy's. One hundred and fifty senior citizens come every day. Over two hundred children come daily for a nutritional-tutoring program. Once a week over five hundred children come for their "doctrina." Yet, everyone was taught a different lesson on a different topic that had nothing to do with the liturgies celebrated. We began to feel that the catechetical value of all that we were doing would be greatly enhanced if we could bring what we were *teaching* to relate directly to what we were *celebrating*. So we made a change. Throughout the week, whatever was taught led directly to and culminated in the Sunday liturgy.

We decided to implement this approach and began on a new venture. From the liturgical-cultural themes chosen, we developed catechetical themes for each week of the year. From these themes, we would derive concrete catechetical goals and objectives. From these we would develop detailed lesson plans for all levels.

We developed plans for Kindergarten-2nd grade, from 3rd-5th grade, from 6th-8th grades, from 9-10, from 11-12, and for adults. In each plan we incorporated an activity that would be brought to the liturgy as a special offering from that particular group. The teachers themselves came together to write the plans. Since the system was our own, we did our own training with the help of MACC (Mexican American Culture Center). In the process, the teachers formed a core group that came to know both themselves and the program they were teaching very well. Even though the experience was difficult, it was also enriching.

Teachers were learning a new discipline. Parents and children were experiencing the same catechetical theme, and all would culminate in the Sunday Liturgy. In the first year of our plan, we developed the liturgical themes that have already been explained. We talked about Jesus Christ the Liberator and about sin as the ultimate root of all injustice and oppression. In the second year of the liturgical-catechetical plan we talked about the mission Church. We stressed that the Church is a community of people bound together in the realization of a mission. The Church is, therefore, a pilgrim Church, a missionary people. In the realization of its mission, the church expresses itself through the culture of the people that are the church and of which Christ Himself is the Center.

We again celebrated Dia de la Raza but this time as a confluence of culture. On Mission Sunday we had a commissioning rite for those who were to serve the community in a special way. We talked about ourselves as a priestly people, as a kingly people, and as prophetic people. We then spent 20 weeks celebrating the sacraments and we celebrated sacraments as liberating forces. We directly related the sacraments to mission and we presented them as sacred moments in life that help liberate the person. We explained the symbolism and in front of the assembly, celebrated each sacrament in our Sunday liturgy. Since that year was the Bicentennial, we closed it with a celebration of LIBERTY AND JUSTICE FOR ALL.

In the third year, we wanted to concentrate in a special way on sacred Scripture. Since most of our people come into contact with much Mormon and Jehovah's Witness proselytzing, many of the people had asked that we develop biblical themes. Remembering the popularity of the themes dealing with cultur-

l and religious heroes and not wanting merely to give our people biblical ammunition to shoot at others, we decided to
develop biblical themes through biblical heroes. We wanted to
show people grappling and coming to terms with their own
faith.

We therefore began the third liturgical-catechetical year
with the creation account. We presented Yahweh as the Crea-
tor who makes man in his image and as his Co-Creator. We
then developed the disruption that followed through Adam
and Eve, Cain and Abel, and the Tower of Babel. The Pa-
triarchs were presented as men entrusted with the re-crea-
tion and building up of the new world. Abraham as the man
of faith was the focal point. Through the Exodus story, we
pointed out the power of God to fulfill His promise to his people by bringing them from slavery to freedom. Moses was presented as prefiguring Christ the savior of his people. The
judges were seen as heroes to give example that Yahweh can
inspire one to do or say things above and beyond ordinary
capacity. We discussed Samson, Gideon and Ruth. In Kings,
we endeavored to convey the lesson that Christians must put
their faith in Yahweh, no matter how powerful men may
seem. The Prophets were presented as the voice of Yahweh.
Since oppression of the poor had become commonplace and
since Yahweh was no longer God but someone to keep in
case of future trouble, the Prophets spoke. Amos, Jeremiah,
and Isaiah were presented.

There was then a lengthy section on the ministry and miracles of Jesus, and the passion, death, and Resurrection. The
year closed with a celebration of the early Church. The focal
points of the celebration were Peter and Paul, Ananias and Sap-
phira, and Aquila and Priscilla.

In our fourth year, we are celebrating as the core-theme of
our liturgical-culture-catechetical process the humanity of
Jesus. Many times the divinity of Jesus so overwhelms us that
the feelings and lessons of his life are lost on us as examples.
We tend to forget that Jesus asks us to be perfect even as our
heavenly Father is perfect. In this year we look at Jesus who
teaches us to pray, at Jesus who celebrated, at Jesus who

123

looked for and found friends, and at Jesus who teaches us to be fair, honest, and just.

The bringing together of liturgy, catechetics, and culture had indeed enhanced the caliber of our evangelization. Not only were we reaching more people but we were also reaching them more intensely and effectively.

In the meantime, those who actually ran the program were developing as leaders who took their place with the leadership core-group of the community. As more people became active leaders in one way or another, we greatly enhanced the ability of our parish to reach out to people. But as we would sit, discuss, and evaluate, all of us felt a disturbing anxiety. It was only after much reflection that we were able to conclude that the anxiety came from feeling we were not doing enough. We would talk about and celebrate the life and freedom that Jesus has given us, knowing that things in the neighborhood would preach the opposite. Everyone would feel that they were masters of their destiny—until they got home or to work or to school.

We wanted to express in action what we knew, celebrated, and believed. We could no longer preach freedom or liberation without practicing it. We could no longer tolerate the deterioration of our homes, schools, streets, and our spirits. Furthermore, if we wanted to reach even more people, then we would have to confront the issues of the community. We would have to become one with the struggle of the community. We therefore made the decision to begin that process.

The leadership core group met and the first decision made was to go to the community and find out what the people were thinking. As we visited and talked, we found that people were bothered most by poor streets, no sidewalks, and no parks for their children. We felt that we could be most effective and most successful first in pursuing a park for our community and our children. There was quite fortunately in front of the parish church a ten acre vacant plot of land owned by the city. We decided in a series of meetings with at least two hundred and fifty people that the vacant lot would be the site of our new park.

Along with that decision came a vague, unexpressed apprehension. It was as if people were saying, "we will give it a try but you can't beat City Hall." People were already preparing themselves for failure. It was imperative that we succeed. In a series of action-meetings with city officials attended by at least five hundred people from our parish who were interested in the park, we were able to acquire the site as a park and we were able to secure the funding from city monies.

Two months after these decisions were made, our parish celebrated the ground-breaking. We first celebrated a Mass of Thanksgiving and afterwards walked to the park-site where along with members of the City Council, the groundbreaking was held. Approximately a year later, the park was completed and we gathered again for the dedication.

There was a Mass and afterwards the dedication. The mayor of the city officiated. Since the city had asked us to designate a name for the Park, we put that decision before the people of the community and the choice was immediate and unanimous: St. Timothy, patron saint of our parish church.

But more beautiful than even the park or its name was the expression on the faces of the people who had never achieved an accomplishment of this magnitude. Never before had the mayor come to this neighborhood. The people felt proud and the entire community noticed.

In fact, about a month after the dedication, a group of residents from one of the housing projects approached us concerning a problem in their project. They had seen our success with the park and asked us for help with their problem. Because of the danger posed to children in the project, the residents wanted the traffic circulation re-routed. They had tried to do this for three years but to no avail.

We cooperated with them and the problem was solved in three weeks. Not only had we helped but now we had an entry into a community we long wanted to get into but couldn't. What had spawned the opportunity was acquiring a park for our children. In doing something significant for the children of the community, we had drawn to ourselves people who now trusted us because we cared for their children. We have continued this effort with street improvements and drainage projects and housing rehabilitation as an intrinsic part of our catechizing and evangelizing.

But we haven't done any of this alone. When we made the decision to address ourselves to the needs of our community, it was a decision shared by many other parish-communities as well. Many churches felt the same anxiety we felt. It was therefore decided to bring all these churches together to form a citizen based organization that would address the capital and social needs of our people. It was also decided that the building unit for the organization would be the parish church.

From money donated by six religious denominations, an organizer was hired to help put our organization together. After a year of initial groundwork in which experiences like ours were duplicated in many parishes, the organization was brought together on a city-wide basis and named Communities Organized for Public Service (COPS).

At our first convention attended by 40 parishes and 2000 people, the structure was decided upon and issues chosen for the coming year. At our second convention we attracted 4000 people and at our third convention 6000 attended.

In these 3 years we have been successful in attracting close to $100 million in capital improvements for our neighborhoods. COPS has also become part of the institutional church insofar as it is the arm through which we reach out into the community and show our concern and love. Because of COPS we have also been able to reverse much of the resentment against the Church. As people see that the Church is genuinely concerned and willing to take risks, they put the past aside in order to help build up the present and the future. As people see that the Church is successful in improving the community, they come in order to be part of something that is effective and concerned. As they come and as they become part of us, we evangelize by what we celebrate, what we teach, and what we do.

What I have shared with you has been a recounting of what I have seen happen at the parish community I serve. While the experiences narrated could never be duplicated anywhere, the principles underlying them are valid and important. Before people can respond more and more to the mystery of the Christ, before people can experience the fulfilling process of conversion, there must be established between people and Church a relationship that is built on acceptance and trust. This acceptance and trust can flow only from a deep and firm respect—respect for who the people are, their traditions and customs, their culture, and above all their struggles.

In my parish, that acceptance and trust was established through a respectful concern for the symbols of the people. Only then were we able to talk of the vital issues confronting the community. When we did so, we did so through moments and events and personages that are culturally important to the people and we incorporated these events, these moments, these persons into the celebration of the liturgy which is the ultimate focal point of the community. Because of this, our faith-year was a liturgical-cultural event that touched many people and brought them into contact with the mystery of Christ.

Later, in order to further enhance our liturgical-cultural calendar, we made our celebration themes our catechetical ones as well. This brought a unity and singleness in direction that was most beneficial and incisive. When people began to see and understand more of where we were going, there was the desire to express our faith and beliefs in a social and even political manner. Through our association with COPS we have begun systematically the improvement of all our neighborhoods. This action not only gives us the opportunity of expressing our faith, but also establishes bonds with other members of the community who came to us because they see in us concern and love for all. It is this concern and love that sparks the conversion to Christ of which all of us are part. I feel the greatest value of this experience is perhaps to help point out how—if at all—the process of conversion can be "institutionalized" or built into the times we come into contact with many people.

In an urban setting many people approach the Church. When they do, those moments should be moments of conversion. Attuning ourselves to their situation, reflecting their life and struggles in what we do and say, playing their music and singing their songs, we can make of those moments saving encounters with Christ. Doing that, the person moves along the pilgrimage of catechumen to a fuller realization of what it is and can be to be a Christian.

Blaine G. Barr

How Can a Large Parish Become A Viable Catechumenal Community?

Blaine G. Barr is pastor of the Parish Community of St. Joseph, New Hope, Minnesota. He is a graduate of St. Paul Seminary, St. Paul, Minnesota, and of Gregorian University, Rome.

As I thought about this question, I kept coming up with the same answer—a large American parish really can't become a viable catechumenal community any more than someone can become a Christian. As a Christian is "made, not born," so too must the parish be formed or changed. Therefore, the question I would like to address is, "How can a large American parish be formed or changed into a viable catechumenal community, and who is going to do it?"

Even with this rewording, the question will not be easy to answer; but at least some possibilities can be seen. The revision of the primary rites of initiation heralds a cry to begin a reform and renewal of the most radical sort. "We are talking about initiation into the church, so the church is the key issue. What one does about initiation will depend on one's theology of the church, one's vision of the church."[1] Therefore, we need as radical a restructuring of our views of church, its mission and ministry, and as radical a restructuring of our parishes, as is the restructuring of the rites of Christian initiation themselves. This will not be something that will be accomplished easily or quick-

129

ly, but with deep faith in the power of the Spirit, much patience, determination and lots of hard work it can be done.

Why do I say this? "Because, first of all, the restoration of the baptismal focus of the paschal season with the adult initiation of catechumens as the central event of the liturgical year presumes a local church which has come to grips with the full meaning of baptism.... Second, such a revision represents a radical change of sacramental symbols and priorities.... Third, such drastic revision and innovation represents a departure in pastoral priorities and perspectives, a departure so radical that it has been unparalleled since the middle ages and well before. The norm of pastoral care becomes the radical transformation of life and values, publicly celebrated as a corporate responsibility....

"Fourth, it assumes that the liturgy will be a manifestation of the real life lived by the church, a life marked by sufficient conversion to be worth celebrating, sufficient conversion and catechesis to perceive that the proclamation of the wonderful works of God is possible because they occur among us, sufficient conversion to ensure that the laity are not the passive recipients of hierarchical grace but that ministry is a mirror of the priestly service of the entire people of God."[2]

It is apparent, therefore, that we are dealing with an ideal and a vision of church, ministry and parish as community that very few in the church have today. And among those who have this vision, fewer still have been able to make it a reality. Why? Because the problems one must face in attempting to develop this kind of model appear almost insurmountable. I would like now to describe five of these problems, as I see them.

First, there are too few pastoral leaders and ministers with the vision, imagination, creativity, courage, living faith, determination and leadership ability needed to achieve this goal. Many of our most creative and able leaders and ministers, both men and women, have left the active ministry and are continuing to do so. The church is no longer attracting as many of the brightest and the best among our young people. Our seminaries and religious orders are still turning out men and women who function relatively well in the church rather than the kind of thinking, visionary and courageous persons we need to effect the radical renewal the revised rites of initiation call for.

Second, we continue to operate generally under the desperate assumption that all ministry must be presbyterial. As a result, in all too many parishes, we still have a sacred few ministering to an indifferent many. What the church needs is not new ministries, but rather a corporate, shared, collegial *ministry* that is as broad, as deep and as pluralistic as the church itself. This is the vision of ministry outlined in paragraph 41 of the *Rite of Christian Initiation of Adults* which says: "The initiation of adults is. . . . the business of all the baptized. Therefore, the community must always be ready to fulfill its apostolic vocation by giving help to those who need Christ."

Third, as Ralph Keifer says, "For most of us the Church is not a dynamic and communal reality. That conversion should be a matter of any kind of experience, much less of corporate experience, is not expected and not really desired. As a result, to speak of initiation is extremely problematic because there is so little to initiate people *into*, and little or nothing to elebrate."

He continues, "The church is not the focus of a strong corporate identity. The focus on institutions rather than persons has resulted in a dependence upon culture to sustain Christian life and Christian identity. Since the presupposition of the established church is that religious identity and meaning will largely be forged by a culture which is conceived to be fundamentally Christian, we are in for serious trouble. The retention of a pattern appropriate to the established church implies the retention of pastoral patterns which presume rather than attempt to evoke its radical conversion; an undirected and uncritical assimilation of the values of the culture as a whole; and the retention of ecclesiastical institutions in an ossified and progressively more ineffective form, accompanied by a progressive erosion of those institutions as the values of the culture are assimilated and work against them."[3]

Fourth, again in Keifer's words, "We have a massive religious problem on our hands because the paschal mystery is, to most people, a near-abstraction. If we are going to do any real initiating, we are going to have to become comfortable

131

with God-talk, gospel-talk, Jesus-talk, and Spirit-talk which is both convinced and convincing. We are, most of us, horribly inept at this, horribly embarrassed by it, so much so that the homiletic and catechetical Christ is usually presented as an absent lawgiver and teacher and example. Unless we can learn to speak of God as a living and present reality, we are doomed (and the word is appropriate) to failure. There is at present no greater pastoral vacuum than the inability to show people the presence of God in their lives. (What we need are) ministers who might be willing to take the kind of risk required to articulate for others one's own experience and understanding of a personal God."[4]

Fifth, we have serious structural problems in that, first of all, we are lacking in models of what a viable catechumenal community could be. Many parish models exist but, by and large, they are irrelevant, out-moded, mostly inoperative ecclesial models. Also, "There is the desperate problem of parochial size. Unless we begin to come to grips with this question, our initiatory rites will continue to have the flavor of the incongruous and the peculiar. It is indeed an incongruity to welcome people into a 'community' of strangers."[5]

By listing these five problems we must face and somehow deal with, I am not implying at all that there is little reason for hope. Rather, I see them as a challenge and with Robert Hovda I believe that true reform and renewal are more attainable than ever before. "We are coming at our problems from many different avenues and movements, but all are signs of life, dedication, rich promises of energy that a more coherent ecclesial life can tap and help flourish. We have persons and groups of persons putting their bodies, resources, talents and time into liturgy planning, catechetical programs, works of social ministry, prayer meetings, protest and witness activities. Every one of these avenues or strands is a hook on which we can hang our hopes; every fragment is an invitation to put a way of life together. That way of life is the local church, and its genesis and formation is the process of Christian initiation—a process that has to be revived in some manner if the local church is to gain any degree of health."[6]

Before describing what we have done in the Parish Community of St. Joseph to attempt to develop the concept and experience of community, I would like to define the terms of the question as I understand them and will be using them.

Since our task is to change a large American parish into a viable catechumenal community, the operative word is *change*. In our environment, dominated by technology, change is the name of the game. Effective management of change is what separates the quick from the dead. "Here below to live is to change, and to be perfect is to have changed often." (Newman)

To change is to grow. To grow means to risk what we know for something we don't know. As one observer has commented, "The Spirit guarantees continued growth, but the Church must take the risk of changing itself if it is to find the fullness of its adult presence in the world." Yet many people in the Church today are firmly fixed on a plateau of faith, afraid to take another step in the direction of growth. "Frightened men, afraid to lose something of the past cannot respond to the Spirit and so they resist development of new forms which can express the Church's servant role ever more creatively." Those who are most in need of change yield most slowly to it.

The object we are dealing with is the *parish*. A parish is a local gathering of people "ecclesia" who associated with the bishop through his pastoral representative, profess in explicit faith that Jesus is Lord and ratify this faith through rites of Christian initiation. A parish is a structure—a community of communities with defined boundaries, leadership and ministerial roles. A parish is a place where Christ lives and acts among his people, but even more than this, *the parish is Christ* living and acting among his people, making God real and immediate to them and giving them what he gave his disciples, that is, his message, his life, his love and a share in his ministry. The parish is a school of Christian formation teaching and forming its members to be true disciples of Jesus and authentic witnesses of his message to others. Finally, a parish is not an isolated unit but a people united to Christ with other people professing the same faith under the spiritual leadership of the pope, the bishop of Rome, and especially the local bishop, with a pastor appointed as his delegate to guide each local community of believers.

Here I am using "large" and "American" to define a typical suburban territorial parish numbering anywhere from 500 to 3,000 households, or from 2,000 to 12,000 persons, predominately white and reflecting the faith, mores, customs and values of more or less average Catholic Americans. Rural, black, chicano, campus, inner city and ethnic national parishes have their own unique characteristics and needs which I will not be able to address in this paper.

Community is the objective we are striving for. Building community. . . . the reason for it all. Community is something that happens among people who keep on making it happen for one another. . . . understanding their sameness and uncovering their differences. True community is like a crystal that will never stop growing outward, always manifesting internal structure by external patterns of expansion. Community, then, is more a quality or happening or experience than an end product. According to this definition, a parish cannot ever be a community but rather it is a group of persons constantly striving for community. In this ongoing process, there must be coordination and direction side by side with dialogue and interchange. There must be planning as well as talking; there must be action as well as intention. The parish that is only "action-oriented" may be as inconsequential as an amateur football team looking for easy opponents, and the parish with great communication and camaraderie may only be celebrating itself.

But, community is also a social form and, as such, it is an intermediate social form somewhere on a continuum between a primary group on one end of the spectrum and an association or organization on the other. It reflects similarities with both of these groups yet it is also different from each of them. In addition, we must recognize the pluriformity of groups in today's parish, all of which can be involved in some way in the process of becoming communities; namely, family groupings, neighborhood groupings, the parish council, committees, staff, choir, etc. Anyone seriously interested in the question at hand should learn all that they can about community. Several of the better presentations I have found on the subject are listed in the footnotes.[7]

And what about "catechumenal"? "If we are going to establish an adult catechumenate for the purpose of making Christians, then we had better have some idea about who a Christian is."[8] The question should be, "What is a Christian community?" It is a sacrament, the place where people meet the Lord and encounter his saving word and action. It is a group of people who express in explicit faith that Jesus is Lord, ratify this faith through rites of Christian initiation, deepen this faith by growing to know and love Christ better through the Gospels, seal this faith in the Eucharist and witness this faith by finding ways to serve Christ in others through practiced application of the Christian message to their daily lives.

A "viable" catechumenal community then is one where this whole process of the adult catechumenate is truly fostered, where it can vigorously grow and develop and where people can meet and experience the Lord.

Our goal or task then is to change, to form, to build a large American parish into a viable catechumenal community. "One of the greatest problems facing .... the Church today is knowing where and how to begin."[9] So, where do we begin? I am firmly convinced that we will achieve this goal only if we begin with strong leaders who have begun their own personal growth and spiritual renewal. Changed people change structures and institutions. Until persons in ministry change by taking their own spiritual renewal seriously and learn how to be truly pastoral leaders, the reforms and renewal called for by the revised rites of initiation will never happen in our parishes. "It is persons who build communities. Communities form around their leaders, and they are usually as strong as their leaders. Without the right persons the whole process cannot get off the ground."[10]

The kind of leader we need, in addition to what has already been said, must know who he/she is, i.e., he/she must have a good self-image and self-confidence in his/her ability to lead. Unfortunately, our seminaries and novitiates have not done very well in developing this kind of leader. On the contrary,

135

they have all too often done just the opposite by producing men who are followers, who function well in an institutional church, unimaginative, docile men, men without vision who can't see any reason to change anything, and if they did, would not have the courage or initiative to do so.

According to the Bishops' document on the Continuing Education of Priests, a priest must exert "prophetic leadership." In order to do this, a priest must feel secure enough in his own person to act autonomously. The findings indicate a large number of priests would experience difficulty in exerting the "prophetic leadership" which is needed.

"Only the man who embodies the Gospel message of reconciliation and freedom in his personhood and in his relationship with others can mediate the good news to a generation that is suspicious of roles! But mediating the good news through personal presence and dialogue demands a high level of ego development. This includes seven qualities found in an integrated way only at the autonomous and integrated stage of ego development, stages which few priests have achieved."[11]

First, the kind of leader we need must know where he is going and why. Second, he must know his theology well—a theology flowing out of Vatican II, and thoroughly understand the goal he is to work toward reaching.

Third, a pastoral leader must know how to get there—how to begin, how to maintain the development once begun and how to achieve the goal.

Fourth, he must really love Jesus, the church and his ministry. I mean he must have real enthusiasm and find sharing in Jesus' ministry the most exciting, fulfilling, exhilarating experience of his life. Such a leader seldom finds his ministry tiring, frustrating or disappointing. He is truly and deeply committed to Jesus and nothing else is more important to him, not even his own personal fulfillment.

Fifth, he must truly love the people he has been appointed to lead and serve and be deeply sensitive to their needs as persons. In a community persons must always be most important. Again, those trained in an institutional church often develop an institutional mentality and are more concerned about good and efficient programs, services and rituals than they are about individual persons. Perhaps we should spend less time on job descriptions, performance reviews and program evaluations and more time learning what the real ministry of Jesus is all about and trying to discover what kind of spiritual growth it is producing. What good does it do to have an efficient farmer plant his seeds according to a well designed program if he doesn't take an interest in fostering that growth.

Lastly, in addition to the knowledge and love, described above, a pastoral leader must have vision and be a dreamer—to be able to say with Martin Luther King, "I have a dream." And with Shaw, "I dream of things that never were and say 'Why not?'" Doers are dreamers who dare. Never to dream, never to have visions, is not to live. He must be always open to the Holy Spirit and expect the unexpected. He must be creative, willing to experiment and to take risks. He must have insight which turns common experiences into revelations. He must have moral courage, determination and fearlessness. Senator Robert F. Kennedy once said, "Moral courage is a rarer commodity than bravery in battle or great intelligence. Yet it is the one essential, vital quality for those who seek to change a world (church) that yields most painfully to change." He must be willing to make many personal sacrifices and to pay the price to see his dreams come true. He must be a man of prayer and of deep living faith. And, he must be foolish enough to believe that a large American parish can, in fact, be changed into a viable catechumenal community. A saying I have on my kitchen wall reads, "Thank God for damn fools, otherwise God's work would never get done."

This is all beautifully summarized in the National Conference of Catholic Bishop's new document "As One Who Serves," "to lead means to exercise a decisive influence on the thought and actions of others. It is an influence which no longer flows automatically from the office or position. Rather, a leader in our day appeals to his own personal experience which, presented as a model, becomes normative to the extent that it helps others understand their own experience, but uses his own experience as a principle of discernment for the service of others.

137

"The truly effective leader in our midst is one who has a zest for life, who can inspire others, who can stir their minds and hearts, who can dream, and who can encourage people to believe in themselves. By embodying in his own pattern of relationships the vision of the Kingdom, priests can inspire men and women to follow on the pilgrimage to that Kingdom."

A serious question, however, still remains. Where do we find or, rather, how do we develop this kind of leader? I am not quite sure. But, I do know that we had better find the answer before it is too late. Otherwise, the next state of the church will be worse than the last. Our bishops and seminary personnel should have it high on their list of priorities to address this issue in a radical way.

It seems to me that three things go into making a leader—stimulating ideas, exciting people and experiences which cause a person to think and to grow. At least that is what did it for me. Seminary courses and theological manuals and text books didn't do much for me in terms of leadership training or getting me excited about ministry. So I looked elsewhere after a wise spiritual director told me that all that I should know as a priest was not contained between the covers of my text books.

In order to stimulate my ideas and my thinking, I read as much as I could about the church, the lay apostolate, Catholic Action, the Young Christian Worker Movement, social action, the liturgical movement, the life of Christ, selected saints' lives, especially St. Paul, and the lives and writings of exciting modern prophets. I read Congar, deLubac, Chautard, Danielou, Holzner, Suhard, Hasseveldt, Michonneau, Guardini, Perrin, Godin, Cardijn, Baroness deHueck, Dorothy Day, de Montcheuil, James Keller and *Integrity* magazine.

As people change institutions so, too, they change other people. There are four men who each had a special and profound influence on my life and on my thinking. I know I wouldn't be where I am at today if they hadn't entered my life. Monsignor Wolf, my seminary psychology professor, taught me to think for myself and be my own person. Father John Courtney Murray, who conducted our retreat in Rome a year before ordination, taught me to never be satisfied with the present but to look to the future with courage and fearlessness. Monsignor Josef Cardijn inspired me with a love for the mission of the church and the lay apostolate and he provided me with a simple methodology which has become part of my daily thought processes—"observe, judge and act." And Monsignor Reynold Hillenbrand from Chicago, perhaps had the greatest influence of all—a man in almost constant pain who spoke so softly one often could barely hear him—taught me quiet determination and perseverance in the face of almost insurmountable odds. Also, he taught me a great love for the Church and especially for its teachings on social justice.

Experience, it is said, is the best teacher. While studying in Rome, I spent my summers visiting every Catholic action, social action and liturgical center I could find, meeting the people there, seeing where and how they worked at ministry. Then when I returned to America I became deeply involved in the YCW Movement as Federation Chaplain in our Archdiocese. These ten years of forming young adults to be responsible Christian lay leaders taught me much about leadership and gave me a learning experience I could never have received anywhere else or in any other way. Sitting at leaders' meetings week after week, sharing in the Gospel inquiry and listening to these young people struggle with their weekly social inquiries gave me an experience of church community and ministry I shall always gratefully cherish.

It was out of this background and with fifteen years experience as an assistant priest that I was appointed pastor of St. Joseph's parish in August of 1967. St. Joseph's was a traditional conservative country parish of 250 families. It was my responsibility to find a way to minister to the needs of the rapidly growing number of people moving into the area. After a realignment of boundaries we suddenly became a suburban parish of 800 families. Today, we number 1,600 families or households, or somewhere between 5,000 and 6,000 persons.

First of all, I began to work at forming the parish into a Christian community by immediately setting out to develop a new model of parish according to the following set of convictions or guiding principles which I had in mind and which were part of my vision and dream of what a parish of the future should be.

1. The parish must be modeled on the teachings of the Second Vatican Council and the theology of church and ministry flowing from that Council.
2. There must be provision made for continued growth, flexibility and experimentation.
3. Developing the concept and experience of community must be the central focus in building parish spirit and structures. To do this the larger parish must be broken down into smaller manageable units.
4. Ministry must be shared both with a pastoral team and with lay members of the parish.
5. The religious education of adults must take precedence and be the first educational priority.
6. Liturgy must be a meaningful communal experience.
7. Parish ministry must lead to Christian social ministry—to the implementation of the beatitudes in our lives.

The next step is to establish your objectives. What needs to be done to achieve the goal? Or, better, *what needs to be changed* in order to have a large American parish become a viable catechumenal community?

There is a process to building something and this is equally true in forming a community. Many efforts in the church have failed because the processes of how to work were not understood. In pastoral planning, what is in itself more important is not necessarily the first thing we must pay attention to. The following objectives, therefore, are not listed in order of importance but in order of attention and in the order we attended to them in developing our parish.

1. To find out what needs to be changed. In other words, to survey the situation and do a needs assessment. You must find out what the parish is like, what kind of liturgy, religious education programs, pastoral ministry, lay involvement and structures exist and what kind are needed. How many people there are and in what age groups, where their heads are at, what needs they have. What kind of facilities there are and whether or not they are adequate to foster the growth of Christian community. At St. Joseph's, we have done population, demographic and various attitudinal studies to give us answers to these questions.

2. To establish a place where people can come together to hear the Word of God and celebrate the Eucharist and one which will help them experience community. This is when and where you have the greatest number of your people gathered the greatest number of times. So, you begin by changing the gathering place.

Within seven months of my arrival at St. Joseph's, I had the church completely remodelled to accommodate a renewed liturgy. The people were consulted, thè plans explained and they voted to go ahead. I also found rental space in a public school to accommodate the increased numbers of people and here I placed the altars (we had to use two rooms seating about 300 each) in such a way that the people could gather around them. At one time we were celebrating fourteen Masses a weekend using three different spaces. As we began plans for a new permanent facility, we used the principles mentioned above and designed it around our concept of parish and ministry. As a result, we have a very flexible, versatile and functional multipurpose parish community center with no pews or kneelers and people seated so that they can see other people's faces. In this way they can experience worship with other persons rather than with a room full of anonymous bodies.

3. To communicate to the people the goal, the vision, the dream. You begin by changing people's ideas of church, parish and ministry.

I used every opportunity and means I could to let the people know who I was, why I had come to St. Joseph's, what I had in mind to do, what I expected of them and what guiding principles I would be using to develop the parish and achieve the goal. I constantly kept before them themes such as church as the people of God, parish as a community of believers, lay involvement in all areas of ministry and Christian social service and ministry as evidence of authentic Christianity. I did this through homilies, mailed weekly bulletins, a monthly newsletter, articles reproduced and distributed, and meetings of all sorts. Very effective was a two-year series of weekly gatherings with groups of about twenty persons each who resided in close proximity to one another. These gatherings began with refreshments and socializing, then people sharing who they were and where they came from, followed by sharing my thoughts and vision, and concluding with time for questions and exchange. These gatherings lasted about three hours.

4. To find others to share in the responsibility and in ministry—people of God who can see the vision, get excited about it and who can do the job. You begin by changing ministerial roles, attitudes and responsibilities.

I began to build a staff immediately. First, a secretary, then a religious education coordinator, and soon another. Then a parish worker followed by a social action coordinator until now we have fourteen persons salaried as ministers and four office staff. The pastoral staff consists of two priests, four religious education coordinators, three sisters who are pastoral associates, a liturgist, two social action coordinators, a professional counselor and a family life director. We work closely as a team, meeting regularly to coordinate our ministry and to improve it as well as to grow in ministry together.

Also, in the beginning, I established an advisory group of twenty lay persons who were involved regularly and directly in all important decision making until a parish council was formed. Today, we have a strong council, active functional committees and several hundred persons involved in all areas of ministry. This has resulted from the application of the principle of reproducibility[12] by all staff members.

5. To develop a structure which will foster and facilitate the experience and growth of Christian community. You begin by radically changing present parish structures.

One of the first things I did was to subdivide the parish into smaller manageable neighborhood groupings. We have twelve currently—each identified by something familiar to the people such as the name of a school or housing development. Each neighborhood elects a representative to the parish council for a two year term, acts as a support group for its members, welcomes new members, occasionally plans and participates in worship together, provides for the needs of its members, holds social activities, provides grass roots involvement and gives feedback to the pastoral team and parish council on the effectiveness of their pastoral ministry.

One of the more successful projects we have initiated to develop our neighborhood structure is our Weekend Liturgy and "Hospitality Program." Each weekend a different neighborhood hosts the rest of the parish at all the liturgies. They greet people, usher, take up the offerings, lector, serve coffeee after Mass, distribute communion, staff the nursery and prepare the collection for deposit at the bank. Men, women and high school students all help. Two years ago when we first invited people to participate in this program 350 volunteered. Last year more than 700 persons volunteered. This gives people a sense of ownership, and enables them to say more easily, "This is my parish, I help there."

Each neighborhood council representative is encouraged to form a team of leaders around himself or herself, each interested in a different area of ministry, whose role it is to coordinate that ministry within the neighborhood so that each neighborhood will become like a mini-parish. In this way many more people will be ministered to and in a much more personal and caring way. This, in turn, will build personal relationships and bonds of friendship which are the foundation of community.

Our parish is governed by a constitution which a committee meeting weekly spent a year writing. It states the purpose of the parish, requirements for membership, the rights and duties of members of the parish, the council and the staff, election procedures and it defines the structure. Our parish has no traditional Catholic organizations, societies or associations. Based on the concept of a parish being a community of communities, our model is that of a wheel with the pastoral team being the nuclear community surrounded by the parish council with ministry flowing through them out into the different neighborhood groups. Committees of lay people work closely with the staff to develop, improve, implement and evaluate the ministry of the parish under the authority of the council.

6. To develop a coordinated and interrelated total parish ministry. You begin by changing the present direction and emphasis of parish ministry, i.e., you must change it from the worship, instructional, institutional model we have had for centuries to a pastoral, prophetic, mission directed, community model. Instead of being directed inward as has been the case for too long, ministry must now be directed outward.

At St. Joseph's we see ministry falling into four areas—all interrelated and interdependent and not one of them being any more or less important than another. Each area of ministry needs the other three and each has something to give to the other three. This is the dynamic of total parish ministry. The four areas are: the ministry of building Christian community; ministry of the Word; ministry of liturgical sacramental worship; and social or pastoral ministry.

John Shea, professor of theology at Mundelein Seminary in Chicago, describes the mission of the local church very simply by saying that, "You gather the folks, you tell the story, you break the bread." And I would add, you send them forth to spread the good news—to minister.

Looking at the mission of the church in this way, the ministry of building Christian community is first in order of attention. "You gather the folks." One cannot have a catechumenal, ministering community until one first has a community. At St. Joseph's we do everything we can to promote the concept and foster the experience of community. I began by changing the name of the parish from The Church of St. Joseph to The Parish Community of St. Joseph. I preach about it and incorporate the idea into my letters to the people and into just about every brochure we publish. Twice now we have published pictorial directories as a way of promoting community. As new members are welcomed, parishioners from their neighborhood share with them their own experience of being involved in a commu-

144

nity oriented parish. Our parish logo is designed around the concept of community and it appears on our stationery and on pins or badges which are given to all new members. The value of every activity is measured by whether or not it builds community. We are currently developing a family growth and enrichment program in order to strengthen the individual family community and we are forming family clusters to develop a stronger sense of community within our neighborhood structure. These are but a few examples of the many efforts we make to build community.

"You tell the story." Through ministry of the Word the parish proclaims the Good News of Jesus Christ. This includes both preaching and teaching. This message is announced as the yeast that is able to penetrate the totality of a person's life. The Word of God speaks to what is happening in the parish community and in the world in which it lives. It speaks to "joys and hopes, the griefs and anxieties of the men at this age" (*The Church in the Modern World*). It helps people interpret the meaning of their lives according to the gospel. In season and out of season the parish community, the local People of God, proclaims who they are and what they are about in this world. The total life of the parish community as well as the total lives of the individuals that make it up proclaim the Good News of the Lord.

Our emphasis at St. Joseph's has been and will continue to be to teach and preach to adults. Each year we offer from fifteen to twenty or more adult education courses. This past year—one thousand adults participated in these courses. Also, we are developing a family centered religious education program (150 families currently enrolled) which requires that the parents become directly involved in and be responsible for the religious education, sacramental preparations and faith development of their own children. We tell them that our role as pastoral ministers is to support them in this endeavor and to help them to do their job better.

As we learn more about the revised rites of initiation and the adult catechumenate we will incorporate this into the life and ministry of the parish. This year we had seven converts en-

145

rolled at catechumens. They went through the whole process—the rite of enrollment in the catechumenate, the rite of election and, finally, the rites of initiation at the Easter Vigil.

"You break the bread." Our parish liturgical ministry includes not only the celebration of the Eucharist but also the development of the worship and prayer life of the people, and their sacramental life. In the sacramental worship life of the Church the people of a parish come together to worship the Father with Jesus their Lord and Brother under the direction of the Spirit; in the great signs of the Christian tradition the community engenders and nurtures the faith. The Rites of Initiation establish the visible community of persons committed to the Christian Life. The Rites of Reconciliation and Healing proclaim the effective power of God in overcoming sin, alienation and fragmentation in our lives and in the world. The Rites of Life-style give concrete expression to Christian vocation.

All of these Rites find their source and summit in the sharing of the Eucharistic Meal; there the Word of God is proclaimed to the assembled community, the parish participates ritually in the redemptive sacrifice of Jesus, and is sent from the Eucharistic meal on its mission to serve the world and one another. Through the sacramental worship life of the Church, especially in sharing the Eucharistic meal, the parish community itself becomes a sign of the unity that the Lord has worked among them, and thus displays in sacramental symbol, before its fellows and the broader community, the resonance, the similarity, and the common power that invests the work and mission of Christ and their own.

"You send them forth to spread the good news—to minister, to serve, to heal, to be witnesses of Jesus' saving Word and Action." Pastoral and social ministry is the proper work of a ministering community and flows out of the other three areas of ministry. Parish communities do not exist only for themselves. They are a people with a mission of service to the world. Not only do they constantly invite all men to join them in the faith, but they also apply their human and material resources to the growth and development of individual persons and the larger human community. "Wherever and whenever a cry is raised in

146

pain from poverty or ignorance, or in the thirst for justice and the truth of God's work it is no longer possible for any man to be deaf to its command." (Synod/69, p. 9.) The local parish is called to be sensitive to the immediate needs of those who suffer. It is also called to constantly seek solutions to the societal problems that prolong social evils and make it so difficult for many to rise above them. It is called to support all those who are engaged in bringing about a better world for people to live in.

We have six members of our pastoral team and several hundred volunteers involved in this area of ministry at St. Joseph's. Three sisters who are called Parish Workers or Pastoral Associates minister directly to individual members of the community in countless and varied ways. They visit homes, the sick, persons questioning faith, people in crisis, those suffering grief or the trauma and loneliness of a recent divorce, the elderly, young single adults, they bring communion to shut-ins, etc. This is one of the most exciting ministries in the church today. I don't know how a parish can afford to do without several such ministers on its pastoral team.

A former Jesuit priest with a Ph.D. in Human Behavior ministers as a professional counselor to those whose emotional, psychological or relational problems require a skilled therapist. He also conducts courses which can help people in a positive way to prevent their personal and family problems or conflicts from reaching crisis proportions.

Also, there are two married women on our team who coordinate the ministry of Christian social service and social action from our Social Action Center—a separate building which also houses an emergency food shelf and clothing rack. It will be impossible in this paper to do justice to all that they and their volunteer lay ministers do. Some examples: Each month they provide some 650 meals, receive and log 1,000 phone calls of which 250 are calls for help, information or referral to outside social agencies and services. Two hundred and fifty volunteers are involved in some way in this ministry of serving the needs of persons both within our community and outside it. Through this ministry many inactive Catholics have come back to the

147

practice of their faith and other persons are being attracted to our church by this witness of Christ's love.

7. To bring about a deeper understanding of Christian commitment and stewardship. You begin by changing the attitudes of people toward church membership and support. "We must bring to life a church where ministry is nothing less and nothing more than the common coin of the community. We have to bring to life a church in which all members are expected to be ministers as a price of their membership. . . . We must form communities that constantly summon people to serve, identify areas of need, discern the talents of their members and put the explicit stamp of Christian ministry on people's attempts to help each other and their neighborhoods. . . .

"We know that lay ministry in some shape or form is going to be increasingly prevalent in the future. Our job now is to raise the consciousness of all the church so that lay persons will at last accept the vocation they took at baptism. This is the dream held out to us by the Fathers of Vatican II when they declared: 'By its very nature the Christian vocation is a vocation of apostolate.' "[13]

Our annual parish stewardship program asks not only financial support but also an offering or commitment of time and talent to the community. This is done publicly at all our Sunday liturgies. We use themes such as "Come, Get Involved in God's Work" and "The Lord Needs Your Commitment." People are encouraged to write down the amount of time they will give and specific ways in which they will serve the Lord during the coming year. At all Masses on one weekend preceeding the commitment date, members of our pastoral team speak during homily time about their ministry and commitment, and on another weekend three lay persons do the same at each Mass—a total of twenty-seven different people.

8. To direct every effort toward the human and spiritual growth of both individuals and families. You begin by changing or renewing the spiritual lives of the people. This objective is really a goal arrived at by a committee of six of our pastoral staff and six lay persons who went through a two year training process with twenty-seven other churches of different denominations called "Viable Futures for Congregations." This was more than an ordinary planning process. It was called a futuring process—a process for planned growth through which a forecasted and inevitable future can be changed allowing us instead to reach our real potential—what we believe could be if we wanted it badly enough. It asks four basic questions: Where have you been as a parish? Where are you now? Where are you going? And, where could you be if the right changes were made?

Although this is the last objective we attended to in developing our parish model, it probably should have been one of the first even though we may not have had as great a response in the beginning and before the people were as excited about the parish as they now are. Last year we conducted a thirteen-week program called GIFT—Growth In Faith Together.[14] One thousand adults filled in a sixty question survey about their faith needs and concerns. Of these, four hundred adults participated weekly in forty reflection groups during five weeks of Lent. Ninety-two percent of the respondents indicated that spiritual renewal was their primary felt need. As a result of this, the people of the parish have been more responsive than ever before to the opportunities we have provided to study scripture, to pray, to learn more about their faith and to grow spiritually. Presently, 130 persons are participating in an eight-week seminar on the Holy Spirit. This fall we plan to offer the Genesis 2[15] program (an eighteen-week spiritual growth program), or something similar, to the entire parish with the hope that even more will participate than did for GIFT.

With this kind of spiritual deepening taking place, achieving the goal of forming a large parish into a viable catechumenal community will become a real possibility. Our next endeavor a year from now will be to conduct a parish wide evangelization program in an effort to reach those whose faith is lukewarm, dying or dead, and the unchurched as well. This will provide an ideal opportunity to implement the adult catechumenate in the way envisioned by the Church in its decree on the Restored Catechumenate and Rite of Christian Initiation of Adults.

□ □ □

Having answered the question of what needs to be done and having provided some description of some of the things we have done at St. Joseph's, the next question is, "How do you do it?" You must develop or employ a planning process and methodology.

The planning process I have used consistently and effectively is the one I learned from Monsignor Cardijn—"observe, judge and act." I ask myself the questions, "What is or isn't happening and what is the situation I am facing?" "What should and could be happening?" "What is the difference between the two?" and "What do I want to happen, what must I do, how will I do it and who will I get to help?" Then I work out the details of a plan of action.

The methodology we have been following to develop community and ministry consists of six steps.

1. Recruit. First we extend an invitation to people. "Come and see." Then we enroll or register them in the parish. Shortly after they are welcomed by a parishioner or couple from their neighborhood. This is followed by a public welcoming ceremony at a weekend liturgy. As their interests and talents are determined they are invited to participate in the ministry and activities of the parish. We still have to develop a better orientation process than we now have.

2. Group. Here we identify all the natural and structured groups of people we have in the parish and determine how we can best foster the experience of community within each of them—families, children, teens, young singles, the elderly, neighborhoods, the council, committees, pastoral team, interest and activity groups such as the choir, prayer groups, study groups, etc. New members are integrated into whichever of these groups they fit, choose to be or are invited to join.

3. Form. Christian formation takes place through the total ministry of the parish as people learn to know, love and serve both God and neighbor and experience the saving Word and Action of Jesus in their lives. Specific skills are taught and

150

knowledge imparted in order to bring people's gifts to fruition for the benefit of the community and the building of the Kingdom.

4. Nourish. When a community is nourished it has vitality, it is alive, it grows. When it is undernourished it grows weak, it stagnates, it dies. We are nourished most directly and most surely when we celebrate the Eucharist. "I am the bread of life. Come to me and I will refresh you." "They gave steadfast attention. . . . to the breaking of the bread and to the prayers" (Acts 2, v. 42).

"The prodigious power of conversion surges initially into a church through catechesis and the water and chrism of baptism into Christ: the power of conversion is sustained in a church through the eucharistic banquet in Christ: all other sacraments, as well as all other ecclesial activity, flow out from here. When one talks of initiation in Christian terms, one is talking therefore of how all else begins and, ultimately, of how all else is sustained. The hinges upon which an orthodox ecclesiology and an adequate pastoral endeavor swing are baptism-in-its-fullness consummated in the eucharist."[16]

It is through the Eucharist that the love of God revealed to us in Jesus is strengthened, continued, celebrated, renewed, sealed. "It is here where we can encounter God and all His brothers and sisters at the same time. This is the only place where egotism is shattered and a genuine community is shaped, a community that never gasps for air but which grows and spreads."[17] If we do not keep the Eucharist as a central reality and sustaining force in our daily lives as we struggle to build Christian community among us, then our efforts are doomed to failure and we will never achieve our goal. "Without Me you can do nothing." Everyone who has a responsibility for building up the community must strive constantly to convey this message and share this conviction with all in the parish both by word and example.

5. Commission. As people's understanding of the paschal mystery and identification with Jesus' willingness to lay down his life for his friends deepens and becomes a strong desire developing into a personal commitment, they will begin to mediate God's outpouring of love to each other. The stronger love for each other becomes, the more clearly is seen his love for all and that this love is best developed through the response to others needs both those living within the community and outside it. Through its efforts to be pastoral and responsive to the needs of others, the parish community discovers that it must become prophetic.

"Local parishes become prophetic when their members decide to follow their Lord, who was nailed to the cross because he took his own prophetic role seriously. As they understand more deeply the nature of the commitments that are required of their members, if they are to faithfully represent Christ in all aspects of their lives, they will become less concerned with new buildings and more concerned with the quality of Christian life and mission. The form of mission must be the life of Christ whose mission was to save the world by the way of servant love. As Christ took on the garb of a particular time and went out as a servant to particular needs, so also must the church.

"As the concept of community begins to shape, form and direct the parish in a new manner, the concept of ministries is not weakened, but rather enhanced and enlarged. For it is not only the priest or the priest and professed religious, who are called to minister, to serve, to engage in completing the works of redemption; it is the entire community. The whole community is called to witness to the resurrection of Jesus and the power of life over death. The whole community is called to minister, to serve. The service of ministry will include the work of reconciliation, healing, teaching, leading, working to improve social conditions and political responsibility. Ministry is action on behalf of the human family."[18]

At St. Joseph's we have public commissioning ceremonies or rituals for lay teachers, council members and others involved in ministry as a witness to the parish members that the call to ministry is for everyone. In our parish bulletin we have a long list each week of opportunities for Christian service and involvement in social ministry. We take every opportunity to bring people to an understanding that life in Christ ultimately in-

152

volves accepting Jesus' commission to minister—to spread the good news, to teach, to heal, to serve, to build up the kingdom.

6. Support. Without personal support, ministers grow weary, lose their enthusiasm and even give up their mission.

All that has been said about changing a large American parish into a viable catechumenal community and how to do it is for naught if careful attention is not paid to how you are going to maintain, support, foster and continue to develop what you have started. Some things you need to have are: personal and regular affirmation of all involved in ministry; an ongoing planning process; open honest two-way communication; constant clarification of goals, objectives, roles and responsibilities; sufficient coordination and administration; a large enough pastoral team so that there is adequate time for study, prayer and personal growth in ministry and, especially, time to experience the community they minister to; someone to relieve the pastor of his administrative burden and manage the parish for him so that he has time to encourage and give support to all who minister, both staff and volunteers alike.

Probably the greatest problem we have in our parish and the main reason that we have not moved closer to our goal is that eighty percent of my time as pastor is taken up with the administration and management of the parish, doing things that a lay person or unordained person could easily do and probably do more efficiently. As a result, I don't have sufficient time to read, to study, to pray, to develop closer personal working relationships with our pastoral team members so that we can share visions, dreams and faith together, to work closely with the parish council in fostering their spiritual formation and growth in ministry, to be available as priest to our people. For example, I had to stay up until 3:00 a.m. almost every night for a month in order to find time to do this paper. To develop the role of parish manager is one of the most urgent restructuring needs we have in the church today if pastors are to be successful in building or changing a large parish into a viable catechumenal community. If I had it to do over again, I would look for such a person as one of the first members of my pastoral team so that I could have given more time to achieving the goals and objectives above.

I was asked originally to also answer the questions "What has worked and what hasn't worked in our parish in building community?" I can say that just about everything we have tried has worked to some extent. Some things with a great deal of success and others with less. When things did not work as well as we had hoped, the problem has been the result of human limitation and not enough faith in the work of the Spirit. At fault were such things as lack of time; inadequate planning; goals and objectives not clarified; poor communications; assumptions made, but not checked out; failure to do adequate needs assessments; failure to train people involved in ministry; and failure to share more of ministry with the lay people and to delegate work and responsibilities.

I hope that this description of our experience at St. Joseph's and our efforts to develop a model of parish as community will be helpful to others in their endeavor to establish the adult catechumenate and implement the revised rites of initiation in their parishes. It is but one limited effort and I feel that we still have most of the journey ahead of us. If we are ever to have significant numbers of parishes which are viable catechumenal communities, then many different models will be needed. But out of our efforts and achievements, our gropings, our difficulties and our errors, the new Church of tomorrow will be able to rise.

> The woods are lovely, dark and deep,
> But I have promises to keep,
> And miles to go before I sleep.

—Robert Frost

NOTES

1. Robert W. Hovda, "Hope for the Future: A Summary," *Made, Not Born* (Notre Dame: University of Notre Dame Press, 1976): p. 153.

2. Ralph A. Keifer, "Christian Initiation: The State of the Question," ibid., pp. 138-139.

3. Ibid., pp. 141-142; 145-147.

4. Ibid, pp. 150-151.

5. Ibid., p. 151.

6. Robert W. Hovda, ibid., pp. 152-153.

7. Max Delespesse, *The Church Community: Leaven and Life-Style*, (Ottawa (Canada): The Catholic Centre of St. Paul University; 1969).

   Stephen B. Clark, *Building Christian Communities*, (Notre Dame, Ind.: Ave Maria Press, 1972).

   Drs. Evelyn & James Whitehead, *Forming a Community of Faith* (Kansas City, MO.: NCR Publishing Co., 1976). Cassette of a talk given at the Convocation on Parish Ministry held at Notre Dame University, Sept., 1976. Three of our pastoral team made the presentation on suburban parish at this Convocation.

   "The Parish As Community," Texas Catholic Conference Working Paper, *Origins* (Washington, D.C.: National Catholic News Service, 1977), Sept. 15, 1977; vol. 7: No. 13, pp. 193-198.

   "Basic Communities in the Church," Pro Mundi Vita Bulletin (Brussels, Belgium, 1976), Sept., 1976, No. 62.

8. Nathan Mitchell, "The Adult Catechumenate in an Age of Pluralism," *Liturgy* (Washington, D.C.: The Liturgical Conference, Jan., 1977), Vol. 22, No. 1; p. 12.

9. Stephen B. Clark, op. cit. #7; p. 173.

10. Ibid., p. 177.

11. "Growth in Ministry Program for Priests of the Archdiocese of St. Paul and Minneapolis," Archdiocesan Profile Report Summary (St. Paul, Minn.: Center for Growth in Priestly Ministry, 1978), pp. 11-12.

12. Gerard Egan, "Reproducibility—A Source of Life in Ministry," *LINK* (Kansas City, MO.: NCR Publishing Co., 1973), Special Feature, Nov. 26, 1973.

13. Donald F. Brophy, "Lay Ministers for Tomorrow's Church," *America* (New York, N.Y.: America Press, 1978) Feb. 4, 1978, pp. 77-78.

14. GIFT, A creative adult education process to stimulate a Growth In Faith Together, ed. by Rev. James R. Schaefer (Paramus, N.J.: Paulist Press).

15. GENESIS 2, A continuing program for spiritual and human development (Santa Monica, Calif.: Intermedia Foundation).

16. Aidan Kavagnagh, "Adult Initiation: Process and Ritual," *Liturgy* (Washington, D.C.: The Liturgical Conference, Jan., 1977) Vol. 22, No. 1, p. 5.

17. Max Delespesse, op. cit. #7, p. 31.

18. Texas Catholic Conference Working Paper, op. cit. #7, p. 198.

Jane C. Redmont

Campus Ministry and the Renewed Catechumenate

Jane C. Redmont was a chaplain at the University of Wisconsin at Madison. She earned her baccalauréat in France, her AB (Religion) from Oberlin College, and her Master of Divinity degree from Harvard Divinity School. A former catechumen herself, she speaks with a special kind of experience.

In this paper, I shall try to provide some information on the role of the catechumenate in the campus ministry, to identify a few important pastoral and theological issues, and to indulge in some speculation about the problems and possibilities we have a the University Catholic Center (St. Paul's Chapel) at the University of Wisconsin at Madison.

CAMPUS MINISTRY: YOUTH, DIVERSITY, MARGINALITY

The age group most widely represented on college and university campuses is the young adult group (ages 18-35). In its early period especially, this is the age of identity formation, which includes the formation of religious identity and the making and breaking of religious affiliations. Simply because of this, there are likely to be significant numbers of adults entering the Church on any campus. Yet studies on the renewed catechumenate have not focused upon the campus as catechumenal community. Neither have many campus ministries, as far as I know, taken a look at the place and role of adult inititation within their ministry to young adults or begun to consider how the renewal of the catechumenate might affect them.

One caution first: national and regional gatherings of campus ministers remind us again and again that it is hardly possible to speak of *the* Catholic campus ministry setting. The university settings vary, as do the styles and the human and financial resources of the campus ministries. Consider the variety of Catholic campus ministry settings in the United States today.

- ■ Catholic colleges and universities with a large campus ministry staff, substantial resources, and a congregation of Catholic students;

- ■ Private colleges and universities with a campus ministry funded at least in part by the educational institution itself and often headed by a "dean of the chapel" (frequently a member of one of the "mainline" Protestant denominations);

- ■ State universities, where campus ministry centers are rarely supported by the university and frequently receive financing from the local diocese or from a religious order;

- ■ Community colleges and technical colleges, a great many of them urban and attended by large numbers of minority students (e.g., Black and Mexican-American students) and older-than-average students (e.g., women returning to school after having raised a family, veterans).

Clearly, one cannot draw the same conclusions about the possibilities of application of the RCIA from all of these situations. Some things are, however, common to all campus ministries. In one way or another, all are involved in the process of higher education, and therefore must confront similar issues and values—the quality of education in a given institution, students' concern about career opportunities and the current economic situation, the nature of financial investment made by a university, and the pressures of academic life, to name a few. All are serving communities bound to the rhythms of the academic year which are not the rhythms of the liturgical year: at Christmas, Easter, and Pentecost, vacations often drastically reduce the size of the worshipping community, so that the culminations of the journeys of Lent, Advent, and the Easter season are rarely celebrated in the presence of all those who have made the journey together.

Another characteristic of campus ministry is its marginal and experimental nature. It is perceived by the rest of the Church, and to a great extent perceives itself, as "outside the norm," which is the parish. While within the Church there are many liturgical communities—hospitals, houses of prayer, prisons, as well as parishes—the current structure and practice of the Roman Catholic Church assume that the parish church is the norm and that all other communities are derivative. This marginality has often been creative: campus ministries have been "on the edge" of the Church in the sense of "being most open to new possibilities." They have had the room and often the resources to experiment with new styles of liturgy, to be flexible in the shape of their ministry, to become involved in social concerns. They are presently employing large numbers of lay people, and have been at the forefront in expanding the creative role of women in the Church.

CATHOLIC CAMPUS MINISTRY AT THE UNIVERSITY OF WISCONSIN AT MADISON: ST. PAUL'S UNIVERSITY CATHOLIC CENTER

Over 30,000 students attend the University of Wisconsin at Madison. The majority of them are natives of Wisconsin, and come from Lutheran and Roman Catholic backgrounds. Eight thousand or so are Roman Catholic. A number of churches have centers and full-time staffs, which tend to be "building-bound," and serve primarily those who come to them of their own initiative. In contrast, a variety of Christian student groups are very active in the dormitories, more involved in direct outreach, and are largely evangelical and fundamentalist. I would venture that these groups (e.g., Campus Crusade, Inter-Varsity Christian Fellowship, Navigators) involve at least as many students as do the "established churches" on campus.

Many students at the UW-Madison are religiously affiliated or involved in a religious search. However, an equal number at least are disillusioned by the faith community in which they were raised and openly oppose the practice of any religion. The administration of the university, on the whole, tends to be suspicious of organized religion (this is fairly common in state universities throughout the country). Many of the students who attend St. Paul's, therefore, come to us seeking a supportive community—a group of people who do not consider religion an aberration and who share their beliefs and values. Another tension between the university and the religious communities on campus—less frequently named but no less present—arises from the fact that the university promotes values contradicting those of the Gospel, such as competition, individualism, and the tendency to view and evaluate the world in terms of production.

St. Paul's has the distinction of being the first Catholic Chapel at a state university in the United States. It has been a stable Catholic presence at the UW-Madison since the first decade of this century. Today it is a large center that serves the needs of a variety of people, most of them young adults. Ten Eucharistic liturgies are celebrated every weekend, drawing a total of 4,000 or 5,000 worshipers. One quarter or so of these are directly involved in programs and activities at the Center, which range from sacramental preparation to education for social justice. Many of those who worship at St. Paul's are not students. St. Paul's has the status of a parish, enabling it to celebrate and record weddings and baptisms. Besides staff and faculty families, some people from the community outside the university are also members, although current policy is that one must be in some manner connected with the university in order to be a registered member.

St. Paul's is unusual in that it is a self-supporting university parish. Working members tithe from their earnings and students contribute—or, at least, are asked to contribute—a dollar a week. This is notably different from other campus ministries, which are for the most part dependent upon their diosese or upon a religious order.

The staff at St. Paul's has changed in the last few years from an ordained and male staff to a staff including lay and ordained, male and female members. Ten people are employed full-time: five chaplains (three dioceasan priests including the administrative pastor, one Jesuit priest, and me, a lay woman), a secretary, an administrative assistant, a program coordinator (all lay people). This year part-time workers have included a Franciscan priest, two pastoral counseling interns (both lay women), several choir directors, and a deacon. Several priests who are students at the university celebrate daily and Sunday Eucharist regularly at St. Paul's.

Some tension exists between the family and student populations at St. Paul's. There are two different "constituencies" with different needs and different lifestyles, which often experience themselves as competing with one another and which the staff often experiences as competing for its time.

Many people who are not offically members attend St. Paul's for a variety of reasons. The chapel is centrally located and is easily accessible from both town and campus. For years it has attracted worshippers from neighboring Catholic parishes, unaffiliated Catholics, and non-Catholics. St. Paul's is a community of faith, a center of spiritual growth and renewal, that attracts students and non-students alike "just by being there." There are at least two factors involved in this attraction: first, the strong faith commitment within the St. Paul's community, reflected in and nurtured by a rich liturgical life, and second, its openness. People feel free to ask questions, to believe, to doubt, to share their journeys of faith together. Different levels and states of participation in the life of the Church coexist in relative harmony. It is an inclusive rather than an exclusive community.

For a variety of reasons which include its self-awareness as a "liberal university community," St. Paul's experiences itself as "different," and the issue of continuity and discontinuity with the rest of the Church that is a pervasive "campus ministry issue" is very much alive here.

THE CATECHUMENAL JOURNEY AT ST. PAUL'S

Lives and journeys I have been privileged to witness and share: Julie was a student of 21, Methodist and Episcopalian in background, whose search became visible when she began attending our "Basic Instruction Series" with her friend Ron, a "born Catholic." I watched them support and respect one another's journey of faith. Ellen was also Protestant in background, a graduate student also working part-time, deeply intellectual and sensitive, divorced and living with her two young sons, slowly discovering the richness of community life in the Catholic tradition and of her relationship with the Lord in prayer. When Carol, a young working woman, announced her decision to receive the sacrament of Confirmation and be formally welcomed into the Church, she surprised almost everyone for she had been active at St. Paul's as a liturgical musician for at least a year. Few people knew that she was not "officially" a Catholic. During the Easter Vigil she spoke about her personal pilgrimage and the meaning of the celebration of her full reception into the Church: "It feels like a marriage," she said, "a lifetime commitment, a public promise to 'make the relationship permanent.'"

And Martin was a young single man who was raised a Roman Catholic. A former user of hallucinogens, disillusioned with the lifestyle he had chosen, he came and asked to be prepared for the sacrament of Confirmation. He had read some, but knew very little of Catholic doctrine or even Catholic practice. He did have a clear sense of having discovered the presence of Jesus Christ in his life and of having entered into a relationship of trust and love. And Maria, nineteen years old and about to begin college, walked into my office and said with determination: "I want to be baptized; what should I do?" Brought up in an atmosphere indifferent to religion by parents who had been raised as Catholics, she was curious about everything from doctrine to parish life, eager to learn how to pray, full of excited questions, yet with a deep calm and peace underneath her ebullience.

162

These are just a few of the people we have been privileged to begin welcoming into the Church here. Most—perhaps a few dozen a year—who seek entrance into the Church here are young adults, and the majority are students. Generally, they were baptized as infants in another Christian tradition and have been in and out of various churches and usually away from organized religion for a time. A few are baptized Catholics who were never catechized or confirmed. Only a handful of those seeking initiation into the Church have never been bapitzed—either coming from a nonreligious (usually formerly Christian) background such as Maria's, or brought up in a Jewish or non-Western/Biblical (e.g., Buddhist) religious community.

The number of interfaith (Christian + non-Christian, particulary Catholic + Jewish) and ecumenical (Protestant + Catholic) marriages has increased noticeably in the last decade. Some of these marriages have resulted in entrances into the Roman Catholic communion. Due to changes in both the Roman Catholic and other churches these "transitions" are no longer seen as necessary and are chosen freely rather than hastily embraced as was more often the case in the past. Among those entering the Church here, many have been inspired by the life of a loved one—friend, spouse, grandparent, teacher.

Like most of the university community, the catechumens are a mobile group, often present at St. Paul's only a few years or even less, absent during a few months of each year, and uncertain of their plans from one year to the next. Also, although this is not true for all or our catechumens, they include a high percentage of intellectually demanding "searchers."

Catechumens on a university campus are very likely to come from a wide range of cultures and countries and add to the diversity already present among the North American catechumens. In the pastoral area, this raises the question of sensitivity to the catechumen's culture and of the expression of this vital element in his or her life in the liturgies of initiation (through music or forms of prayer).

Another group of people needs to be added to the description of "catechumens" at St. Paul's, although they are not cat-

163

echumens in the strict sense. They are people who received the sacraments of initiation as children and who, having moved away from the Church a long time ago are undergoing a process of conversion, a transition to adult faith. They are at least as numerous as those seeking entrance into the Church. Their search and the stages they pass through are remarkably similar to those of the catechumenate proper, with one major experiential difference: in the case of "born Catholics," there exists a need to reflect upon their experience of Church, and often to name the pain associated with that experience. Both groups share a need for discovering the reality of shared prayer, deepening a personal relationship with Jesus Christ, evaluating the relationship to the Church as an institution, becoming acquainted with and involved in different forms of Christian service, and, after a decision to make a commitment, celebrating this in some visible way with and within the faith community.

All of these journeys have in common the lived mystery of Christ and his Church. For each person there is a growing awareness of the presence of God in his or her life—and particularly of the presence of Jesus, incarnate, crucified, and risen. There is as well a growing conviction on the part of each that his or her relationship with God is better able to grow, nurtured by the sacramental, spiritual and social life of the Roman Catholic communion.

THE CATECHUMENAL JOURNEY AT ST. PAUL'S

For the most part, adult initiation at St. Paul's has not been celebrated in the public and communal way to which the RCIA calls us. Yet catechumenal processes were already present at St. Paul's. Many of the principles and beliefs underlying the restoration of the catechumenate have been present here for several years and very much taken for granted. St. Paul's, as a community, has a growing sense of faith as journey; a growing commitment to sharing and celebrating the crucial passages and times of growth in this lifetime journey; and a strong belief in the ministerial vocation of all baptized Christians, reflected in active lay involvement and leadership in sacramental preparation, retreats, service projects, social activities, and Life in the Spirit Seminars.

Curiously, we have approached adult initiation almost apart from these trends until now—without relating the reality of initiation into the Church to our emerging vision of Church and the common life it has begun to inspire. However, the resources already present within our university parish, as well as existing programs and the processes which deal with the initiation of adults, point to a readiness for an explicit catechumenate and already function as "catechumenal processes."

A. What a Modern Catholic Believes

"What a Modern Catholic Believes" is a six-week educational program. It focuses on basic beliefs of the Catholic Church, particularly as they relate to the sacramental life of the Church. The series has become a tradition at St. Paul's. It is offered at least five times a year with fifty people or so in attendance each time. The series provides ample space for those attending the sessions to share their questions and experiences with one another.

No assumptions are made about how participants in "What a Modern Catholic Believes" will follow up on the series. Some of these participants are interested in becoming Roman Catholics but are still in the "inquiring" stage; for them the series functions as a sort of precatechumenate. Others have already made the decision to become Catholics, but have not much knowledge of Catholic doctrine, or wish to learn about certain areas of belief and practice. Still others are young men and women who are engaged to marry Roman Catholics and who wish to understand their future spouse's faith (both members of the couple are encouraged to attend and usually do so). Finally, a growing number of participants are those who speak of themselves as "Catholics in need of renewal," who want "to know about the changes," and who sense their own need to mature into an adult faith commitment.

B. "Instructions" Following the WMCB Series

For those who wanted to deepen their search and study with the intention of being received into the Church, participation in the Basic Instruction Series was followed by individual "instructions" with one of the chaplains, with little formal participation by the rest of the community in the process of initiation. While some waited until the Easter Vigil to celebrate the sacraments of initiation in the midst of the community, many entered the Church at a liturgy during the year—often on a weekday. The community has not been absent from the process of initiation—usually the person being received into the Church had shared his or her journey with a few friends who attended St. Paul's, attended Sunday and weekday liturgies, and taken part in some of our programs and activities. But none of this was celebrated or formalized. The journey itself was not celebrated—only the culmination of the journey. Most of the time, the process of welcoming someone into the Church was so private that the chaplain who had been "giving instructions" was the only staff member of St. Paul's aware of a given person's journey of conversion.

C. The Confirmation-Reaffirmation Program

In process and structure, the confirmation-reaffirmation program is the closest we have come to a catechumenate at St. Paul's. It was begun in 1976 as an experimental program independently of the Basic Instruction Series and individual instructions, and was intended neither to replace them nor to compete with them. Two groups of people were involved in the Confirmation-Reaffirmation Program:

1. Baptized Christians (approximately one half Roman Catholic and one half Protestant) who had not received the sacrament of confirmation. (Some were teengaers from our parish families who were admitted to the program with the understanding that this was an adult venture in which the same commitment was asked of them as of the other participants.)

2. Catholics who had received all the sacraments of initiation, but wanted to re-examine their faith. They came into the program with the option of reaffirming publicly at Pentecost what had already been expressed in their Baptism and Confirmation but never claimed in their adult life.

The program was presented as a chance to "take a look at what faith is for me" and to consider what it might mean to express faith in Jesus Christ in the Roman Catholic tradition. Participants were asked for a commitment to a process of one whole academic year, a year of searching focused on faith experience, with reflection on doctrine within the context of the discovery and sharing of faith experience. They were called to prayer and reflection—alone and in small groups—and to involvement in service. At St. Paul's, the entire parish was involved through selected themes woven into Sunday liturgies. A few special celebrations were held during the year, including a blessing by the worship assembly before the group's midyear retreat, and culminating in a liturgy of confirmation and "reaffirmation" at Pentecost. The RCIA was not used in the celebrations, although some were remarkably like the liturgies of enrollment and blessing of the catechumenate.

The liturgy was designed to avoid confusion between the conferral of the sacrament of Confirmation and the gesture of "reaffirmation," but in a manner that celebrated the reaffirmation of faith by those already baptized and confirmed as children in a sufficiently public and visible manner.

Pastorally, one of the most interesting and astute aspects of this program is the linking of the journey of faith of two groups of people—those who have not received all the sacraments of initiation, and those who did receive them long ago, but who struggle with the same call to conversion, the same questions, the same issues of faith, of commitment to life in Christ, and of relationship to the community called Church.

D. The Life in the Spirit Seminars

I mention the "Life in the Spirit Seminars" briefly in this description of catechumenal processes at St. Paul's because the

Seminars (offered at least once a year by members of the very large and active charismatic prayer group at St. Paul's) exhibit a format and a spirit which take into account the individual's continual call to conversion and growth in faith, and the need for this call and growth to be shared in community. The Seminars have often performed the function of "welcoming to the Church" or of "welcoming back to the Church." They provide a setting for people to talk and pray in small groups—often the first experience of sharing faith and prayer that the participants ever had. As such, they can be spoken of as "catechumenal."

TOWARD A CATECHUMENATE AT ST. PAUL'S

A. A New Direction in Adult Initiation: Lent-Easter

It seems to me that, practically speaking, the renewal of the catechumenate calls for a double transformation in the pastoral practice of initiation.

1. Private *"instruction"* by a priest or a lay catechist must become *initiation into the life* (faith and practice) of the Catholic Christian community—an initiation covering four areas: learning the tradition, beginning to live with the death and resurrection of Jesus as one's reference point, liturgical initiation, and the Christian apostolate (*RCIA*, No. 19).

This initiation is to be performed by the community itself—specifically, by many members of the local church: "welcomers," sponsors, catechists, and small prayer groups. The teaching and nurturing presence of a variety of people more accurately reflects both the Church's daily struggle to be faithful to our Baptism and the pluralism present in the Church, than does a series of conversations with a single person, ordained or not.

2. The one celebration of initiation—usually a rather private event—must become a series of celebrations rejoicing in the catechumen's faith journey and culminating in the celebration

of the sacraments of initiation with the local Eucharistic assembly during the Easter Vigil.

Both of these transformations presuppose a fundamental transformation in the local church community's self-understanding. First of all, it must understand itself as church *community*. Further, neither of these two transformations is possible if this community does not experience itself as called to a process of conversion as the catechumens are and capable of exercising actively the ministry of God's "priestly people."

This past Lent saw the first attempt to work toward the first part of this double transformation with a very small experiment. A handful of people—all of them baptized Christians wishing to become Roman Catholics—had been seeing me individually for study and spiritual direction in preparation for a profession of faith, reception of the sacrament of Confirmation and First Eucharist. After encouraging them to wait until the Easter Vigil to celebrate their entrance into the Church, I gathered them together two or three times during Lent with their sponsors. In these Lenten gatherings, we shared the stories of our journeys of faith with one another, talked about the meaning of what the "catechumens" were celebrating at Easter, particularly the sacrament of confirmation; and prayed together. Although this was more of a "band-aid solution" than anything else, the fruits of these small gatherings were numerous.

For all those present and particularly for the catechumens, the group afforded a sense of common journey, and of being received into a community of faith made up of many diversely gifted—and wounded—men and women. It reminded and taught us how much the faith of each one of us is nurtured by the faith of others in the community. It also clarified the role of the sponsors and gave each of them a chance to affirm and celebrate their place and role in the journey of each of the catechumens. At the final session, all of those who attended the meetings expressed the need for some kind of post-Easter "mystagogical" gathering.

□ □ □

Our Easter Vigil was planned and designed by several people and groups of people. I was responsible for planning the Liturgy of Water and Baptism/Confirmation. An infant was to be baptized during the Vigil, which posed a challenge to me as I tried to design a liturgy containing both infant and adult rites of initiation that would make sense theologically and aesthetically. In the end, I designed a liturgy of infant and adult initiation which contained two significant variations from the traditional celebration:

1. After the common renunciation of sin and renewal of baptismal vows—which served as the traditional profession of faith for the parents and sponsors of the infant, as well as for the catechumens—and the infant's baptism, and before the celebration of Confirmation, each of the confirmands gave a brief personal profession of faith. These statements, spoken after the confirmands had professed with the community our common faith (and received baptismal candles together with the parents of the infant), singled out the unique and precious gift that each one brought to the Church at St. Paul's that night. Statements of what each had received and felt ready to share with others were deeply moving for the gathered community—calling all of us to realize that we were not simply "offering something" to new members of the Catholic community, but receiving the gift of their life and faith, and with them, being graced by the presence of the Spirit in our midst.

2. The second "alteration" was a change in the role of celebrant of the liturgy of initiation. Since I had been the principal "contact" with St. Paul's for most of the people who were being initiated into the Church, both they and I needed to express liturgically what our relationship had been in the last weeks and months, which posed another challenge. Taking into account my limitations—the chief one being that I may not preside at Eucharistic celebrations not being a priest—we have been trying to experiment at St. Paul's with styles of presiding and celebrating that reflect liturgically the nature of the pastoral reality at St. Paul's (i.e., that we have male and

female staff members who minister to, and with, male and female parishioners).

This year's Easter Vigil was one of the most harmonious experiences we have had in this area, with no sense of artificiality, and a real sense of "flow" between the priest's role and mine. Specifically, I gave the introduction to the rites of initiation and a brief "running commentary," asked the questions of renunciation of sin and profession of faith, offered prayers, and gave a gesture of welcome in the name of the community at the end of the rite, together with our pastor, who was the confirming minister.

B. A Pilot Program at St. Paul's

After coming to know St. Paul's and observing the catechumenal processes I have described, I presented to the staff for discussion a proposal for a catechumenate at St. Paul's that attempted to bring together the norm of the RCIA and our lived pastoral situation.

The proposal suggested devising a mode of follow-up on the Basic Instruction Series which would be a one-year catechumenate. The process would be primarily communal, although catechumens would have opportunity for individual spiritual direction, and would involve sponsors and "sponsor families." Such a program would have the community teach in the four areas set forth by No. 19 of the RCIA: 1. learning the tradition; 2. living the mystery of Christ's death and resurrection; 3. celebrating various rituals; 4. ministry outward. In all four of these areas, various members of St. Paul's would be involved as catechists, liturgists, companions in prayer and in service, and simple "welcomers."

The first and second areas would be taken care of by weekly gatherings for prayer and study in small "sponsor groups."

We would commit ourselves in the third area to celebrating the stages of the catechumenal journey during the liturgical year, from the enrollment of the catechumens in September or October until Easter.

We would try to cover the fourth area by asking that the cate-chumens become involved in some aspect of Christian service with the help of members of the community who could wel-come and introduce them to these activities.

The proposal, presented this spring to the staff of St. Paul's, was accepted. I will be coordinating the catechumenate, and am making the following assumptions: We shall link the catechumenate with the Confirmation-reaffirmation program either by combining the two programs, or by keeping them sep-arate and assuming that they meet different pastoral needs. Al-though we have not yet made this decision, I suspect we will choose the latter option (Confirmation-reaffirmation seems bet-ter to meet the needs of "born Catholics").

Only two or three of our ten weekend Eucharistic communi-ties will be chosen as communities of celebration of the RCIA—"pilot communities." The catechumenate program will be a "pi-lot program." We will set it up and try it for one year, evaluate what we have lived together a year from now, and make further decisions and commitments accordingly. We will not require all people who wish to be received into the Church to take part in the catechumenate, although we will encourage them to do so. To require such a process of all potential catechumens, to declare immediately a stop to all private instruction, is not real-istic, given the differences among the "catechumens" (some of them coming to us are almost ready to enter the Church and others need a longer process of initiation). The staff of St. Paul's also needs time to "grow into" this model of Christian initiation.

In such a transitional and pluralistic community as this, we may never be able to offer a single model of adult initiation. At least for now, it is good for more than one model of adult initia-tion to exist at St. Paul's.

The liturgical and academic years conflict. If we are to have a viable catechumenate in this university community, we may have to adjust the celebrations of initiation to fit the academic schedule. The challenge facing us is that of remaining faithful both to the liturgical season in process and to the human expe-rience of growth in faith which the liturgy helps us to celebrate.

C. Pastoral and Theological Problems: Confirmation and Eucharist at St. Paul's

One of the pastoral/theological issues raised for us at St. Paul's both by the Confirmation-reaffirmation program and by the large number of baptized Christians from other confessions seeking reception into full communion with the Roman Catholic Church is that of Confirmation. To put it briefly: we have not "resolved" the Confirmation issue at St. Paul's. (Has anyone?) What is Confirmation? The definition given in early Christian tradition is changing as the age of reception of Confirmation advances. It is difficult to explain it as inseparable from Baptism when in fact it has been separated.

As in virtually all American parishes today, the traditional order of the sacraments of initiation has been changed. Our children make their first communion quite early and we have no annual First Communion Sunday. Rather, first communions are celebrated at Sunday Masses throughout the year as family celebrations. The religious education program here is increasingly family-centered, operating on the principle that the parents are primarily responsible for their children's faith development.

In contrast, Confirmation occurs at a much later date with less family involvement. At this point we have no special Confirmation class for our teenagers, and most of the parents who felt they were able to share their faith with younger children do not yet see themselves as primary teachers of high school youngsters. Last year some of these young people chose to enter the Confirmation-reaffirmation program. It is not clear how we will help to prepare them for Confirmation in the future. Confirmation has become, whether we like it or not, a rite of passage for teenagers—a sort of Catholic *bar mitzvah/bas mitzvah*. There is a clear human need for some kind of ritual during the teenage years (preferably the early teens) to mark the beginning of a new stage of growth in faith that coincides with a new stage in human development. The question is: should this ritual be the sacrament of Confirmation?

In the same way, there appears to be a growing pastoral need—at least here at St. Paul's—for a young adult rite of reaffirmation of faith and commitment to living that faith within the Church community. If we celebrate the sacrament of Confirmation with a focus on that experience, at that stage of life, have we strayed too far from the traditional meaning of Confirmation? Or are we to take as fact that the meaning of the sacrament has significantly changed?

Further confusion about Confirmation is occasioned by the tendency in past years to celebrate the initiation of adults in the same jumbled order as the initiation of children, with first Eucharist, the sign and reality of full membership in the Church, sandwiched between Baptism and Confirmation. Frequently adult "converts" at St. Paul's have made their first communion in one celebration, and only later celebrated Confirmation as a further stage of initiation and personal growth in faith. It seems that if the pattern of the RCIA were followed, the need for marking stages of growth and conversion would be fulfilled by the liturgies of the catechumenate and the sacraments of initiation might be celebrated in the traditional order with Eucharist as the culmination of the celebration.

The issue of Eucharist is another unresolved pastoral question in the process of adult initiation at St. Paul's. The fact is that students who do not celebrate their initiation into the Catholic communion in stages, but simply celebrate a profession of faith and Confirmation at some point, frequently do not wait until that date to begin sharing fully in the Eucharistic meal with the rest of the congregation. Thus, the value of the Eucharist as a sacrament of initiation is lost. The fact that it is a sacrament of initiation is forgotten, partly due to the fact that "catechumens" attend our Eucharistic liturgies and that they and other non-Catholics choose in good conscience to receive communion. While it is impossible for us to decide who can and cannot share in the Eucharistic meal at St. Pauls's we cannot—and, I think, do not want to—run a check on 5,000 people in order to declare some of them "certified" Roman Catholics. I suspect that if we begin to formalize and celebrate the catechumenal process, some of the ambiguity and confusion would disappear. The hunger for Eucharist makes the celebration of full communion with the Body of Christ all the more of a celebration. But it needs to be supported and celebrated and valued. We are not doing this at the present time.

Small wonder, then, that we are left with this "undifferentiated" situation where some catechumens receive communion and others do not, where there is no visible sign that distinguishes catechumens from members in full communion with the Church. (I use the expression "members in full communion" since catechumens are already members of the Church.) We will have to find ways at St. Paul's to celebrate hunger for the Eucharist both reverently and realistically. Returning to the notion and practice of the "Mass of the Catechumens" is one idea. It remains to be seen whether the catechumens will feel comfortable with this. I suspect it will be difficult for them to accept the procedure, and for us on the staff to encourage them to accept it.

VI. CONCLUSION

We have begun. St. Paul's is a privileged community that may have more catechumenal resources than most. It is also a university-related community, with a transitional population that has yet to be called to an intense and continuous form of ministry. We shall spend the summer inviting various groups and individuals at St. Paul's to be involved in welcoming the catechumens next year. Together we shall plan the structure and content of the sponsor groups; we shall reflect on some of the theological and pastoral issues mentioned in this essay; and we shall determine ways to inform and educate the larger St. Paul's community about our new venture in the fall.

I have no illusions that the catechumenate will solve all our problems. It will not "single-handedly" bridge the family-student gap, make of us more active members of the church community, immediately transform our lifestyle, resolve our differences, or even solve all the questions we have begun to raise about adult initiation.

What it will do—whether we count it as "success" or "failure" by the end of next spring—is to challenge us. It will challenge us through the visible presence of the catechumens in our midst, to consider our own journey of faith and to reflect on the meaning of our own baptism; to be people of hospitality who cannot help but share what they have received, whose faith is not confined to the search for personal fulfillment; to ask questions, not just about Christian initiation, but about the life of the Church today; and to begin to live these questions in a vital and creative way, with the help of the Holy Spirit. It will challenge us to be a different kind of learning community on the UW-Madison campus.

Beyond the question of the catechumenate for young adults in a university parish is the broader and deeper issue of youth and the Church. Many young people are leaving the Church. And many who have never been in the Church remain on the outside because they do not find in the Church anything to nourish their hunger for God and for community or anyone who might live their questions with them. Is this not, at least in part, because we, in our haste to be proclaimers of the Word, have forgotten the first step of the ministry of the Word, which is *listening*? We cannot proclaim unless we have heard. Are we taking the time to invite youth to share their questions with the broader Church community, to challenge it, to speak God's Word to it?

The problem is not merely to find a better way in incorporate young adults into the Church, but to welcome these new members with the awareness that they bring something precious and irreplaceable with them, to realize that, in receiving them as baptized brothers and sisters, we may be transformed in ways we have not even begun to imagine.

James B. Dunning

The Stages of Initiation
I. Inquiry

James B. Dunning is Executive Director of the National Organization for Continuing Education of Roman Catholic Clergy. He is also Director of Continuing Education of Priests for the Archdiocese of Seattle. He has his Ph.D. in Religious Studies from the Catholic University of America.

Note: The subject matter under this title will be treated in the next three articles by Rev. James Dunning, Rev. Thomas Ivory, and Rev. James Parker.

"The rite of initiation is suited to the spiritual journey of adults, which varies according to the many forms of God's grace, the free cooperation of the individuals, the action of the Church, and the circumstances of time and place" (*RCIA*, 5).

"It is my task now to build a new life. . . . The thought of where I shall go from here lurks in my consciousness. Will it be to a nursing home, or to a hospital, or will I go directly, with no stopovers? Whichever it will be, I shall look upon it with no dread. . . . As I travel on toward the unknown, the winds of change sweep through vast areas, and I am aware of the death agonies of an obsolete civilization. While my confidence in many of my old beliefs is crumbling, I cling to the belief that the destiny of man points upward. When the bell tolls for me, I shall go willingly, with no bitterness, but with tenderness toward my fellow travelers on my long journey" (Mrs. Polly Francis, age 91).

The Copernican revolution launched by the *Rite of Christian Initiation of Adults (RCIA)* is that initiation is no longer

177

primarily introduction to a book, to a catechism of doctrines, but introduction to a community of "fellow travelers" on our long spiritual journey. If that introduction leads to close bonds and lasting commitment, we can depend on that community to be with us at the critical stages of that journey to support us and challenge us to deeper levels of conversion, even to the point of "building a new life" at age 91 like Mrs. Polly Francis.

In fact, for some time in spiritual direction and adult education I have been offering a process which I now discover contains the ingredients incorporated in the RCIA. The process begins with story-telling—the sharing of our personal pilgrimage, especially the important events in that journey—which leads to a questioning, an inquiry, a search for meaning about the significance of our stories. That leads to reflection upon the stories and faith of the Christian community to discern whether or not Jesus' story and the stories of his followers bring depth and help people interpret their own story. Jaroslav Pelikan has said that traditions are the dead faith of living people and tradition is the living faith of dead people. This second stage is exposure to the community's tradition as the living faith of living and dead people. The third stage calls for faith-interpretation. Regardless of how other people understand their pilgrimage, how do I interpret the meaning of my personal journey? Do I see my life as a gift, as grounded in more than my own fragility and in more than the gifts shared in human community? In other words, do I enter the conversion moment when I see my story as God's story and the community's story as God's story?[1] Finally, do I discern God's presence in my story, in time of both pain and joy, that leads to Eucharist, to thanksgiving, to celebration, and to sharing the Good News with others in the ministry?

I offer two conclusions from the above. First, these stages need not happen in chronological order. They are rather dimensions in a process of conversion, and people, in their own uniqueness and freedom and according to the call of the Spirit, will move in and out of those dimensions in their own way. It is helpful, however, for a spiritual director or catechist to be aware of all those dimensions in order to help people integrate all that is happening in their lives.

Second, this is a paper on catechetical suggestions for the RCIA in the United States. In view of the above, these should be seen as suggestions for all the important times of adult growth and conversion even until age 91. We can hope that adults initiated through such a process will continue their journey with new questions, deeper incorporation into the living tradition of the community, more intense conversion, and new cause for celebration and ministry. With the insights of this process, we can also hope in post-baptismal catechesis that adults who did not clearly begin their spiritual journey by pondering and entering into these stages may do so now and come to see their story as God's story.[2]

The RCIA speaks of four periods of investigation and maturation in the process of a catechumenate: (1) precatechumenate (a period of inquiry and evangelization); (2) catechesis and associated rites; (3) purification and enlightenment (preparation for and reception of the sacraments); and (4) post-baptismal catechesis (comparable to what we speak of as "ongoing" religious education). These four periods occur within three great stages of development: the stage of inquiry, the stage of more profound incorporation into the Christian community through the catechumenate, and the stage in which spiritual preparation is completed and the catechumen celebrates the sacraments by which a Christian is initiated.

I. THE STAGE OF INQUIRY

First, we shall reflect upon the place of story-telling during the stage of Inquiry. Second, we shall consider the importance of questioning and searching for the meaning of those stories in terms of our own lives, the lives of the Christian community, and the life of Jesus. Third, we shall suggest some resources and ministries which might assist in the process of story-telling and questioning.

A. Story-Telling

In a remarkable study, conducted through interviews at St. Columba's Episcopal Church in Washington, D.C., Jean Haldane explored the personal religious journeys of a number of individual church members and the impact of the institutional church upon those personal religious stories. Her conclusion:

> The private nature of the journey is partly responsible for the fact that it appears to "occur on the side" in the church. It is not talked about there. There is a veritable "conspiracy of silence" about it. It is peripheral to, not parallel with the church. It is simply there, untapped and unrecognized, an underground of experience that is the personal context for what happens to each person in the church. Another fact that discourages people from talking about the religious journey is that no one in the church ever asks about their personal faith and practice. Several spoke of fear of judgment and not measuring up to some standard image of a church-goer or Episcopalian.[3]

Her suggestion:

> I am struck by the fact that the church does seem to be concerned with *telling* and not with *listening* . Although telling is a central task of the church as it proclaims the good news, this study tells us clearly that we must pay attention to what happens to the lay people who do the listening and receiving most of the time.... They were dissatisfied because there was "no place and no one" with whom to talk it over. (And they do not mean the traditional "inquiries' class"—they are not looking for "telling" but for dialogue about meanings, in *relationship* to doctrine and their own pilgrimage.)[4]

Haldane's study, and the *RCIA* as I understand it, certainly do not signal the death of doctrine nor retreat from the possible stretching of our own story through dialogue with the stories of the Tradition. They do insist that doctrine should have something to do with our personal pilgrimage, in an approach which Karl Rahner has termed "theological anthropology" (talk of "Theos" has something to do with talk of "anthropos" and is not the rarified abstractions of theological "space cadets"). Or what Gregory Baum has called the shift from extrinsicism to intrinsicism (doctrine which is intrinsic to and which unveils

180

the meaning of human existence). Or what Andrew Greeley has named the shift from apologetics to hermeneutics (from proving credibility of doctrine to interpreting through Tradition the meaning of our stories).[5] I stress this because sometimes the call to story-telling has been heard as a summons to reject intelligence, to mindless "show-and-tell" sessions or "group-gropes" with room for infallible feelings but little room for less-than-infallible thinking, or to a privatism in which we turn in upon our own story but in what has been called the "new narcissism" refuse to ponder what the journeys of others might reveal for us (one wag claims we have become expert "navel observatories"!). No, the summons is to tell the stories and doctrines of the Tradition in ways that dialogue with a person's own religious journey; it is not a call to be iconoclasts regarding the community's accumulated wisdom.

The summons, however, is also to listening before/with/after telling. The *RCIA* states that this precatechumenate period is "a time for hearing the first preaching of the Gospel" (No. 7); I am saying that the document should more clearly say that this is also a time for hearing the personal story of the inquirer. It does mention that during the time of the precatechumenate the faithful should be "ready to open up the spirit of the Christian community to the candidates, to invite them into their families, to engage them in private conversation, and to invite them to some community gatherings" (*RCIA*, No. 41).

Let these times be moments of hospitality and friendship. Let them not be too "churchy," with an ecclesiastical imperialism which suggests that conversation is religious only when it sounds religious. Let us respect the need for all sorts of gestures of human friendship and small talk before people trust each other enough to share their lives. But then let there be listening; and let there be "big talk" about our lives, about our times of pain and joy, our wounds and our times of healing, our death and resurrection. Let the inquirers and the faithful share their stories of dying and rising in their personal pilgrimage. After all, the *RCIA* also states: "Together with the catechumens the faithful reflect upon the value of the paschal mystery, renew their own conversion, and by their example lead the catechumens to obey the Holy Spirit more generously" (No. 4). If the paschal mystery is to be effectively an experience of theological anthropology, and of an intrinsicism and hermeneutic which truly unveil the meaning of our lives, people need the opportunity to translate that language about death and resurrection by telling about their own experiences of pain and healing. Then seeds of the first preaching of the Good News of Jesus can fall upon ground prepared to hear of the surpassing healing and resurrection offered by his Father to those who journey with him and unite their stories to his.

First, then, when trust has been established, inquirers and members of the community will share their stories. What do we mean by story?

> Objectively speaking, story is simply a narrative that links various sequences. Subjectively and to the point, to have a story is to be a person. Or to turn the phrase, to be a person is to have a story... Without my story, I have no identity. I do not know who I am, or what I am about. "If you have no story, how do you know where you're going; and if you're going somewhere, how will you know when you get there?"
>
> A story is made up of steppingstones along the footpath, markings up the side of the mountain, curves and detours along the highway of life. A story is not a four-lane "superslab" (CB jargon for highway) without stops, turns and returns. A story tells about struggle, without which life is boring. My personal story tells of the zigzags in my life—the transitions and transformations.[6]

By telling the tales of those curves and detours, those stops, turns and returns, the inquirer can gradually discern the patterns and rhythms in the journey. He/she can listen to the pilgrimages of others, including Jesus', for echoes of those patterns and rhythms. Are there recurring strains of death and life? Are these stories in harmony? Might the story of Jesus and his exodus through death to resurrection offer the resounding theme upon which all of our stories are variations and which grounds our lives with meaning? If so, perhaps the inquirer will ask for membership in the community of those whose patterns and rhythms he/she shares.

I suggest two critical reasons why the Inquiry period should be rooted in story-telling. First, the Church will be experienced initially by the inquirer (and perhaps for the first time by other members of the Christian community) as a "we" not a "they," a community of persons with stories to share and not as a thing. Isn't it the experience of most inquirers that they were first attracted to the Church by persons, perhaps persons with whom they had lived for many years? Somehow we gave the impression in the inquiry class, however, that the Church was something else. It was those officials "back then" or "over there" who gave us this catechism to learn, these ceremonies to use, and these laws to follow. Story-telling will attempt to ground catechisms, ceremonies, and laws in the lives of real people who are companions with us on our journey, in past and present, who have identities as persons because they have stories to tell.

Doctrines, rituals and commandments, then, are part of their very identity; because they are expressions of what they believe, worship, and value. When the inquirer moves on to the catechumenate to learn more completely about the Tradition, if the initial experience has been of persons with tales to tell of why they believe, worship and value, perhaps the Tradition will not become an "it" and the Church will not become a "they" or a "thing." Perhaps the Church will remain a "we," because we are a community of persons all of whom understand, celebrate, and value our stories in the light of Jesus.

Colman McCarthy is not writing expressly about Church community in the following lines, but he beautifully summarizes what I'm trying to say:

> To have companions of any kind—inner or outer—suggests that a journey is being made, as indeed with all of us there is. It should be a traveling toward gentleness, integrity and joyfulness, a destination all of us long for but hesitate to imagine ourselves reaching, lest on arrival we be given new obligations to love. But if we can travel with a band of inner companions, what tests can prove too demanding? It is not that the chosen companions of our interior, at least not the ones whom I have taken into my life, are meant to teach us matters of power and might—how to earn a living, how to make sense or make progress. Those are the most handily mastered of life's chores. Instead, we need them to share with us the wisdom of the obvious, to repeat and repeat for our stubborn minds what we never quite get right—that all of us are fragile, that

the wealth of the planet should be shared justly and that nothing matters unless it is done with a perpetual fidelity of love.[7]

Granted the problems of immense urban and suburban parishes which offer more anonymity than companionship. Granted the problems of mobility in America where we journey too fast and too often for anyone to stay with us.[8] Nonetheless, the ideals evoked by the *RCIA* of self-knowledge through dialogue, of personal spirituality and conversion, of respect for the uniqueness of each spiritual journey, and of the immense value of traveling on that journey with a community of "inner companions" are not simply ideals of a new ritual but imperatives of an integrated spirituality as such. One way to enflesh that imperative is to foster communities of trust in which stories and faith are shared.

A second reason to ground the Inquiry period in story-telling is that from the very beginning the inquirers should know that, unlike the people interviewed by Haldane, we hope that they will experience their personal journey not "on the side" in the Church surrounded by a "conspiracy of silence" but as heart and center of being Church. That which most deeply grounds the Church is the Mystery of God's Presence to his people. That is what they bring to the community: their own unique experience of that Presence revealed through their story.

That is why the rest of us listen—not for an exercise in group dynamics nor Rogerian client-centered therapy, but for an unveiling of the Presence of the Lord. It will take time for that unveiling to happen in the process of initiation; but from the very beginning inquirers need to hear the message that the Church is not "over there" and the Church does not bring God to them. The Church is "in here," and God has always been present to their journey. The members of the Church are here simply to help the inquirers tell their story and in faith to discern God's Presence there. At all stages in the process we invite inquirers to see themselves not as passive receivers but as active participants in their own story now, and later, if they choose, in the stories and life of their fellow travelers in both Church and world.[9]

Along these lines, Ralph Keifer writes:

Unless we can learn to speak of God as a living and present reality, we are doomed (and the word is appropriate) to failure. At the present time there is no pastoral vacuum more serious than the inability to show people the presence of God in their lives. . . . For all our discussion of the possibilities of ministry in the church today, what is truly remarkable is the low priority assigned for any effort to form ministers who might be willing to take the risk required to articulate for others their own experience and understanding of a personal God.[10]

Ultimately, then, the process of story-telling with inquirers and with members of the Christian community is preparation for ministry of the Word: to help people discern and "articulate for others their own experience and understanding of a personal God." To assist that process we need to identify those experiences; those who have reflected upon religious experience help us zero in on key experiences in which many people have discerned God's Presence. William James has his "varieties of religious experience." Langdon Gilkey identifies secular experiences which contain "dimensions of ultimacy" (experiences of contingency, relativity, temporality, autonomy and freedom in contemporary life). Peter Berger calls these dimensions "signals of transcendence" and "rumors of angels" and ties them to experiences of order, play, hope, evil, and humor.

Paul Tillich, with German pessimism, will see the anxiety of fate and death, emptiness and meaninglessness, and guilt and condemnation as experiences when persons look for the "courage to be" and perhaps discern God's Presence on their knees. Dietrich Bonhoeffer, with German optimism, will see our experiences of power and responsibility and creativity as "men come of age" who discern God's Presence with standing tall.[11]

All of these attempts are simply reflections by theologians of our times to do what Augustine and Thomas, Kierkegaard and Schleiermacher did in their times: to identify the paths which lead humans to God. In the end, however, it is left to the discernment of those in conversation with the inquirers to raise the questions which most often today stimulate the sharing of stories in which people may discover the Presence of their God.

The mention of questions brings us to the second dimension of the period of inquiry.

B. Questioning

From the world of literature, Kurt Vonnegut has a delightful passage about how God creates us as questioners and searchers:

And God said, "Let us make living creatures out of mud, so the mud can see what We have done." And God created every living creature that now moveth—and one was man. Mud-as-man alone could speak. God leaned close as mud-as-man sat up, looked around and spoke. Man blinked, "What is the purpose of all this?" he asked politely. "Everything must have a purpose?" asked God. "Certainly," said man. "Then I leave it to you to think of one for all this," said God. And He went away.[12]

From the world of psychology, Maslow, the father of humanistic psychology, proclaims the importance of questioning, especially questioning what we cherish as values.

The final and unavoidable conclusion is that education—like all our social institutions—must be concerned with final values, and this in turn is just about the same as speaking of what have been called "spiritual values" or "higher values." These are the principles of choice which help us to answer the age-old "spiritual" (Philosophical? humanistic? ethical?) questions. What is the good life? What is the good man? The good woman? What is the good society and what is my relation to it? What are my obligations to society? What is best for my children? What is justice? Truth? Virtue? What is my relation to nature, to death, to aging, to pain, to illness? How can I live a zestful, enjoyable, meaningful life? What is my responsibility to my brothers? Who *are* my brothers? What shall I be loyal to? What must I be ready to die for?[13]

From the world of philosophy, in slightly more technical language, John E. Smith identifies three kinds of experiences which can move us beyond the values identified by the humanists to the ultimate questions which can lead us to God.

The three occasions are: the awareness of the contingent character of one's existence and the question of, and concern for, the ground or the *from whence* of life; the awareness of the limit of existence in non-existence or death and the question of, and concern for, the goal of ultimate destiny of life, the *to whence* of life; and the awareness of being a responsible being and the question of, and concern for, the moral direction and quality of the self in its concrete, historical existence.[14]

And in the world of fundamental theology, in Thomistic language too rarified for our purposes here, Karl Rahner identifies man as man-the-questioner whose questions about beings are within the horizon of Absolute Being. Questions, then, become the entry into the transcendence of self and of finite beings and can lead to God.[15]

Humans differ from brutes in that we can stand back from our stories, reflect upon them, search out the meaning of our experiences, and ask Smith's ultimate questions. What is the source of my life? Where is my life going? What are my responsibilities to life? The overwhelming challenge and critical task of the Inquiry period is to prompt those kinds of questions. If the inquirers are not really inquirers and seekers after Truth, then the Tradition experienced during the catechumenate stage runs the risk of becoming traditions, the dead faith of living people. The journey ceases to be a personal story of times of death-resurrection which causes us to raise our own questions about the source, future, and responsibilities of our lives.

The task of raising questions is a challenge because we need not be sanguine about the readiness of many so-called inquirers to truly inquire. When the most important question before choice of job is, "How much can I make?," and when the pressing question before marriage is, "Can we throw rice?" and when the over-riding question upon meeting a new neighbor is, "What's in it for me?" we are challenged to help people move the surface of their lives to questions they have suppressed, perhaps because they feared to face them alone.

If Kohlberg is any place close to the mark, if most Americans are truly arrested at their third and fourth stages of moral development, this also challenges other Americans to press them with questions which help them integrate values into their personal story. Kohlberg does assert that people like to hear discourse at one level (and no more than one) above where they are themselves. On the other hand, a fascinating study by Peatling suggests that formal education in America is not doing a very good job in encouraging adults to grow. Using Piaget's categories of authoritarian and equalitarian morality, he found that the more formal education enjoyed (if that is the word) by adults, the more authoritarian their pattern of responses.[16] I mention these developmental psychologists only very briefly, but I do so to encourage those charged with raising the level of inquiry in Church and world (and in some ways that includes all of us) to become aware of the problems which confront us and conscious of the need to stimulate the search for values and meaning.

What is true for inquirers is also true, of course, in post-baptismal catechesis for the so-called initiated. Preoccupied with "churchy" questions, sometimes we find questions arising from people's more pressing pains. Nathan Mitchell comments:

> While we were out to lunch planning strategies for renewal, the world was busy raising more basic questions of survival and humanity. While Idi Ami was torturing fellow-Ugandans and making fools of Western diplomats, we were creating renewal committees to "celebrate life." While hordes of believers were turning away from each other's altars, we were debating whether or not Hans Kung is really a Catholic. While millions of Americans sat in superlative apathy before political rapists, we were wondering whether or not the pope will resign. While Linda Ronstadt began singing ballads of violent unhappiness, we kept on nursing punctured pride about the decline of church music.[17]

There is a bit of overkill there, but at least he prods us to question the questions themselves. Are the questions raised in our church auditoriums and our civic chambers convenient ways to avoid facing the critically important questions of death and life in our culture and in our personal stories?

Finally, the challenge to press questions and live with the questions is also more compelling during a decade in America in which we experience both the gnostic answers of gurus, astrology charts, tarot cards and ouija boards and the fundamentalist answer of "born again" Christians. After the turmoil of the political 60's we have moved, to some degree, toward the escapism of the mystic 70's. I believe every time is Dickens' "best of times and worst of times." Every generation will experience its own peculiar mix of sin and grace, the demonic and the divine. In terms of inquiry, at least the 60's offered an atmosphere for questioning, perhaps excessive at times but at least stimulating. My judgment is that in response to the fragmentation produced in part by the questioning of the 60's, people yearned for stability and a "place to be," a community of support, in the 70's. The best thing about the communities surrounding the gnostic gurus and the fundamentalist evangelicals is that they offer those communities of support. Paradoxically, that is the best experience offered by the *RCIA*. The question will be, unlike these other communities, can those brought to birth through the *RCIA* offer people enough support and challenge so that they can continue to pursue their own personal pilgrimage and their own unique questions?

I agree with Andrew Greeley that "the basic religious needs and functions have not very notably changed since the late Ice Age; what changes have occurred make religious questions more critical rather than less critical in the contemporary world."[18] I am saying that the Inquiry period needs to stimulate questions which unveil these needs at times when our culture and individuals seek to suppress them. Greeley goes on to say.

> I am not arguing that all men experience these needs in any very powerful way, save at certain times in their lives, nor am I denying that some men apparently experience none of these needs in a particularly vigorous fashion. What I am asserting is that these needs are inherent in the human condition and that there is no reason to believe that they are any less widespread or less powerful today than they were among the prehistoric painters of France.[19]

Bruce Reed of London's Grubb Institute speaks of people when they do experience these needs.

> A person going about his normal human affairs sooner or later becomes conscious of a threat to his sense of well-being. . . . This con-

dition may come about gradually as the troubles and uncertainties of life around him seep into his inner world; or it may come suddenly as in a crisis, accident, or the receipt of bad news. It may be due to exhaustion after a period of growth and creativity, or the aftermath of some conflict. The need is to regain his bearings and to find a way of reordering his inner world. The person does this by seeking for something or someone outside himself on which he can concentrate or focus. That is, he allows himself to become dependent, and he is prepared to become more and more dependent until he can locate an idea, a person or an object which satisfies his requirements, and thereby can support him in his need. In religious terms, he is seeking something which can be god to him.[20]

Perhaps the threat of technology in the Nuclear Age is different than the threat of wild animals in the Stone Age; but in any age both threat and triumph cause people to raise questions about dependency, about whether they are the source of their own lives, the goal of their own existence, and whether they are responsible only to themselves. As Lonergan asserts, because we are more than brute, goaded by our search for meaning, our "inner light" raises question after question after question until they move us from self-centeredness to self-transcendence.

It is the inner light of intelligence that asks what and why and how and what for and, until insight hits the bull's eye, keeps further questions popping up. It is the inner light of reasonableness that demands sufficient reason before assenting and, until sufficient reason is forthcoming, keeps in your mind the further questions of the doubter. It is the inner light of deliberation that brings you beyond the egoist's question—What's in it for me?—to the moralist's question—Is it really and truly worth while?—and if your living does not meet that standard, bathes you in the unrest on an uneasy conscience.[21]

Our hope is that the questions raised by our "inner light" during the inquiry stage will lead to a surpassing illumination during the conversion stage. If inquirers are surrounded by "inner companions" at this stage of their journey, companions who have also experienced illumination, we hope they will have the courage and support to ponder their stories and continue their journey toward the surrender to which their questions may lead them. We now turn to the ministries and resources which may help inquirers know their stories and live their questions.

C. Resources

I have divided these resources into people, publications, and processes, with only brief indications of the possibilities.

1. People

From what has been said, it should be clear that the people involved at this stage are the inquirer on his/her spiritual journey and ideally the entire Christian community who are available as "inner compansions." The ministry of the wider community will be to create a context in which stories can be shared, questions explored (arising both from individual lives and the wider culture), and the Good News proclaimed. That presumes a mission-minded community of faith, conscious of their responsibility to evangelize. That presumption is unwarranted in almost every American parish.

In practice, therefore, in an informal way, the "inner companion" will often be a spouse, a friend or neighbor with whom the inquirer shares stories and questions, often for many years, and in whose life can be discerned the Gospel. If the inquirer decides to pursue the questions with the wider Christian community, certainly this close companion will accompany the person during the original contacts to assure hospitality. In a more formalized situation, hospitality is also the watchword. Perhaps the parish will have identified certain people noted for their hospitality who offer their homes as gathering places for a number of people at the initial stages of the inquiry period. There a catechist might also meet with the inquirers and also with other selected members of the Christian community who are living the Gospel as a personal spiritual journey. Then the catechist can lead the group in discussions which help them tell their stories, raise their questions, and begin to hear what Jesus' story has to say to their stories. Here the inquirer also ministers by sharing his/her personal journey and raising questions perhaps new to the group.

2. Publications

Aside from references already given, there is a growing bibliography in the area of story-telling. In the footnotes I have listed those which offer theory about the process[22] and those which offer practical exercises and strategies.[23]

I would like to highlight two of those publications because they so well follow the principles suggested in this presentation. The first is Andrew Greeley's *The Great Mysteries: An Essential Catechism.*[24] I might quibble over some of the details of the approach, but the general approach is excellent. Greeley sets up a dialogue between the person's spiritual pilgrimage and the great mysteries of the Tradition. These mysteries are seen in relationship to the questions people raise out of their death-life experiences:

Is there any purpose in my life? The Mystery of God
Are there any grounds for hope? The Mystery of Jesus of Nazareth
Is it safe to trust? The Mystery of the Spirit
Why is there evil in the world? The Mystery of the Cross and Resurrection
Is human nature totally depraved? The Mystery of Salvation
Can our guilt be wiped away? The Mystery of Grace
Is it possible to have friends? The Mystery of the Holy Eucharist
Can there be unity among humankind? The Mystery of the Church
Can we live in harmony with nature? The Mystery of Baptism
Can we find our sexual identity? The Mystery of Mary the Mother of Jesus
Why is life not fair? The Mystery of Heaven
Will we ever find peace? The Mystery of the Return of Jesus

The book itself might be used as a resource in the inquiry period or perhaps more properly during the catechumenate. The approach, however, should mark every period: a balance between the person and the community, the individual story and the stories of the Tradition, a balance between telling and listening.

Another resource, again recommended for the overall approach rather than some of the individual sections which may be a bit sophisticated in language for some inquirers, is Thomas Downs' *A Journey to Self Through Dialogue: An Excur-*

sion of Spiritual Self-discovery for Individuals and Groups.[25]
The title should indicate how well the book fits the suggestions of this paper. The book offers essays on Personality and Soul, Relationship and Scripture, Ritual and Liturgy, Value and Virtue Clarification, and Self-Actualization and the Christian Way, surrounded by instruments for determining learning objectives, for personal reflection and conversation starters.

Once again the approach is to set up conversation between the inquirer's personal journey and the great themes of the Christian Tradition. I believe the book itself serves as an excellent basic resource if there are formal sessions during the inquiry stage.

3. Processes

I have already indicated that the choices here are between the less formal and the more formal. If the parish orchestrates the kinds of resources in people and publications suggested above, whatever process is chosen for a given person or situation, most likely there will be a happy blend between person and community, listening and telling. If those resources are not carefully chosen, the danger is that we shall fall back into a classroom situation with too much telling.

In some cases, because the person has journeyed for some time and has a good grasp of both story and questions, the inquirer may be ready for a few sessions proclaiming the heart of the Good News and then will be able to make a decision regarding the catechumenate.

In other cases, where there is little sense of personal journey and where questions are feeble, much time should be spent with some "inner companions," perhaps using a resource like Downs, to deepen the experience of pilgrimage.

William Bauman describes a more structured process including initial contacts, readings and general meetings, followed by an eight-week program treating general themes of Christianity (much like Greeley), concluding with personal interviews and possible enrollment as a catechumen.[26] That may be most appropriate in some situations; for most people I would lean toward more informal gatherings in homes (if gatherings are deemed appropriate) using resources more explicitly aimed at story-telling and questioning.

In addition to these general processes I would recommend a few more particular processes which might be used during the inquiry period. I believe the process of reflection followed by life review used by the "Jesus Caritas Priest Fraternities" might offer a model for others attempting to deepen their spiritual pilgrimage.[27] Some dimensions incorporated into the Journal Workshops inaugurated by Ira Progoff might be helpful, since journal-keeping is an extremely effective instrument for this period. Finally, retreats, prayer sessions and liturgies where appropriate, offer environments where personal stories can be celebrated in dialogue with the stories of Scripture and the living community.

CONCLUSION

Let me conclude with reflection upon him who is at the center of all Christian journeys as our "inner companion"—Jesus the Christ. With our rediscovery of Jesus' humanity, we are discovering a man like us in all things but sin, flesh of our flesh and bone of our bone, who enters the human drama, shares our journey from beginning to end, and leads us on pilgrimage through death to resurrection. The pilgrimage, however, is through death. We find in Jesus a vigorously assertive man, who on his journey faces constantly the temptations in the human desert, searches out the meaning of his life, and dies asking a question—"Why have you abandoned me?" He enters our emptiness, our abandonment, and shares our questions. He also dies in hope—"Into your hands I commit my spirit!"—proclaiming the Good News that his Father will not allow such a life to come to a dead end.

He also vigorously questions us. After asking Peter, "Who do men say that I am? Who do all those other guys say that I am?" he looks Peter straight in the eye and asks, "Who do *you* say that I am?" That is what he begins with inquirers and continues with the rest of us in the process described in the *RCIA*. "Who do men say that I am?" Dialogue with the Tradition. But in the end, the question which rings on in our ears is, "Who do *you* say that I am? Who do you say that you are? What is your personal journey, and do you find Good News for your story by experiencing my story."

NOTES

1. For the language, I am indebted to John Shea, *Stories of God: An Unauthorized Biography.* Chicago: Thomas More Press, 1978.

2. For an interesting description of people's journey as a periodic "oscillation" between feelings of weakness and power, cf. Bruce Reed, *The Task of the Church and the Role of Its Members.* Washington, D.C.: The Alban Institute, 1975.

3. Jean M. Haldane, *Religious Pilgrimage.* Washington, D.C.: The Alban Institute, 1975, pp. 10-11.

4. *Ibid.,* pp. 16, 17.

5. cf. Karl Rahner, "Theology and Anthropology," in *The Word in History,* ed. by T. Patrick Burke. New York: Sheed and Ward, 1966, pp. 1-23; Gregory Baum, *Man Becoming.* New York: Herder and Herder, 1970; Andrew Greeley, *The New Agenda.* Garden City: Doubleday and Company, 1973.

6. Tom Downs, *A Journey to Self Through Dialogue: An Excursion of Spiritual Self-discovery for Individuals and Groups.* West Mystic, Conn. Twenty-third Publications, 1977, p. 66.

7. Colman McCarthy, *Inner Companions.* Washington, D.C.: Acropolis Books, Ltd, 1975, p. 18.

8. As usual, Andrew Greeley questions the conventional wisdom about the lack of community in America; cf. his *Unsecular Man,* chpt. 5, "Religion and Community." New York: Schocken Books, 1972, pp. 125-50.

9. For a clarification of how persons relate to both Church and world, cf. Bruce Reed, *op. cit.*

10. Ralph Kiefer, "Christian Initiation: The State of the Question," *Worship,* Vol. 48, No. 7, p. 403.

11. cf. William James, *The Varieties of Religious Experience.* New York: Modern Library, 1943; Langdon Gilkey, *Naming the Whirlwind: The Renewal of God-Language.* New York: The Bobbs-Merrill Co., 1969; Peter Berger, *A Rumor on Angels: Modern Society and the Rediscovery of the Supernatural.* Garden City: Doubleday and Co., 1969; Paul Tillich, *The Courage to Be.* New Haven: Yale University Press, 1952; for a treatment of the movement from *angst* to responsibility, cf. Thomas Ogletree, "From Anxiety to Responsibility: The Shifting Focus of Theological Reflection," in *New Theology No. 6,* ed. by Martin E. Marty and Dean G. Peerman. London: Collier-Macmillan, Ltd., 1969, pp. 35-65.

12. Kurt Vonnegut, Jr., *Cat's Cradle*. New York: Delacorte Press, 1963, pp. 214-15.

13. Abraham Maslow, *Religions, Values, and Peak-Experiences*. New York: The Viking Press, 1970, p. 52.

14. John E. Smith, *Experience and God*. New York: Oxford University Press, 1968. p. 151.

15. cf. Karl Rahner, *Hearers of the Word*, chpt. 9, "The Question." New York: Herder and Herder, 1969, pp. 111-20.

16. John H. Peatling, "Research on Adult Moral Development: Where Is it?" in *Religious Education* (March-April 1977), p. 218.

17. Nathan Mitchell, "The Adult Catechumenate in an Age of Pluralism," in *Liturgy: Journal of the Liturgical Conference* (January, 1977), p. 12.

18. Greeley, *Unsecular Man*, p. 1.

19. *Ibid.*, p. 16.

20. Reed, *op. cit.*, p. 3.

21. Bernard Lonergan, "Theology and Praxis," in *Proceedings of the Thirty-Second Annual Convention of the Catholic Theological Society of America*. Mahwah, N.J.: Catholic Theological Society of America, 1977, p. 11.

22. For theory on story-telling and biography as theology, cf. Donald Capps and Walter H. Capps, *The Religious Personality*. Belmont, CA: Wadsworth, 1970; Stephen Crites, "Narrative Quality of Experience," *American Academy of Religion*, 39 (1971), 291-311; John S. Dunne, *A Search for God in Time and Memory*. New York: Macmillan, 1967; *Journeys*, ed. by Gregory Baum. New York: Paulist Press, 1975; Alfred Kasin, "Autobiography as Narrative," *Michigan Quarterly Review* (Fall, 1963); James Wm. McClendon, Jr., *Biography as Theology: How Life Stories Can Remake Today's Theology*. Nashville: Abingdon Press, 1974; James Olney, *Metaphors of Self, The Meaning of Autobiography*. Princeton, N.J.: Princeton University Press, 1972; *Religion as Story*, ed. by James B. Wiggins. New York: Harper and Row, 1975. For a description of a college course based on sharing autobiographies and biographies, cf. Elena Malits, "Theology as Biography," in *Horizons: The Journal of the College Theology Society* (Fall 1974), pp. 81, 87.

23. For some exercises and strategies, cf. Sam Keen and Anne Valley Vox, *Telling Your Story: A Guide to Who You Are and Who You Can Be*. Garden City: Doubleday and Co. 1973; George Simon, *Journal for Life, Part One: Foundations, Part Two: Theology from Experience*, available with cassette program and kit. Chicago: Life in Christ, 1975 and 1977; Ira Progoff, *At a Journal Workshop*. New York: Dialogue House Library, 1975.

24. Andrew Greeley, *The Great Mysteries: An Essential Catechism*. New York: The Seabury Press, 1976.

25. Downs, *op. cit.*

26. William A. Bauman, "An Experiment in the New Rite of Adult Initiation," in *Liturgy: The Journal of the Liturgical Conference* (January, 1977), pp. 26-28.

27. A Directoire describing the "Jesus Caritas Priest Fraternities" stimulated by the life and ministry of Bro. Charles de Foucalud, is available from: Jesus Caritas, Fr. Tom McCormick, 1220 University Ave., Fort Collins, CO 80521.

Thomas P. Ivory

The Stages of Initiation
II. The Catechumenate

*Thomas P. Ivory is the Director of Religious Edu-
cation for the Archdiocese of Newark, New
Jersey. He has his doctorate in theology from the
Catholic University of Louvain, Belgium. He is also an adjunct professor at Immaculate Conception Seminary, Darlington, New Jersey.*

BASIC COMPONENTS OF THE CATECHUMENATE

Many of the ecclesiological perspectives of the Second Vatican Council can be found incarnated in the *Rite of Christian
Initiation of Adults (R.C.I.A.).* Considering her present situation
in the contemporary world, the Church seems willing to leave
behind outmoded pastoral principles and practices. This document approaches the new era with a catehumenal process
which promotes renewal for the entire Christian community.
With creative pastoral planning, certain developments on the
American Church scene can be effectively integrated within the
catechumenal catechesis envisioned by the *R.C.I.A.*

But first we should spell out some of the outmoded presuppositions which could weaken the thrust of this document's vision. Aidan Kavanagh warns us of five dangerous
presumptions:

> We have presumed that conversion is something unto itself that
> takes place largely apart from the local Church and is incommuni-
> cable in public. We have presumed that the sacraments are quite

199

separate things which can be manipulated independently of each other for educational, pastoral, theological, or disciplinary ends. We have presumed the Church itself to be little more than an institution among others, if more inept than others, lying apologetically on the periphery of the real world. We have presumed that evangelization will take care of itself in our culture, since we have also presumed that culture itself to be Christian to the core.[1]

The value of the restored catechumenate may more readily be appreciated by the so-called mission countries, but the American Church would do well to emulate the example of the Church in France which has already recognized the need for a long term process of communal induction. As early as 1943, Abbé H. Godin had heralded the concept of catechumenate in his famous book, *France, pays de mission.* In 1969 Frederick McManus of the Catholic University of America wrote with concern about the American situation: "If the current signs of dechristianization are sound indicators and if the next generation is simply and unapologetically non-Christian, we had better become concerned with the formation of Christian believers." [2] He goes on to acknowledge the necessity for flexibility in the rites of the catechumenate, so as to adapt them to our urban and mobile civilization, as well as to recognize the fact that our culture retains a certain degree of the Christian worldview.[3]

In the first part of this article we will discuss the importance of community, the elements of catechesis and the development of ministries required for successful implementation of the R.C.I.A. in the United States. In the second half of the article, we will examine some approaches to pastoral planning for this goal.

A. The Importance of Community

Johannes Hofinger, S.J., reminds us that what the ordinary person experiences as Church is the local Christian community:

The universal Church, with its magnificent conciliar documents and social encyclicals, does not impress him (her) at all—or impresses him (her) unfavorably—if the pastor and the local community fail to live the teachings contained in these texts.[4]

The crucial importance of the local community of faith has been stressed by many authors who have been actively involved in promoting the catechumenate.[5]

Americans living in an urbanized, technological and computerized culture cannot be expected to have the same experience of community living as did the early Christians. Yet there is the intrinsic need for some kind of communal support at critical moments, and there are the subtle influences which persons considered to be significant exercise upon other persons in their environment. Although we live in a mobile society, we should not lose sight of the dynamics of interpersonal relationships which are valid wherever we may move. Bernard Lee paints the phenomenological picture:

> I will let someone into my life who has made good sense to me. That "good sense" might come from a thousand different quarters. Human relations develop when people make good sense to each other. When I make a *full* decision to let someone into my life, I give that person leave to unpack his life here in mine. When that life has been unpacked, I give particular attention to that part of the baggage that helps account for the good sense which he made to me in the first place. Or, to put it in another way, the central symbols in that person's pattern of significantly organized experience get unpacked in my life. They are the symbols which I have experienced as valuable though I may not have sorted them out yet; but because they are what makes sense out of my friend's life, I have already decided that I like them. When I let someone into the becoming of my own life, in that self-same decision I let into my life the dynamics of his becoming. When I prehend someone because he makes sense to me, the "what makes sense" of him imposes itself upon me. As I increase the number of people I let into my life who have similar and related symbols central to their various patterns of life, I begin to accumulate in amount in my own life the key elements that have gone into making sense out of their lives. The more those lives become central to my own, the more I develop patterns of significantly organized experiences which reflect theirs, or supplement theirs, or complement theirs—but in any event, relate organically to theirs. Of critical importance, therefore, to becoming a Christian is the need for a milieu of Christians who make sense out of life, in some way or other because they are Christians; and the

dynamics by which Christians unpack their own lives in each other's lives in important ways.[6]

Much therefore depends upon the quality of the faith community which evangelizes and catechizes. Father Hofinger gives us the *status quaestionis:*

> A community that does not truly live the Christian life is a great obstacle to evangelization. And it is generally conceded that many individual communities within the institutional Church today are more of a hindrance then a help.[7]

While the traditional parish structure may still be viable in the rural parts of America, those who live in cities do not tend to form societal units in terms of geography. We have evolved beyond ethnic and geographical parishes to communities expressing a certain theological and liturgical vision. "Small is beautiful," and large parishes are discovering the value of forming smaller groups within the larger community. Greater communication and sharing can take place. Sociologists and group process experts can offer a valuable service to parishes trying to become more effective communities.

The whole faith community can become involved in the process through establishing a network of prayer on behalf of the catechumens. The teamwork of the parish staff should be evidenced by their praying, planning, and working together. In the formation of catechists and sponsors, the principles of andragogy should be taught. The presence of the sponsors throughout the catechumenal sessions can prove very helpful and supportive to the catechumens. Likewise, the personal witness of community members of all age groups and backgrounds can benefit the formation process. Senior citizens ought to be especially valuable in sharing their faith stories.

B. The Elements of Catechesis

Within a healthy community environment, catechumenal catechsis unfolds in many dimensions. We have gained some excellent insights from specialists in adult education, and our programs should be based on sound andragogical principles.

Before the inquirer becomes a catechumen, the basic disposition for faith should be discovered. If this is not present, religious instruction will impart only notional and not real knowledge. During the catechumenate, the candidate benefits from a triple presence of the Church: a presence of teaching, of worship, and of the Church to the world.[8] The catechumen is called to a deeper conversion of heart, becoming liberated from selfishness and growing in friendship with God and His people. Berard Marthaler has recently offered a fairly comprehensive description of what is involved in the process of conversion:

> Increased awareness, changed attitudes, and new behaviors correspond to the steps that spiritual writers identify as *metanoia*— change of heart. Horizons are broadened inwardly and outwardly so that we look deeper into ourselves and become more sensitive to the universe in which we live. Conversion results in a change of attitudes toward self, and the relationships we have with others (spouses, children, friends and co-workers) and with groups (family, community, parish). Finally we acquire new skills in communication and modify our own behavior so that it reflects the changes in our awareness and relationships. Conversion is a complex reality which affects every nerve fiber and blood cell in our bodies. Intellectually, conversion means we discover fresh dimensions to the world in which we live. At one level we come face to face with the mystery of existence and find that it is as real as what we see and feel and touch. At another level we come to grips with our feelings and find that they can be trusted. Morally, conversion means revising our values and re-ordering our priorities. We acquire the courage to make decisions in terms of principle and not simply to conform to what people expect of us. We expand our horizons beyond personal gain and satisfaction, taking into consideration the public good and the needs of others.
>
> Religiously, conversion means a shift in the center of gravity in our lives. Eternal and transcendent considerations supercede temporal and transitory concerns. For Christians, this means that . . . Christ becomes a partner in our decisions and actions. While it is possible to experience religious conversion without deepening our intellectual insights or becoming more sensitive to issues of peace and justice, the mature person sooner or later finds that conversion is a package. A person does not acquire a new awareness of reality and a different focus for his or her life without it showing up in one's manner of thinking and behavior.[9]

If we really want to help catechumens to break with selfishness and to grow in love, then we should assist them in realizing the pilgrim nature of becoming Christian and in the responsible development of Christian freedom. The sacraments of Christian initiation are presented as part of the process of the Christian's historical journey, as Alexander Ganoczy has suggested in his treatment of baptism:

> From this participation in Jesus' own history, Christians harmonize their own actions with his. Their pilgrimage may undergo radical changes in the course of a lifetime, but they remain fundamentally linked to God's plan; the influence of Jesus on their lives has a permanent and stable quality that continues with them.... In their pilgrimage in Christ the baptized find that God's plan for temporal and relational living give a permanent and stable quality that continues with them.[10]

If "telling one's story" is a valuable factor in the inquiry stage, then this second stage ought to involve the dialogue of one's story with the stories and history of Christian Tradition. We invite the catechumen to listen to the story of God's love revealed in the Old Testament events, along with an appreciation of the faith stories of Israel's heroes. As biblical themes such as call, exodus, and covenant emerge, the catechumen can be led to make the connections between personal experience and Church doctrine. Special concentration is placed upon God's love revealed in Jesus and his followers, and the witness of contemporary Christians will foster the dialogical process of reflecting on one's own story in conjunction with our understanding of God's story.

Each catechumenal session could benefit from having four components which might vary in order from one week to the next:

1. doctrinal instruction, based on the scriptural themes, in connection with personal experience and correlated to the liturgical year;
2. audio-visual presentation on the theme;
3. discussion period;
4. prayer with scripture.

If doctrinal information is correlated to the liturgical year, the entire community, as well as the catechumens, can benefit from the teaching of doctrine within the context of praying together. The history of salvation ought to be presented in such a way that each catechumen comes to realize a personal vocation and relationship with God and his people. In 1959, Joseph Lécuyer wrote a very fine article in which he presented the central themes of the Church Fathers' teachings regarding Christian initiation.[11] Rooted in God's philanthropy, humankind is invited to respond both personally and communally. The historicity of Baptism, the obstacles to growth in faith, the process of initiation into the prayer and life of the Church, and the significance of Easter were among the patristic themes.

The inter-relationship of the different parts of the message should be shown in order to be faithful to the Gospel. An analogy provided by Father Hoffinger makes this point clear:

> An agent is engaged to assist in the transfer of a beautiful home to a new owner. Before he delivers the house, however, the agent demolishes it and hands over to the owner "faithfully" all the stones and lumber and other material of the old construction. Would this not be a crime of faithlessness? Who would not want to send the agent to prison, or, better yet, to an asylum?
>
> As this poor agent acted, so does a "faithful" messenger of the Gospel who correctly transmits the particular doctrines of faith but without clearly showing the main meaning and the interrelationship of the whole message. . . .
>
> God does not just desire by his revelation to provide us with a long list of unconnected truths; he wants to challenge us through this plan to a new life in union with him.[12]

Much is able to be said in favor of picturing the catechumenate as a paschal journey.[13] The catechumen should be assisted to grow in those interior dispositions which are in rhythm with the Paschal Mystery. Alexander Ganoczy feels that the entire educative process related to baptism should be marked by the cross. This "calls for a realistic attitude in accepting crisis and conflict as normal phenomena in creating the future."[14]

One possible outline for the development of catechetical content is the following:

1. Old Testament themes, showing God's love and the responses of faith-heroes.

2. New Testament study of Jesus:

- His personality revealed in relationships and situations;
- Parables helping us to understand the Father's plan for his Kingdom;
- Miracles stressing the Lord's compassion and healing power;
- Moral teaching, seen in the context of responding to God's love, and living responsibly as a disciple of Jesus.

3. New Testament study of the Community of Jesus—the experience of the early Church.

4. Church History—emphasizing the saints who served as prophets, calling the Church to greater holiness.

5. Overview of the Church today—its evolved structure but its same basic desire to grow in fidelity to Jesus.

6. Overview of sacramental theology, as well as a familarity with the formal prayers and sacramentals of the Church.

Ritual and symbolic activity help Christians to unfold their experiences for each other along their pilgrimage through life. Liturgical celebrations at various stages of the catechumenate should foster, as Bernard Lee puts it, "the unpacking of lives so as to turn loose 'out there' the operative holds of the Jesus-event in contemporary life, making the Jesus-event not just neutrally available, but waiting to leap into life." [15] Michel LeGrain reminds us that when it is true, the liturgical rite is dialogue and communication; it celebrates life; it renews us interiorly; it makes us less self-centered.[16] The catechumens should be carefully instructed about the biblical antecedents of liturgical signs, and should be helped to understand the use of symbolic language and activity in our worship.

In addition to supporting the catechumens through the conversion process, teaching them the doctrines of faith within the context of God's loving initiative throughout the history of salvation, and celebrating their progress in response to God's Word in liturgical rituals, the local faith community should involve the catechumens in the practice of the spiritual and corporal works of mercy. By utilizing these opportunities for apostolic service, the catechumens can "learn by doing." Emerging from these experiences, the prayer of the catechumens becomes more personal and authentic.

C. Development of Ministries

The catechumenate calls forth many diverse ministries from the Christian community. In fact, Aidan Kavanagh maintains that "the nature of ministry in its formal sense takes its inception from the natural and form of the catechumenate." [17] The catechumens themselves exercise a corporate, proto-sacramental ministry in the local Church, witnessing to the conversionary nature of Christian life.

Laity, religious, deacons, priests and bishops all have their distinctive but complementary roles in the catechumenate. Someone with an understanding of the whole process and with administrative skills should serve as director of the local catechumenate. Training sessions can be conducted to help in the formation of sponsors and catechists. At least one person or committee should be entrusted with the special ministry of extending hospitality by means of the environment and dynamics of the meetings.

The entire local Christian community assumes a communal sponsorship in terms of responsibility for the catechumens. In addition, each catechumen is entrusted to a personal sponsor who serves as a witness to Christ and a guide to the usages and customs of the Church.[18] The sponsor's role has been summarized as one who must teach by personal example, lead by being a model, lend support in difficulties, and be prepared to vouch for the godchild when asked for a judgment.[19]

Catechists should also strive to become model Christians, lest they lose their credibility. They ought to be drawn from people of prayer who are willing to be prepared for this ministry by participating in a course of instruction. Both content and method, respecting the principles of andragogy, will be throughly explained in this course. The director of the catechumenate will supervise periodic evaluation and continuing education of the local catechetical team members.

Certifying catechists for adult catechesis will mark a healthy new stage in the history of religious education in the United States. Although lip service has been paid to the primacy of adult catechesis, this has not been reflected in our budgeting of resources. Implementing the *R.C.I.A.* will bring us to a more mature understanding of both catechesis and ministry.

PASTORAL PLANNING

The ideal of leading catechumens to an adult act of faith and to active membership in the Christian community seems to be so much in line with the essential mission of the Church that we might wonder how it ever came to be so obscured. In our haste to correct our negligence, we might rush into the establishment of a catechumenate without effective pastoral planning. Long-range goals as well as short-range objectives ought to be discerned by as many members of the local faith community as possible. Members must be willing "to pay the price," "to buy into" the responsibilities which a catechumenate will demand of them.

Some authors have pointed out that the *R.C.I.A.* is contrary to American culture, and therefore runs the risk of being relegated to a bookshelf or filing cabinet. Ralph Keifer has stated the question clearly:

> The attempt to reform the rites of initiation has issued in the promulgation of rites which are, historically and culturally speaking, a massive rejection of the presuppositions both of pastoral practice and of most church goers regarding the true meaning of Church membership. This is a revolution quite without precedent, because the Catholic Church has never at any time in its history done such violence to its ritual practice as to make its rites so wholly incongruous with its concrete reality. Such an act is either a statement that rite is wholly irrelevant, or a statement that the Church is willing to change, and to change radically, that concrete reality. Such an approach is either suicide or prophecy of a very high order.[20]

Aidan Kavanagh puts it more succinctly: "Certainly it is contrary to our American experience and culture. Were it otherwise, it would be unfaithful to a gospel which is not exactly coextensive with our culture."[21] The situation of Christians in East Germany offers an extreme example of what might be demanded of Western Christians to preserve their faith in an hostile environment.[22]

What, then, are some theological principles which will guide us in this new venture? Geoffrey Wainwright draws the following principles from the witness of the New Testament:

> Liturgical initiation should bring out the primary work of Father, Son and Holy Spirit in the salvation which it sacramentally mediates; it should give a proper place to the human response for which God calls from those with whom He deals graciously; it should express the way in which the Christian life already represents in the midst of the world the first-fruits of the final kingdom in that it is a life of righteousness in the unity of the Body which tastes by anticipation the joy of the age to come.[23]

André Aubry suggests that the goal of our catechumenal ministry is working with a small community, poor or in the situation of the diaspora, and building it up to become the Body of Christ. The intermediate objectives are the bringing together of interested people in a spirit of dialogue, announcing the Word of God through effective catechesis, and celebrating the sacraments. He pictures the catechumenate as the space and the time for the blossoming of a young Church.[24] This calls for the planning of a dynamic process which moves through the stages of evangelization, entrance into the catechumenate, illumination and ongoing adult catechesis. American Catholics might do well to examine the initiation process of other Christian denominations.[25] Hopefully, the R.C.I.A. will be an incentive rather than an obstacle to the spirit of ecumenism. In these concluding sections, we want to examine the call to evangelization, the paradigm offered by the R.C.I.A., and the formation of neo-catechumenate communities.

A. Evangelization

The important ministry of evangelization is a crucial complement to the catechetical ministry which we have been discussing. The catechumenate serves as the vital link between the missionary apostolate (evangelization) and the community life of baptized Christians. Aidan Kavanagh levels quite an indictment against the inadequate evangelizing efforts of the Church in America:

> We must learn that the absence of unbaptized adult catechumens in our churches is not just an embarrassing statistical problem. It is a judgment of God upon our easily accepted and quite general evangelical bankruptcy.[26]

Americans live in a society where the Gospel has been preached, and yet over eighty million Americans remain unchurched. Although, the United States is not a missionary church, strictly speaking, we must turn our attention more fully to the ministry of evangelization. Johannes Hofinger urges us to promote "evangelizing catechesis," making certain that all religious instruction has been an evangelizing dimension. More creative utilization of the electronic and mass media might lay the groundwork for follow-up efforts at evangelization on the local level. What is basically at stake is the attitude of the local faith community. Either catechesis and sacramental celebrations are directed toward an apostolate of evangelization or the community will continue to diminish in vitality and membership.

B. Paradigm Offered by the R.C.I.A.

The catechumenal process of initiation is constitutive of the life of the Church. The adult catechumenate serves as a paradigm insofar as it describes the goal to be achieved: adult faith in a believing community. Richard Reichert suggests a total pastoral approach:

> A well functioning parish realizes that its membership is at various levels of conversion and requires various forms of catechesis. Since virtually all were initiated into the church without benefit of an adult catechumenate the whole parish experience can be viewed as a continuous catechumenate, constantly calling each individual to conversion, offering instruction, challenging to service, providing litirgical experience.

The R.C.I.A. has great value in bringing focus to such pastoral work within a parish, clarifying what such a "continuous" catechumenate is striving to achieve and the stages of growth to be anticipated. In this sense virtually every parish's pastoral program can be understood in part as a remedial catechumenate, providing the context for conversion and growth in faith for those already initiated.[28]

During the past ten to fifteen years, we have seen the growth of various renewal programs such as Cursillo, Charismatic Renewal and Marriage Encounter. We continue to maintain traditional parish societies, which seem at times to be struggling for a purpose to exist in face of the more dynamic renewal movements. The R.C.I.A. can provide the "umbrella" for all the healthy developments we have been experiencing since the Second Vatican Council, and at the same time it can give a new sense of purpose to the so-called traditional parish organizations. Through careful planning and coordination, the R.C.I.A. can indeed become the paradigm for our faith communities.

C. Neo-Catechumenate Communities

One approach to preparing a faith community to organize a catechumenate for the non-baptized is to face up to the empirical fact that many baptized persons, baptized years ago in infancy, do not have "the faintest existential notion of the worship, fellowship, service and mission involved in the Christian life." [29] Although people have been sacramentalized, many have not been throughly evangelized and catechized. It is not as though only the fourth stage of the catechumenal process, mystagogia, were absent from their formation; in effect, their reception of the sacraments of initiation has been isolated from the entire catechumenal process. Adrien Nocent has wisely suggested that the R.C.I.A. can be adapted for the catechesis of those who have already been baptized.[30] Johannes Hofinger recommends Lent as the most convenient time for helping Christian adults to deepen their appreciation for their faith and to understand the true meaning of Christian commitment.[31] Sunday homilies may still be our most accessible medium for reaching these adults and forming them.

Needless to say, religious education programs for children and adolescents should be adapted within the context of a "post-baptismal catechumenate," including all its dimensions: doctrinal, liturgical, apostolic and communal. Parental involvement is necessary, and vibrant adult education opportunities should complement the efforts to catechize the young people.

A more radical approach was begun in Spain in 1962 by Kiko Argüello, founder of neo-catechumenal communities. These have spread throughout Europe and South America, and to Japan and Kenya. More recently, they are being formed in the United States. Pope Paul VI had encouraged this apostolate, saying: "Many people feel attracted by these neo-cathecumenal communities, because they see that there is a sincerity, a truth in them, something alive and authentic, Christ present in the world." [32]

Kiko Argüello explains the purpose of generating these neo-catechumenal communities within the structure of the local parish community:

> It is a question of persons who wish to rediscover Christian life, live it fully with the essential consequences derived from their baptism, by means of a catechumenate which proceeds in stages, like that of the early Church, but adapted to their condition as baptized persons. These communities have consequently the mission of being, in the centre of the parish, the sign and sacrament of the missionary Church; of offering a concrete opening for the evangelization of the "distant" by presenting—to the extent to which faith is developed—the signs that call pagans to conversion; that is, love with the dimensions of the Cross and Unity.[33]

The neo-catechumenal process lasts for several years, with periodic assistance from specially trained catechists from the international leadership group. Kiko Argüello describes the results perceived:

> Where the experience develops, one catches a glimpse of a new structure of the local Church. The latter would be formed of small communities and would thus present itself as an organic body which, to the extent to which the faith blossoms there, causes charisms to mature and postulates ministries.[34]

212

If such a process seems overwhelming for the average parish, then a more modest pastoral plan might be adopted. In order to assist in the religious socialization of previously baptized but poorly initiated adults, the parish leadership team could plan a seven point process:

1. Beginning with the parish liturgical celebrations, observe what category or type of parishioner participates least. Is there a need?
2. Seek out, possibly through home visitation, those who have become alienated or who were never really converted to their Christian faith. Who are the people in need?
3. Assist these adults, through dialogue and patient listening, to diagnose their own needs regarding the Christian life. What are their needs?
4. Utilizing sound andragogical principles and techniques, offer adult education programs which meet these needs. Are their needs really being addressed?
5. Involve the witness of committed parishioners in the program, allowing the participants to be touched by their acts of charity and service. Are their needs being socialized?
6. Guide the maturing Christian toward the spiritual and apostolic movements prominent in the Church today. Are their needs being constructively channeled?
7. Accept their insights in helping to improve the ecclesial environment. Are their needs being healed and fulfilled?

□ □ □

On the diocesan level, the Archdiocese of Newark has launched a three year program of spiritual renewal for parish faith communities. One of the principal benefits of this effort is envisioned to be the formation of catechumenates in viable environments. Two semesters of six weeks apiece have been designated each year for this coordinated effort. Diocesan agencies are collaborating with parish leadership people in preparing the program and in avoiding counter-productive scheduling of programs at the same time. The six semesters are divided as follows:

1. Leadership Formation (motivation and training in skills)
2. The Call of the Lord
3. Our Response-Conversion
4. Empowerment by the Holy Spirit to live justly
5. Discipleship
6. Evangelization.

Parishes are being offered four components, and 80% of the parishes seem to be choosing all four:

1. Sunday liturgy material, including theme development, homily outline, prayer of the faithful and recommended music;
2. large group activity, designed for other occasions;
3. take-home materials, so as to include the sick and shut-ins;
4. small group discussion material, with several options sensitive to both the urban and suburban character of the diocese.

The establishment of a prayer network is the first responsibility of the parish leadership team, and ecumenical cooperation is sought. A diocesan spiritual director for the program is working closely with pastoral leadership and deanery support teams. An extensive evaluation systems will lead to whatever adjustments are necessary in the program's content. Material is prepared one semester in advance and can take these evaluations into consideration. Although renewal is experienced at the parish level, such diocesan cooperation and support is certainly welcome.

D. Conclusion

We begin with the believing community admitting that it is incomplete and in need of renewal to fulfill its mission more effectively. We respect the contributions and talents of all God's People, and seek to celebrate the sacraments within the context of a growth process. Reflecting on the quality and density of presence of the Jesus-event in the local faith community, Bernard Lee writes: "Every person who participates in a Sacramental experience has something to do with the density of presence which accrues." [35]

We have the talents and resources to make the *R.C.I.A.* one of the greatest instruments of renewal for parish communities to emerge from the Second Vatican Council. We can envision the core leadership on our parish staffs working in close harmony to serve their parishioners—by their praying together, by their discerning and planning together, by their promoting of the gifts and ministries of all in the parish family. We can hope that some of the eighty million unchurched Americans will become attracted to such faith communities—wanting to learn more about this group of believers, wanting to participate in whatever gives them such a sense of purpose and loving responsibility for one another. We can foresee the happy blending of catechesis and evangelization, of spirit-filled liturgical celebrations and unselfish social action, on Christian formation and vibrant communities of committed faith-filled adults.

NOTES

1. Aidan Kavanagh, "Adult Initiation: Process and Ritual," in *Liturgy* (January, 1977), p. 8.

2. Frederick R. McManus, "The Catechumenate: Liturgical Initiation," in *American Ecclesiastical Review* (April, 1969), p. 263.

3. *Ibid.*, p. 277.

4. Johannes Hofinger, S.J., *Evangelization and Catechesis* (New York: Paulist Press, 1976), p. 140.

5. For example, cf. Jean Letourneur, "Christian Initiations in France," *Lumen Vitae*, XII, No. 3 (1957), pp. 478-79; Louis Lochet, "Community of Catechesis," *Lumen Vitae*, XII, No. 3 (1957), pp. 427-44; Jacques Cellier, "Catéchumènes et Communauté Chrétienne," *La Maison Dieu*, 71, No. 3 (1962), pp. 146-48; F. Coudreau, "The Catechumenate in France," *Worship*, 42 (April, 1968), pp. 227-29.

6. Bernard Lee, *The Becoming of the Church* (New York: Paulist Press, 1974), pp. 260-61.

7. Hoffinger, *op. cit.*, p. 108.

8. F. Coudreau, *art. cit.*, p. 236.

9. Berard Marthaler, "Catechetical Dimensions of Marriage Encounter," *Origins*, Vol. VII, No. 9 (August 11, 1977), p. 131.

10. Alexander Ganoczy, *Becoming Christian* (New York: Paulist Press, 1976), p. 78.

11. Joseph Lécuyer, C.S.S.P., "Théologie de l'Initiation Chrétienne d'après les Pères," *La Maison Dieu*, No. 58 (2e trimestre, 1959), pp. 5-26.

12. Hoffinger, *op. cit.*, p. 52.

13. Xavier Seumois, P.B., "The Catechumenate: A Paschal Journey," *Lumen Vitae*, XV, 1960, pp. 667-85.

14. Ganoczy, *op. cit.*, p. 95.

15. Lee, *op. cit.*, p. 262.

16. Michel LeGrain, "Les ambiguités actuelles de satus catèchuménal," *Nouvelle Revue Theologique*, 95 (January, 1973), p. 52.

17. Kavanagh, *art. cit.*, p. 10.

18. Michel Dujarier, "Sponsorship," *Concilium*, Vol. 2, No. 3 (February, 1967), p. 29.

19. F. Coudreau, *art. cit.*, p. 239.

20. Ralph A. Keifer, "Christian Initiation: The State of the Question," in *Made, Not Born* (Notre Dame: University of Notre Dame Press, 1976), pp. 149-50.

21. Kavanagh, *art. cit.*, p. 10.

22. Geoffrey Wainwright, *Christian Initiation* (Richmond, Va.: John Knox Press, 1969), pp. 74-75.

23. *Ibid.*, p. 80.

24. André Aubry, "Le Projet Pastoral du Rituel de l'Initiation des Adultes," *Ephemerides Liturgicae*, LXXXVIII, 1974, Fasc. III, pp. 186-87.

25. Cf. Wainwright, *op. cit.*, pp. 80-84. Also Laurence H. Stookey, "Three New Initiation Rites," *Worship*, 51 (1977), pp. 33-49.

26. Aidan Kavanagh, "Christian Initiation for Those Baptized as Infants," *The Living Light*, Vol. 13, No. 3 (Fall, 1976), p. 395.

27. Richard Reichert, "A Catechist's Reponse to the Rite of Christian Initiation for Adults," *The Living Light*, Vol. 14, No. 1 (Spring, 1977), p. 140.

28. *Ibid.*, p. 144.

29. Wainwright, *op. cit.*, p. 72.

30. Adrien Nocent, O.S.B., "L'Ordo Initiationis Christianae Adultorum: Lignes Theologico-Liturgiques du Catéchumènat," *Ephemerides Liturgicae*, LXXXVIII, 1974, Fasc. III, p. 172.

31. Hofinger, *op. cit.*, p. 13.

32. Pope Paul VI, Address to the General Audience of January 12, 1977. Translated in *Christ in the World*, XXII, No. 2 (1977), p. 79.

33. Kiko Argüello, "To renew Christian life in parishes," *Christ in the World*, XXII, No. 2, (1977), p. 95.

34. *Ibid.*

35. Lee, *op. cit.*, p. 277.

James Parker

The Stages of Initiation III. Purification and Enlightenment

James Parker is pastor of the Church of St. Paul, Silverton, Oregon, and Lecturer in Dogmatic Theology at Mt. Angel Seminary, St. Benedict, Oregon. He has his doctorate in theology from the Catholic University of Louvain, Belgium.

Three "R's"—reality, reflection, and ritual—are all wrapped up in the single process of becoming a Christian. We can't separate them: reflection is part of reality, reality is found in ritual, and ritual is reflective. Nevertheless, what we can't separate, we can and do distinguish.

First, then, there is the reality. That reality is conversion, the change of mind and heart and soul that occurs as one enters, step by step, into the life of the risen Lord that is lived in his Church. Second, there is reflection upon that reality. That reflection is catechesis that seeks to understand, guide, and encourage the spiritual journey of conversion. More like guidance than informational instruction, it is, in the apt phrase of Aidan Kavanagh, "conversion therapy." [1] Third, there is ritual. And that ritual is, of course, the complex of rites that celebrate, and, by celebrating, intensify conversion.

Restoration of the Church's structured process of becoming a Christian has begun with the promulgation of the *Rite of Christian Initiation of Adults (RCIA)*. Of that triad—reality, reflection, ritual—ritual is the easiest place to begin. Excellent workshops have adapted the *RCIA* to the American and local scene.[2]

There is a danger, however, that renewal might remain on the ritual level. Without conversion and catechesis the rites will be nothing but exhibits of liturgical archaeology, oddities that will soon slip again into oblivion. The pressing need in the United States is for the development of a contemporary catechesis and a re-direction of pastoral efforts along missionary lines that promote the reality of conversion.

It is beyond the scope of any article or book to develop a full-blown catechesis or to detail pastoral activity that will call forth and sustain the reality of conversion. What we can do is to reflect on the nature of the conversion process and on the formal elements of its catechesis.

We have noted that conversion and catechesis occur in stages. The stage of conversion that is celebrated in admission to the Church is lived out and appropriated during the period of the catechumenate; the stage of conversion that is celebrated in election for the sacraments is experienced and recollected during the time of Lent; the stage of conversion that is celebrated in Baptism, Confirmation, and Eucharist is reflected upon during the Easter season. Conversion and its catechesis are alternating steps in the journey by which one becomes a Christian.

My present concern is the conversion stage of "election" and its "catechesis" during the time of purification and illumination which is Lent. The quotation marks signal what is distinctive about this conversion stage and its "catechesis." For, as the introduction to the *RCIA* states clearly, the time of preparation for the paschal liturgy "involves spiritual recollection more than catechesis" (*RCIA*, No. 25). And, what is to be recollected is that most fundamental dimension of conversion, the experience of being chosen by the Lord through his Church's call or election. The immediate preparation for the paschal liturgy is not, therefore, a forward looking catechesis concerning the sacraments of Baptism, Confirmation and Eucharist soon to be received, but a retrospective reflection upon what has happened when, after their enrollment on the first Sunday of Lent, the catechumen is addressed by the Church as "the Elect."

I would like to begin, then, with brief biblical and theological remarks on the theme of election. After that I will situate the experience of election in the process of unfolding conversion. Then I will be ready to comment on the "catechesis" appropriate to Lent and, finally, to offer some pastoral suggestions.

ELECTION

God's election is what constitutes the identity of Israel. Yahweh has set his heart on this people and made them a people peculiarly his own (Dt. 7:6). No merit of Israel, a "no nation" and the smallest of peoples (Dt. 7:7), but only the love of God can explain such favor. Moreover, this election is for service, not privilege. Israel is to make known the justice and mercy of God. The mysterious person who stands for the whole people and whose sufferings sum up their entire history is called by God, "my chosen one," and, "my servant" (Is. 42:1).

God's election is what constitutes the self-awareness of Jesus. The Father has chosen him (Mk. 1:11), and he has come not to be served, but to serve and give his life as a ransom for many (Mk. 10:45). In turn, Jesus instructs his disciples that they have not chosen him, but that he has chosen them (Jn. 15:16). Their election is for the sake of proclaiming to the ends of the earth the good news of the coming of God's reign in his resurrection.

The experience of election, then, is an experience of grace and of mission. "It is not we who choose to awaken ourselves, but God who chooses to awaken us." [3] This is the meaning of grace. And, election is not for our sake alone, but for the sake of others. This is the meaning of mission.

B. Election and Conversion

I have claimed that conversion occurs in stages marked and celebrated by rites such as those provided in the *RCIA*. Surely conversion is an event with its time and place, but it is also a process with its beginnings, development, and maturity. Surely, too, conversion is of the whole person, but since we can distinguish in the whole person understanding, acting, and believing, so we can speak of intellectual, moral, and religious dimensions of conversion.

Conversion is first experienced as searching. The inquirer is moved by some restlessness in his heart and by some questioning in his mind. He may be confronted by his need to face the inescapable mysteries of life and death, or by his need to belong to a community, or by his need to live a life of commitments, or by his need to share the inner world and outer involvements of a spouse. Though often enough he can't find words for it, he is looking for life in greater fullness. And, if he turns to the Church, he asks for the faith that he has come to perceive as holding the promise of that fuller life. At least in a rudimentary way, he has come to acknowledge that life is a mystery to be lived rather than a series of problems to be solved, and that this mystery of life is the mystery of a personal God revealing himself in Jesus who, as risen, is present in the Church.

Once a member of the household of faith, the catechumen, as he is now called, experiences conversion primarily as a transformation of mind and morals, or, the gaining of a "sufficient knowledge of Christian teaching and a sense of faith and charity" (*RCIA*, No. 23). The catechumenate allows him the opportunity to integrate and solidify his conversion in its intellectual and moral dimensions. It allows conversion to become a change in the way he percieves the world, the way he lives his life, the way he interacts with others, the way he performs his job. Living within the Christian community and reflecting upon his life in the light of Scripture, the catechumen becomes more capable of articulating the cognitive elements of his faith and more sure of himself as one whose commitments, public and private, are less and less in terms of personal satisfaction, more and more as responses to Gospel values.

How, then, does the "elect" experience conversion? In his searching as an inquirer and in his learning as a catechumen, he has been experiencing conversion as something of his own making, the product of his several choices. *He*, after all, has discovered life as meaningful, God as personal and manifesting Himself in Jesus, the Church as his home, and the Gospel values as his way of life. This initiative of his in conversion is emphasized in the rite of admission to the Church: he presents himself as a "candidate" seeking faith and the eternal life faith promises.

Somewhat less dramatically does he experience conversion as God's gracious choice of him. There comes a time, however, for him to experience conversion as just that—the work of God, the work of one who has sought him out, found him, and grasped him. Such an experience is what is meant by religious conversion, or conversion it its specifically religious dimension. It is the experience of being grasped by ultimate concern, of God's love flooding our hearts.[4] Religious conversion, in short, is the experience of conversion as election.

The whole process of conversion, then, is experienced at the time of liturgical election as having been God's work. That election comes through a Church and is announced in the voice of the bishop or priest: "You have been chosen for initiation into the sacred mysteries at the Easter Vigil" (*RCIA*, No. 147).

Election, however, is not only gracious but also purposeful. It involves mission and ministry. The "Elect" is called to minister as priest, prophet and king. At the time of his election he is to experience the truth that while all men and women are called to the banquet of God's reign, he is chosen for the service of that banquet, getting out its invitations and waiting at its tables.[5]

C. The Catechesis of Election

Lent, according to the introduction to the *RCIA*, is a time of spiritual recollection. Just as catechesis shapes and structures conversion in its intellectual and moral dimensions, so a retreat gives form to conversion in its religious dimension. For a retreat, in the pithy definition provided by Thoreau, is an occasion "to front only the essential facts of life." And the essential fact of life, as discovered by Israel in the desert is that we move not by our own strength but by the empowerment of a God who, "as a man carries his child," (Dt. 2:31) carries us on our journey. In the desert experience of a retreat, one should come to know his dependence upon the loving choice of God. He is uncentered of himself and re-centered in God.

Ideally, then, Lent is a time of retreat. A little "armchair anthropology" might add to our appreciation of this. Lent is to be like the solo venture required by some American Indians of their youth. Before a young man took up his position in the tribal enterprise, he was led away from camp so that he might have the vision of his guardian spirit. So the Lenten retreat is meant to throw one back upon his own deepest resource in God and thus prepare him for his part in the corporate mission of the baptismal priesthood.

Bernard Tyrell provides us with a valuable analysis of the dynamics of a retreat whether they be found in sessions for the healing of neurosis, or in meetings of Alcoholics Anonymous, or in the Ignatian exercises.[6] His analysis helps us lay bare a structural identity underlying present day pluralism on the American retreat scene with its directed Ignatian retreats, Marriage Encounters, *cursillos*, and "Life in the Spirit Seminars," to name only the most well known. To understand that identity may help us in making creative use of these many retreats and in designing special retreats for the Elect.

A retreat, according to Tyrell, is comprised of alternating moments of "spirit feasting" and "spirit fasting." It begins with the message of God's love for me, a love which is the precondition for any change or conversion of my life. The alcoholic is made aware of the concern of the group, the neurotic of the care of the therapist, the married couple of the truth that "God doesn't make junk," the "Life in the Spirit" participant and the Ignatian retreatant of the truth that he is infinitely loveable.

In the light of such love, one can move on to face his condition of need. He can uncover the block to his growth. This is the moment for "spirit fasting," a moment of negativity during which one acknowledges his non-being so that he may be rid of it. The alcoholic acknowledges his addiction and the neurotic those habits of thinking and acting that have been his undoing and have made him feel miserable. In the "I" stage of the Marriage Encounter, the couple explore their negative self-images, in the "We" stage their faulty communications, and in the "God" stage their defective notions of God. The "Life in the Spirit" participant acknowledges his need for salvation and the Ignatian retreatant enters into the "First Week," or the consideration of the "hell" in which he lives.

"Spirit feasting" follows quick upon such "spirit fasting." One experiences again, but now in a more intense way, the pull of love upon his life. This is the moment of positivity, during which he discovers his state of authentic "being." It is the moment of healing and reconstruction. The alcoholic and neurotic uncover the basically healthy dynamisms of human life that have, in their cases, gone astray. The "Life in the Spirit" participant couple in the "I" stage learn the importance of positive self-images, in the "We" stage the means for healthy expression of feelings, and in the "God" stage the name of a God with whom one can "fall in love." The Ignatian retreatant enters into the "Second Week" with its consideration of the banner or standard of Christ.

"Spirit feasting" climaxes in a moment of election. The alcoholic and neurotic are moved to take the responsibility for their attitudes and behavior that will change their feelings. The Marriage Encounter couple decide to love (themselves, each other, and God), for love, ultimately, is not a feeling but a decision. The Life in the Spirit participant asks for baptism in the Spirit and the Ignatian retreatant commits himself to Christ in that moment that Loyola himself calls "the Election."

The alternation of "spirit fasting" and "spirit feasting" continues as long as a retreat lasts. The "Life in the Spirit" participant, for example, goes on to consider what is necessary for his growth in Christ (fasting), and then receives his commission to witness to God's love (feasting). The Ignatian retreatant goes on to consider his part in the passion of Jesus during the "Third Week" (fasting), and dwells with his risen Lord during the "Fourth Week" (feasting). This continuing alternation is reflected in the Lenten scrutinies, designed, according to the introduction to the RCIA, with a "twofold purpose: revealing anything that is weak, defective, or sinful in the hearts of the elect, so that it may be healed, and revealing what is upright, strong, and holy so that it may be strengthened" (*RCIA*, No. 25).

I have spoken of a retreat as a "desert" and as a "solo" experience. Essential to the self's becoming decentered and recentered in God is drawing apart from the daily engagements that too often submerge us in a "taken-for-granted" world. A retreat demands its own time and place.

The setting of a retreat, important as that is, is not all that is suggested by the words "desert" and "solo." Also essential to a retreat is the feeling of being personally addressed and existentially involved. The alcoholic and neurotic are cured not by theory but by caring relationships. The encountered couple's marriage is improved less by communication theory and more by dialogue. The "Life in the Spirit" participant hears God calling him and the Ignatian retreatant is thrown alone upon God for the long conversation we call prayer.

The emphasis upon "desert" and "solo" should not, however, suggest isolation or individualism. A last and most important element in a retreat is the presence of the community. A good retreat is very much the result of an active presence of one or more communities—the community that first invites a person to the retreat, the community that makes possible the retreat by providing baby-sitting and transportation and meals, the community that welcomes the retreatant, the community of fellow retreatants who, even if they are not engaged in conversation, give the reassurance that comes from fellow-feeling, the community of those who give presentations and witness from their own experience, and, finally, the community of those who assist with prayer and palanca.

D. Pastoral Suggestions

At the very least, Lent should be a time for a retreat designed to prepare the Elect for the Easter Vigil. But we are not interested in minimalism. Lent should be, as well, a time of retreat and a time for retreats for the whole community of those baptized as infants for whom conversion and its catechesis follow rather than precede ritual celebration (Cf. *RCIA*, No. 21). Lent is for all of us.

The Lenten retreat weekend for the Elect might be a diocesan event, but, where the elect are many, it is best a parish affair. It should involve the pastoral staff, the sponsor/godparents, the catechists, and, perhaps, the recently initiated or received parishioners. These, along with other interested parishioners, are valuable not only for their presence, but also for the witness they can give in a concluding "spirit feasting" session on "What life in Christ in St. Philomena's parish is and could be for me."

Such a retreat would be followed up, ideally, by regular spiritual direction. There is increasing interest in America in personal direction, and this might be provided by the pastor and/or godparent. At the same time, much spiritual direction seems to be occuring in small reflection or prayer groups. This type of direction, more informal and spontaneous, is possible if communities such as those gathered on a Lenten are perduring groups.

Pastoral strategy for the parish at large should be aimed at making Lent a time of retreat and a time for retreats. Strikingly simple is an idea being implemented in some parishes of calling halt to "business as usual" during the Lenten season. No parish council meetings, no school board meetings, no CCD meetings, no finance committee meetings. Nothing. Nothing, that is, but a parish retreat or, perhaps, a retreat rather than business meeting for each of the organizations or groups. American parishes that are highly organized, hyper-active, and task oriented can give them impression of activism. Halting business as usual takes an axe to the root of this heresy and makes it possible to realize the point of all activity—that God, if we let him, is bringing about his Reign through us.

Besides making Lent a retreat, we must see Lent as the time for retreats. The priest must be engaged in pastoring, noticing who is ready, at this time of his life, for a deeper appropriation of his baptism during the renewal site of the Easter Vigil. These individuals might well make a directed retreat, some a "Fully

Alive Weekend," one couple a Marriage Encounter, another couple a weekend at the Trappist Abbey. The year doesn't go by without some people a making passage in life and others undergoing a life crisis. These passages and crises are occasions for conversion, and Lent is the time for seeing the gracious and purposeful hand of God in what has happened.

Parish adult education groups, whose regular sessions are more catechumenal than Lenten in nature, might be invited to experiences that resemble a retreat. The parish discussion group on Death and Dying in America, for example, might be invited to a day of recollection on one's own death and resurrection.[7] The parish organizations involved on social concerns might be invited to make a retreat in weekly installments on the hungers of the world.[8] The parish council members, freed from regular business obligations, might be invited to shared recollection and prayer along the lines of the *Ashes to Easter* program.[9]

The key to all these retreats is the experience of election. The retreat for the Elect provides an experience of election that prepares his initiation in the Easter Vigil. So also, every parish Lenten retreat should provide similar experiences of decision that will prepare and give sense to the ritual of renewing baptismal vows during that same liturgy.

E. Conclusion

Rosemary Haughton, in her study of fairy tales and the spiritual search, claims that folk and fairy tales are very much in line with the Gospel insistence that the power of human effort and know-how, of whatever kind, cannot of itself provide the answer to life and the way to salvation.[10] These tales, often about a youngest son who is ill-equipped, ignorant, a maker of hairraising mistakes for which he suffers, but always upheld by the knowledge that he is loved and sent to succeed, speak of human existence as charmed and meaningful. If, as Fr. Dunning has suggested, catechesis consists in telling one's own story and listening to the story told in faith by the Christian community, when we might look upon the "catechesis" of Lent as a matter of re-telling and re-listening to those stories in order to hear them as the folk and fairy tales they are. One's own story, so often told as serious and even woeful, is, just like that story of Jesus, an improbable tale of the graceful and purposeful election of God.

NOTES

1. Aidan Kavanagh, "The Norm of Baptism: The New Rite of Christian Initiation of Adults," *Worship*, Vol. 48, No. 3, p. 151.

2. One such workshop was the Southwest Liturgical Conference, January 23-26, 1978, Pueblo, Colorado. Taped proceedings of this conference are available from *Hosanna*, 10581 Livingston Dr., Northglenn, Colorado 80234.

3. Thomas Merton, *New Seeds of Contemplation* (New York: New Directions, 1961), p. 10.

4. Cf. Bernard Lonergan, *Method in Theology* (New York: Herder and Herder, 1972), pp. 106 and 240-42.

5. Cf. Nathan Mitchell, "L'Zikkaron," *Liturgy*, January, 1977, p. 16, as well as similar remarks in his unpublished but taped addresses to the Southwest Liturgical Conference.

6. Tyrell's analysis, presented at the convention of the Catholic Theological Society of America, June, 1977. Tyrell deals only with these three therapeutic situations. The extension of his categories for the understanding of the whole American retreat scene is my own.

7. Such a day of recollection has been designed and presented very effectively in the Archdiocese of Portland in Oregon by Ms. Mary Chandler of Mt. Angel Seminary, St. Benedict, Oregon 97373.

8. Such a serial retreat has been published by the Oregon Center for Peace and Justice, 126 NE Alberta, Portland, Oregon 97211.

9. This program is available from the Liturgical Conference, 1330 Massachusetts Avenue, N.W., Washington D.C. 20005.

10. Rosemary Haughton, *Tales from Eternity* (New York: Seabury Press, 1973), p. 31.

James B. Dunning

The Stages of Initiation
IV. The Sacraments of
Initiation and Afterwards

"The sacraments of baptism, confirmation, and the eucharist are the final stage in which the elect come forward and, with their sins forgiven, are admitted into the people of God, receive the adoption of the sons of God, and are led by the Holy Spirit into the promised fullness of time and, in the eucharistic sacrifice and meal, to the banquet of the Kingdom of God" (*RCIA*, No. 27).

"After this last stage has been completed, the community and the neophytes move forward together, meditating on the Gospel, sharing in the eucharist, and performing works of charity" (*RCIA*, No. 37).

The journey continues. Now the pilgrimage is marked by celebration and dancing along the road, and by helping hands extended to fellow travelers so that all may share the Good News. The new Christians celebrate their election and conversion in the great rituals of passage from death to life during the Easter Vigil, in the eucharistic celebrations of Easter Week, and the other eucharists from Easter through Pentecost. In fact, one of the first Gospels which they will hear, the reading for Wednesday of Easter Week, proclaims the message which launches them into this next stage of their journey. Jesus is with them on the road. He comes to them, as he did to the disciples on the way to Emmaus, to assure them that just as the Scriptures have said, he is with them in all those times whey they will trip and fall and once again enter into death. He is with them in the breaking of the bread. And he sends them forth with "hearts burning inside" to share this Good News with their companions on their journey (cf. Luke 24:13-35).

The *Rite of Christian Initiation of Adults* summons the new Christians to deepen and celebrate their conversion by entering into the Emmaus story, by pondering the Scriptures and breaking the bread especially at the eucharists of the Easter season, and by performing works of charity. As Father Parker suggests, the spiritual direction and discernment of the Lenten season unveils the gifts of their God in their lives. These gifts are celebrated at eucharist and shared in ministry. I suggest that celebration through listening to the story of our people in Scripture and breaking the bread, and ministry to our fellow travelers are the two ways in which new Christians continue the Emmaus story and journey with Jesus on the road.

A. Celebration

The final chapter in the conversion stories in the Gospel is so often celebration. "Rejoice—the coin is found, the lost sheep is back home. Give thanks—all you latecomers to the vineyard will be overpaid. Zacchaeus, get out of that tree—let's have dinner together at your place. Put on your white garments—the king is throwing a banquet. And perhaps most consoling of all, my son, put on this ring, these sandals, this fine robe—let's kill the fatted calf and have a party."

The entire initiation process can be seen as a discernment process—a discerning on God's Presence and his gifts in my life, a discerning that I am the one who was lost and is found, wandering and now back home, starving and now welcomed back to a banquet. God has grasped me and elected me to sit at his table. This is the discernment which brings me to the celebrations of the Paschal season. This is also the discernment which brings me to all Christian celebration.

Once again, the *Rite of Initiation*, then, offers a model for all sacramental preparation. We need to tell our stories, raise the questions about the meaning of those stories, ponder the stories of others and the Good News of Jesus. Then we make the personal response of faith. We are converted. We turn from ourselves as the source of our life, and we turn to God who elects us to His gift of life which we experience in the Christian community. We celebrate those gifts in Baptism-Confirmation-Eucharist. We also turn to God in faith when those stories reveal that it is God's gift of shalom which heals us, and we celebrate in the sacrament of reconciliation. It is God's gift of fidelity and love which bonds us, and we celebrate in the marriage sacrament. It is God's gift of compassion and care which calls us to service, and we celebrate in the sacrament of orders and initiation into other ministries. It is God's gift of healing which binds up the wounds of body and spirit, and we give thanks in the sacrament of the sick.

This is the change, this is the conversion from self-sufficiency to thanksgiving and dependence on God which brings the new Christians to celebrate. This is also the real change and conversion which should bring all Christians to all sacramental celebrations. Sacraments express in word and gesture our faith, our celebration of being graced. If liturgies in some parishes remain dead and deadening, the problem is not just that the new "changes" have not been explained. It is primarily because people have not gone through the real change, the conversion, which we expect of people in the new *Rite of Christian Initiation*.

The rite suggests that sacramental catechesis for new Christians happens primarily at the Easter liturgies themselves.

> This new frequenting of the sacraments enlightens the neophytes' understanding of the holy scriptures and also increases their knowledge of men and develops the experience in the community itself (*RCIA*, No. 39). Since the nature and force proper to this period came from the new, personal experience of the sacraments and of the community, the main place for the postbaptismal catechsis or mystagogia will be the Masses for neophytes, that is, the Sunday Masses of the Easter season (*RCIA*, No. 40).

Until this time, the rite suggests that ordinarily the catechumens "should be dismissed in a friendly manner before the eucharistic celebration begins" (*RCIA*, No. 19). This certainly strikes a new note for most American parishes, and perhaps the wisdom or impracticality of such a change will emerge only from experimentation. But if it takes place, the exit of catechumens certainly should jolt the people who remain to question why they are worthy to stay. The practice also suggests that real sacramental celebration occurs only after discernment of gifts and conversion to God, and that sacramental catechesis happens not just through talk about sacraments during the catechumenate but primarily through experience of sacramental word and gesture during the period of mystagogy. The catechesis of the prior stages is largely a dialogue of our personal story with the stories of the Tradition. The liturgies celebrate acceptance into the community and the gradual movement away from the evil of self-centeredness, sin and death toward the acceptance of Good News. It is the celebrations of the Easter season that celebrate the Good News of God's election and his gift of resurrection. The catechesis, which is more appreciation than information, happens in the liturgies themselves.[1]

Let me add two cautions, one about initiation into Scripture and the other about initiation into breaking of the bread. First, if the sacramental preparation of the first three stages of this rite has been grounded in storytelling—the stories of the new Christians, of the Christian community and the Tradition, and God's story—then the new Christians are prepared to listen to the language of Scripture which is the language of myth (in the widest sense). My assumption is that for every Christian this is a process for a lifetime, because we continue our own journey and our story "turns and returns." We also continue our journey with the companions of our Tradition, living and dead; and the richness of their stories forever continues to challenge and stretch our own. We hope that the initiation process has communicated to the people that storytelling never ends, and we need to take the time outside liturgies to reflect on these stories.

More than that, my assumption is also that the language of story and myth often falls on deaf ears in America. Our culture sometimes systematically drills us to think in abstractions, not in story-form. Some psychologists distinguish between primary process thinking and secondary process thinking. The former is thinking we do with our intuitions and feelings, with our imagination. It is also called left-handed thinking, arising from the left side of our personality and our body, which some claim is controlled by the right lobe of the brain. This is the source of "gut-level" reactions, of our most creative efforts in art and poetry, of hunches and lucky guesses, of our reflection on those things we feel most deeply which emerge in myth and story.

Secondary process thinking is one step removed from our primary experiences. Where left-handed thinking deals with the inner world of feeling, the unconscious, mystery and eternity, right-handed thinking deals with the outer world of space and time, conscious life, logic and reason, and analysis. Left-handed thinking creates stories about our fears and hopes during times when we face those ultimate questions of death and life, our "from whence," "to whence," and our responsibilities. Right-handed thinking produces theologies which systematically critique and analyze the meaning of those stories.[2]

Let me cite just one example of the need for left-handed thinking when listening to the stories of Scripture. The great Jewish storyteller (and left-handed thinker), Elie Wiesel, tells the story of Isaac not as the story of one figure in the Jewish past but as the story of the entire people which illuminates the personal story of every Jew who survived the holocaust.

> Why was the most tragic of our ancestors named Isaac, a name which evokes and signifies laughter? Here is why. As the first survivor, he had to teach us, the future survivors of Jewish history, that it is possible to suffer and despair an entire lifetime and still not give up the art of laughter.
>
> Isaac, of course, never freed himself from the traumatizing scene that violated his youth; the holocaust had marked him and continued to haunt him forever. Yet he remained capable of laughter. And in spite of everything, he did laugh.[3]

Let the right-handed thinkers exegete the passage for all the various literal and typical senses that they can find there. Those who would hear the Word and let it grasp them and bring meaning to their own lives will have to be left-handed thinkers who are open to the realm of mystery.

A technological culture of measurement and analysis such as that of America, more open to what Martin Heidegger calls "calculative thinking" than "meditative thinking,"[4] can systematically rob us of the ability to think of mystery and to enter the world of myth and story. It need not. Scientific thinking itself these days is more open to hunch, intuition, and mystery.[5] But many of our contemporaries have not yet heard about that scientific conversion, and they may need to be goaded beyond analysis into mystery and story. Perhaps for many people during the period of mystagogy we need to offer gatherings outside liturgies which continue the experience of storytelling and myth begun during the earlier stages. I hope that added effort would encourage the new Christians toward left-handed thinking and the telling of tales for a lifetime.

My second caution is about what may be needed in our culture to deepen people's experience of the breaking of the bread, their experience of the power and ritual gesture and symbol. The experience of symbol also depends upon left-handed thinking, on imagination, on our union with primary experiences of life and the good earth. Michael Novak writes:

> Religious studies derive from roots sunk in the concrete earth: from dance, exultation, song, despair, pain. At the origins of all great religions are sweat, sperm, a woman's cry, soil, grapes, tears, blood. . . . Around the edges of all religious worship have been orgies, feasting, fertility rites, purpled feet pressing grapes, the joys of a sweaty harvest-time. . . .When their tie with earth is cut, they die.[6]

John Shea writes of three paths to God: mystical rapture (which at least thinks it leaves earth behind to enter transcendent light), rationalism which begins with the concrete but abstracts through logical steps toward an Unmoved Mover (right-handed thinking), and sacramental awareness:

> A middle way, between mystical rapture and lock-step proof and the one which seems both the richest and most available, is the way of sacrament and feeling. Everyday awareness has two points. For example, I (1) see a bird (2) Sacramental awareness has three points—I (1) see a bird (2) and in and through this interaction become aware of the dimension of Mystery (3) Gerard Manly Hopkins sees a windhover fighting the currents of the wind and in his strug-

gle he is plunged into the mystery of human redemption. Two people are in love; and in their love for each other they become aware of a larger love in which they participate, the source of their own care. This is sacramental awareness. . . . The sacramental way is the way of the poet and novelist.[7]

The same culture which cripples left-handed thinking for story and myth may cause our imagination, our poetic sense and sacramental awareness to hobble a bit. Once again, if storytelling has marked the earlier stages of initiation, we might process with firmer steps into poetry and liturgy. As Karl Rahner has said, the poet is the one who has radically faced who he is.[8] Perhaps, once again, for many people during the time of mystagogy we shall need to gather to do some left-handed thinking which deepens our capacities for sacramental awareness, not just during liturgies but throughout lives which we bring to liturgies. Then liturgical celebration may give thanks to a God whose Presence we have discerned in all the times when our lives become transparent to Mystery.[9]

Such gatherings might be primarily prayer sessions which expand imagination and sacramental awareness. I won't go into the many methods available today which stimulate our capacities both for myth and sacramental awareness. In some ways, all of them are variations, sometimes with very helpful new insights, upon St. Ignatius' "composition of place." If sessions are held to deepen understanding of the roots of myth and ritual, I recommend just one resource which I believe is written in language easily understood: The Rites of People, by Gerard A. Pottebaum.[10]

B. Ministries

There is some concern today about a flabby use of the word, ministry, sometimes stretched to include even bartending as ministry.[11] For that reason, some would restrict ministries to ordained service such as priesthood and diaconate or officially installed ministries such as lectors. I would rather use the term broadly to include any service we offer which gives witness to the Gospel and to add that the community officially recognizes those who serve well so that they might serve the entire community and give witness to what we all should be in our own way: celebrants, ministers of God's Word, servant ministers of healing, and builders of community.

The United States Bishops' Committee on the Liturgy takes this expanded approach to ministry:

> In the 1960's, we saw the development of *lay ministry* which is built on the premise that ministry is the privilege and responsibility of the total Church and everyone is called by baptism to exercise it, each in his own way and according to his own call and gifts.
>
> As a result of this more recent emphasis on the theology of ministry the five main functions of ministry—teaching, preaching, celebrating, organizing, and individual pastoral care—are no longer the exclusive domain of the ordained minister although some aspects require the Sacrament of Orders.[12]

Although the signs of the times offer exciting testimony that many lay persons understand their Christian vocation as lay ministers (and have acted as ministers for years, without using the word), the language of the bishops' document must sound foreign to many cradle Catholics. It should not sound foreign to adults who have experienced the new *Rite of Christian Initiation*. From start to finish the rite has been a process of helping people discern the gifts of God in their lives, to discern how their story is God's story and an epiphany of his Presence in human history. As Father Parker has observed, the new Christian experiences God's Presence and the election into the Kingdom as an election to mission.

I suggest that this mission is fundamentally grounded in what Vatican II in *Lumen Gentium* described as the Mystery of the Church. That Mystery is God's Presence to his people. Paul VI said in his opening address at the second session of the Council: "The Church is a mystery. It is a reality imbued with the hidden presence of God." Just as the entire Church is sacrament of God's Presence, so the discernment process of the *Rite of Initiation* has helped the new Christian to see himself or herself as the image of that same Presence, a sacrament, a sign lifted up, the salt of the earth and light of the world. I suggest, therefore, that Christian ministry is basically offering images of God's Presence. This is the mission of the new Christian.

Various authors have identified the ways in which the Church through the centuries has imaged God's Presence. Perhaps the most familiar have emerged in Avery Dulles' models of the Church and Bernard Cooke's identification of five basic ministries.[13] I am more comfortable with the four dimensions of Christian mission identified by the National Federation of Priests' Councils in its "Ministry in a Servant Church": ministry of the Word ("kerygma"), ministry of community-building ("koinonia"), ministry of celebrating ("liturgia"), and ministry of serving and healing ("diakonia").[14] Other theologians have suggested that these are four fundamental Christian ministries, and I have written extensively of these elsewhere so I shall not do so here.[15]

I shall suggest, however, that these four ministries may be of special help to new Christians searching to discover ways in which they might share God's gifts in ministry, because they parallel the four stages or periods in the process of the *Rite of Christian Initiation of Adults*. Also, although each Christian may discern special gifts which summon her/him to one of these ministries, the process of initiation should communicate that in some way every Christian is called to continue these four stages in service to the human family. The process of sharing stories and faith continues (ministry of the Word). In family, neighborhood, parish, and in larger communities, each Christian continues to build what might be called neocatechumenate communities (ministry of community-building). Every Christian continues to celebrate conversion and passage through death to life (ministry of celebrating). All Christians are summoned to share that life and God's gifts in ministry, especially to the most wounded and unloved (ministry of serving and healing). In all these ways, each Christian continues to image Jesus who is *the* image of the invisible God, Jesus and who *is* the Word of God, one in community with the Father and with us, our Eucharist and thanksgiving to the Father, and the Suffering Servant of God.

This approach to the mission of the Church may also expand the lay ministry of new Christians beyond just "churchy" occupations. The language of Word, community-building, celebrating, and serving-healing might move people to see such possibilities for service in the world, beyond church doors. Dr. Donald P. Warwick writes in a study of the organizational effectiveness of the Catholic Church," ... the emerging layman of today is much more concerned with the significance of faith for his secular existence than with participation in parish councils, school boards, and similar structures." [16] After her interviews with members of St. Columba's Episcopal Church in Washington, D.C., Jean Haldane writes:

> My feeling is that the interviewees assume their home is in the world and they come to the church to reflect upon the world to be renewed for going back to where they belong.
>
> I got the feeling that a new attitude is around in the church—that many "so love the world," if I may borrow that phrase, that they are giving themselves for it in many ways. They are in many ways "preaching the gospel to every creature" but it doesn't look like church-sponsored social action and community service. In other words *the laity are being the church in the world.* They are the leaven within. They may be showing the church where its primary task lies. [17]

She goes on to make some judgments on how well the institution has encouraged the laity to be the church in the world.

> The Gospel message has always included living out a life of service in "our daily lives," but behaviorally the institution's message is to equate church organization work with "real" lay ministry—and the rewards are for those who do this. The recognition of service within the institution is given in many ways, most significantly by the clergyman through his expression of thanks and even more through his closer working relationship with those who are there on vestries committees and in church organizations. It ought to be possible to validate membership in the church and *ministry in the secular sector* as being bona fide lay ministry—an outreach of the church. After all, the laity are uniquely equipped to "go out into all the world" and have more credibility than a clergyman in most instances. We do not have to manufacture programs of lay ministry—it is *already happening* as lay people interact with the world day by day. [18]

240

Haldane said that when talking of lay ministry, her interviewees for the most part talked about church work. When she helped them expand this to include daily living of a Christian life, one person said, "You mean, taking care of my mother these last 20 years could be a part of my ministry?"

I emphasize this understanding of ministry beyond church doors, because I fear that with its stress on active participation, the *Rite of Christian Initiation* could become primarily a way for weary pastors and church workers to recruit helpers or replacements. Certainly these new Christians will know that it was through the support of Church companions on their journey that they came to understand where they were going and discover God's Presence with them. They may choose to be such companions for others who come to the Church for nurture and vision. But it is in their daily lives, their marriages, their secular vocations, their neighborhoods and communities that they will spend most of their time living out poverty of spirit, fullness of mercy, thirst for justice and the making of peace. The catechesis during the period of mystagogy should help them see, if not already seen, that these are the environments of ministry.

In addition to liturgical celebration, then, the time of mystagogy might also offer strategies which help the new Christians clarify how they might offer their gifts in ministry.[20] Already, during the catechumenate stage, they should have experienced Christian service, in church organizations such as the St. Vincent de Paul Society, and in the daily lives of the "new type of catechists" referred to by Aidan Kavanagh:

> Catechists of the "new sort" might better be old people who know how to pray, the ill who know how to suffer, and the confessor who knows what faith costs than young presbyters with new degrees in religious education.[21]

Through such exposure, the new Christians may see the possibilities of ministry in church and world. The mystagogical time would be a time to help them make some formal commitments. Such commitments might also be celebrated in liturgy during what some parishes identify as "Commitment Day" when all the members of the parish publicly choose and celebrate their participation in Christian ministries.

After commitment is made, there may be the need to offer programs which offer increased vision of and skills for ministry. Ordinarily that would not take place during the period of mystagogy, but parishes which take active participation seriously will be attentive to the needs of ministers who want to continue to clarify their gifts and talents for service to the Church and to the members of the human family. The godparents, who remain close to the new Christians during the period of mystagogy, to celebrate the joy of conversion with them at Eucharist and to introduce them more fully to members of the Christian community, might also help them come closer to their commitments to Christian ministry and help them find ways to prepare themselves for more effective service. It would also be fitting that the bishop gather all the newly baptized in the diocese for Eucharist on Pentecost at the cathedral, both to celebrate their communion with the wider Church AND to call them to share their gifts in ministries.

Let me add one caution. Our custom in America has been to pour the water, wipe our hands, and go our merry way leaving the newly baptized to care for themselves, as if to say that the conversion process is complete, the baptized fully in the Church. Now we can forget them.

Of all the stages in the RCIA, the mystagogical period perhaps call for the most change in pastoral practice. If we spend the other periods initiating people into a community of celebration and ministry, that community must stay with them during the Easter season to help them reflect on what has happened and to help them make decisions for the future.

Even more, I would take the stance that so many values in secularized America conflict with Gospel values that to continue to grow in faith the newly baptized need to have some regular contact with a small prayer community which will also provide support. I have already suggested (during the Inquiry period) that the monthly meetings of Jesus Caritas groups offer a model of prayer together, as well as of life review and discernment of responsibilities that would provide the needed support and challenge. That is a necessity for every Christian in our culture. If we have truly helped the newly baptized to experience what it means to be a Christian, they will see the need to such support.

In any event, if the *Rite of Christian Initiation of Adults* has effectively introduced these new Christians to an Emmaus journey which will last a lifetime, they will continue their pilgrimage raising new questions about the events which happen along the way, reflecting upon the stories of their "inner companions" in neo-catechumenate communities with a living tradition, experiencing again and again election by their God who makes their story his story. They will celebrate their gifts at the table of the Lord from which they leave to share those gifts in ministry. Their journey on that road to Emmaus with the Risen Lord will again and again take them to Jerusalem to experience Pentecost, where as young men and women his Spirit will reveal to them new visions and as old men and women will move them to dream new dreams.

This time of mystagogy has initiated them as celebrant and ministers of the mysteries of death and resurrection which unites their story to the Mystery and story of their God. Such stories can only lead to new visions, new dreams, new celebrations, and new ministries.

NOTES

1. Many liturgists object when catechists supposedly use liturgy to teach. I believe their objection is based upon a narrow view of education which is limited to a teaching model which imparts information. Here I am speaking more of a broad view of education which fosters growth through appreciation and celebration.

2. For a more extended analysis of this theory cf. Urban T. Holmes III, *Ministry and Imagination.* New York: The Seabury Press, 1976, pp. 89-93; and Tom Downs, *A Journey to Self through dialogue: An Excursion of Spiritual Self-discovery for Individuals and Groups.* West Mystic, Conn.: Twenty-third Publications, 1977, pp. 37-42.

3. Elie Wiesel, *Messengers of God.* New York: Random House, 1976, p. 97.

4. Martin Heidegger, *Discourse on Thinking.* New York: Harper and Row, 1966, pp. 43-57.

5. cf. Ian G. Barbour, *Myths, Models and Paradigms: A Comparative Study in Science and Religion*. New York: Harper and Row, 1974; Michael Polanyi, *Personal Knowledge: Towards a Post-Critical Philosophy*. New York: Harper and Row, 1958; Ian T. Ramsey, *Religious Language: An Empirical Placing of Theological Phrases*. New York: The Macmillan Co., 1957.

6. Michael Novak, *Ascent of the Mountain, Flight of the Dove*. New York: Harper and Row, 1971, p. 24.

7. John Shea, *Stories of God: An Unauthorized Biography*. Chicago: The Thomas More Press, 1978, p. 18.

8. Karl Rahner, "Poetry and the Christian," in *Theological Investigation, Vol. IV*. Baltimore: Helicon Press, 1966, pp. 357-67.

9. For a book containing exercises which help people develop their imagination and their capacity for left-handed thinking, cf. Daniel O'Connor and Jacques Jimenez, *The Images of Jesus*. Minneapolis: Winston Press, 1970.

10. Gerald A. Pottebaum, *The Rites of People: Exploring the Ritual Character of Human Experience*. Washington, D.C.: The Liturgical Conference, 1975.

11. For a concern about this extended use of the word, ministry, and for an approach which differs from my own, cf. an unpublished talk by James Coriden, available on cassette from Daniel Danielson, Office of Clergy Education, 5562 Clayton Road, Concord, CA. 94521.

12. Bishops' Committee on the Liturgy, *Study Text 3: Ministries in the Church*. Washington, D.C.: United States Catholic Conference, 1974, pp. 20-21.

13. Avery Dulles, *Models of the Church: A Critical Assessment of the Church in All Its Aspects*. Garden City: Doubleday and Co., 1974; Bernard Cooke, *Ministry to Word and Sacraments: History and Theology*. Philadelphia: Fortress Press, 1976.

14. National Federation of Priests' Councils, "Priests/USA: Serving in a Ministerial Church." Chicago: NFPC, 1976.

15. cf. my eight articles in *PACE 8*. Winona: St. Mary's Press, 1977-78.

16. Donald P. Warwick, "Personal and Organizational Effectiveness in the Roman Catholic Church," *Cross Currents*, Vol. XVII, No. 4 (Fall, 1967), p. 414.

17. Jean M. Haldane, *Religious Pilgrimage. Washington, D.C.: Alban Institute, 1975, p. 20*.

18. *Ibid.*, p. 19.

19. *Ibid.*, p. 22.

20. For a book which offers exercises to determine values and gifts for ministry, cf. Roland S. Larson and Doris E. Larson, *Values and Faith: Value-Clarifying Exercises for Family and Church Groups*. Minneapolis: Winston Press, 1976.

21. Aidan Kavanagh, "Initiation," in *Simple Gifts: A Collection of Ideas and Rites from Liturgy, Vol. Two*. Washington, D.C.: The Liturgical Conference, 1974.

Theophile Villaca and Michel Dujarier

The Various Ministries
in Christian Initiation

*Fr. Dujarier has already been introduced. Rev.
Theophile Villaca is in charge of catechesis and
the formation of Catechists for the Archdiocese
of Contonou, Benin. He has studied at the Institut de pastorale catéchétique in Strasbourg,
France.*

The principles justifying the restoration of the catechumenate go back to the very origins of the Church. Among these
principles, the conciliar decree, *Ad Gentes*, has particularly
stressed that the catechumenate must be "a training period for
the whole Christian life" and "an apprenticeship ... in the
practice of gospel morality" (No. 14).

But who is responsible for this vital formation? In this same
decree, the Council clearly states: "This Christian initiation
through the catechumenate should be taken care of not only by
catechists or priests, but by the *entire community of the faithful*,
especially by the sponsors. Thus, right from the outset the catechumens will feel that they belong to the People of God" (No.
14).

Thus, far from being the reserve of a few individuals—priests,
catechists, or sponsors—catechumenal education is primarily
the responsibility of the entire Christian community because it
is this community that "with love and solicitude" embraces the
catechumen as its own (*Lumen Gentium*, No. 14).

And this is why the *Decree on the Ministry and the Life Priests* reaffirms with the same insistence that "The local community should not only promote the care of its own faithful, but filled with a missionary zeal, it should also prepare the way to Christ for all men. To this community in a special way *are entrusted catechumens and the newly baptized,* who must be gradually educated to recognize and lead a Christian life" (No. 6).

By emphasizing so strongly the educative role of the nommunity itself, the Council wants to reorient us towards the perspective of the primitive Church. To perceive more clearly its importance, we shall first consider how the early Christians took up this role and how, unfortunately, it has happened that what ought to be everybody's concern has become the province of a few specialists. In the second part, we shall turn to the ways that are opened to us by the new Rite of Christian Initiation of Adults in order that the fraternal community may better take up the responsibility for this initiation via various offices and ministries.

EVOLUTION ON THE PERSPECTIVES DURING THE FIRST CENTURIES

The Church, like a family, is a community that lives and grows thanks to the participation and the contribution that each member brings to it in accordance with the diversity of the charisms received from the Holy Spirit (Eph. 4, 11-13).

How numerous and varied the charisms might be, it is the life of the body that is essential. So, before we describe how the various catechumenal ministires arose, let us first sketch the educational function of the community as community.

A. The Educating Community

One of the characteristics of the Christian community is the concern that the "brothers" have for each other. It was only the Apostle or the elders who were charged with "warning" and "teaching" every man in all wisdom to render them perfect in Christ (Col. 1,28). All the members of the Church have the mission to "teach and admonish each other" (Col. 3,16).

These two aspects of catechesis moral guidance and teaching—do depend on those in authority, but every one participates in them. In the Epistle to the Collossians, St. Paul insists that all the Christians must "warn and correct each other" (cf. 1 Cor. 4,14; 1 Thes. 5,14; 2 Thes. 3,15), as they also must "encourage one another and build one another up" (1 Thes. 5,11; see also the very beautiful text of Heb. 10,20-25).

It was in this context of reciprocal educational concern that the first Christians placed their care for their brothers, the catechumens, and even for their pagan friends.

This concern was manifested first of all by *constant missionary zeal* in the family and in professional life. We note two well-known witnesses of this from the second century. Around the year 140, Aristide of Athens, in describing the life of the Christians, emphasizes the apostolic sense that they had at that time within their own families:

> "They persuade their servants, male and female, if they have them, or their children to become Christians because of the love they have for them. And when they have become Christians, they call them simply 'brothers.' "

Forty years later, Celsus, a pagan, gives us a vivid description of the apostolate that the Christians, men and women, workers and merchants, spontaneously exercised where they worked. These people, without instructions, taught "knowledge of the truth" to women and children and showed them "how one must live." And there were many who thus came "in the women's apartments, in the cobbler's shops, or in the dyer's store, in order to learn there the perfect life."

To the concern for announcing the Good News was added that for *instruction by living example.* Significant in this regard is the prescription given in two pastoral texts from the first half of the third century.

In the *Apostolic Tradition,* after having pointed out what ought to be the daily prayer of the Christian, Hippolytus takes up Paul's counsels to the Colossians and extends their application to the formation of converts:

"Therefore, you the faithful, if you remember this and if you practice it by mutually instructing each other and by giving example to the catechumens, you can neither be tempted nor lose when you always remember Christ."

This is the same invitation that the author of the *Didache* offers when, after having encouaged the Christians to hold fast in persecution, he recalls the educational value of their witness:

"By acting thus, it's not only your soul that we snatch from Gehenna, but we shall learn to act in the same manner towards those who are new in the faith and to the catechumens, and they will so live before God. If, on the contrary, we fall away from the faith in the Lord, . . . we lose not only our soul, but we also kill our brothers with us. For, when they will see our apostasy, they will think that they have been taught a false doctrine; they will be scandalized, and we shall be responsible for them, as each of us will be responsible for himself before the Lord and the Day of Judgment."

What is true of catechesis and of the witness of life is equally true of liturgy. Without depreciating the role of the president, the first Christian writings always insisted on the role of the community not only in the baptismal celebrations, but also in the catechumenal celebrations.

The most ancient documents state that the days preparatory to the initation are times of community prayer.

The *Didache* invites the Christians to fast with the catechumens for one or two days: "Before the baptism, let the baptizer, the baptized, and the others who can first observe a fast."

Still more explicit is the description given of baptismal initiation by Saint Justin:

"They [the candidates] are taught to pray and to implore God, by fasting, for the remission of their past sins, while we pray and fast with them. Then we lead them to where there is water. . . . After having bathed him who believes and who joins us, we lead him to where those whom we call brothers are assembled and we fervently pray in common."

But it is not only at the moment of baptism that the community is present. Its active presence is also met in the course of the catechumenal stages as they are described by Hippolytus. To prepare the entrance into the catechumenate, the catechists and the sponsors perform the preliminary examinations, but "all the people come" to the liturgy itself. Catechesis also done during the assemblies, when the catechumens mingle with the faithful even if, being non-initiated, they cannot yet give each other the kiss of peace.

Thus, during the second and third centuries, the entire community participated in three functions that the following centuries tended to distinguish by clericalizing two of them. Catechesis, witness of life, and liturgy were not yet three reserved functions but three aspects of the way in which the one Church exercised its maternity with regard to the converts. And these three aspects, even if they always imply the presence of the president, were assumed by the assembly of the brothers, each trying individually to be at once catechist, witness, and celebrant.

This perspective must be kept in mind from the very beginning. It matches astonishingly the desires of Vatican II mentioned above. Even when specialized ministries develop, it must never be forgotten that it is first of all the whole community that assured the initiation of the catechumens in these three dimensions.

B. The Specialization of Ministries

In time, that which was done by everyone was confided to more specialized and more clericalized personnel. Let us follow the major stages of this evolution through the three principal kinds of ministry that are implied in catechumenal formation: the Ministry of the Word; the Ministry of Accompaniment; the Ministry of Sacramentilization.

C. The Ministry of the Word

The proclamation of the Word of God has always occupied an essential place in the education of converts.

D. The Ministers: Catechists and Teachers

From the very beginnings of the Church, the term "didaskalos," or teacher, and "catechist" occur frequently. Numerous studies in recent years have attempted to delineate the functions they represent. Without taking up the question of whether or not they received the imposition of hands or another form of official recognition, we want to stress their essential role in the community and their being subject, in a certain way, to the authority of the apostle of the apostle or the bishop, the guardians of the "deposit" of the faith.

During the second century, catechesis was done by the "doctors" (teachers) many of whom were laity. This is evident for the masters who, like St. Justin at Rome or Pantaenus at Alexandria, "held schools." But it was also the case for the teachers who taught catechumens and the faithful in the assemblies who, Hippolytus tells us could be either clerics or laymen.

From the beginning of the third century with the development of the heresies, the hierarchy tended to exercise stricter surveillance over catechesis. Even where the catechetical school was still directed by a layman as at Alexandria, this task was delegated by the bishop, and it was soon taken over by a priest. In North Africa around the year 250, the Church of Carthage seems to have reserved the catechetical function to "doctores audientium" who were priests and were usually aided by "lectors." These "lectors" were already clerics. The same evolution can be noted in Syria. The oldest levels of the Clementine texts still speak of "catechists" alongside the clerical functions. The corrections of the third century make no mention at all of lay ministry.

This movement accelerated when the priests themselves were forbidden to preach toward the end of the third century, this function becoming the prerogative of the bishop. At the end of the fourth century, it would be a novelty to see Augustine giving homilies while still a priest. But outside the liturgical assemblies, it was not rare to see deacons such as Deogratias of Carthage assuming the responsibility of catechesis for individuals who came to them. In spite of this regrettable clericalization, for a long time there were still lay apologists and theologians.

E. The Requirements of This Ministry

One must also stress the pastoral and spiritual perspectives that guided these catechists and teachers. The capital importance and the dignity of their mission was always emphasized, along with its exigencies. The first requirement of this ministry, obviously, was to know well the Word of God to be transmitted. Here is what the author of the Epistle of Clement required in the second century:

"The catechists may not exercise their function until they have been catechized themselves, for they are the guides of men. He who guides the others in the way of the doctrine must adapt himself to the various sentiments of those he instructs. It is therefore necessary that the catechist be endowed with irreproachable knowledge, be very skilled and clear, and be full of the qualities that you will find in Clement."

This text speaks already of the second and still more fundamental requirement: to live authentically according to the Gospel one preaches. This is what St. Cyprian demands of the "lector" who has to proclaim the Word of God to the catechumens: He must be "an example in the Church" in order that one may "imitate the faith of the lector."

F. The Catechist as Educator

If the life qualities of the lector and of the teacher are insisted on so strongly, it is because catechesis is more than teaching, it is a "pedagogy" and envisages educating the *whole* man.

The holy Bishop of Carthage expressed this in a lapidary formula: he who comes from heresy to the Church "comes in order to learn, learns in order to live."

In the same sense, St. Augustine counseled the catechists who presented the history of salvation:

"Therefore, propose this love as the end to which you will relate all your words. And everything that you tell, tell it in such a manner that your hearer will believe through hearing, hope through believing, and love through hoping."

Following Christ, who is the true "pedagogue" and the sole "Master," the Alexandrians praised the dignity of the doctor:

> "By word and action he assumes, on earth, the office of dispensing that which is the sovereign good, and so he mediates the union and the communion with God."

The dignity comes from what is involved in causing growth in order to be saved: the teacher "teaches, makes, transforms, and renews in the order of salvation the man he catechizes." [1]

An entire spirituality of the function of the catechists is being described here. Whether the doctor be bishop, priest, lector, or layman, he must be very much aware of the vital importance of his role and the necessity of the witness of life that is attached to it.

This is the same witness of life that we shall find in the function of accompaniment.

G. The Ministry of Accompaniment

Sponsorship of catechumens is an essential element of the pedagogy of initiation.[2] But it must be clearly understood that this is not to be confused with the sponsorship of infants baptized at birth which, unfortunately, is often more artificial than real.[3]

Originally, sponsorship was exercised spontaneously by Christians who, in their life milieu, were concerned with *attracting* their relatives, friends, and neighbors to Christ. It was not an institutionalized function requiring recognition or mandate, the best proof of this being that this responsibility was exercised for a long time without having a particular name or being the object of canonical prescriptions.

The ancient texts consider this person-to-person evangelization to be completely normal. At this period, those whom we now call sponsors were in fact those who helped their friends to conversion and presented them to the community. Hippolytus speaks of them as "those who bring" the candidates to the faith and thus to the Church and who will "witness to their subject [so that one may know] if they are capable of hearing [the Word]."[4]

Before being the presentors, the guarantors at the moment of entry into the catechumenate—and in order to have this role—we can say that they were the "converters," if this word need not be reserved to the Holy Spirit. If they were the witnesses for candidates before the Church, it is because they were first witnesses of the Church and of Christ before men.

And this primordial role they fulfilled of their own accord, without being forced by any particular prescription. Still less was it necessary to delineate the qualities necessary to accomplish this task! It was only in the fourth and fifth centuries, i.e., at the time when this mission was no longer taken seriously, that the canons had to specify that "the presentors must be of a certain age, faithful, and known to the Church." [5]

The second characteristic of this primitive sponsorship was that the Christian-converters *accompanied* their protegés not only to the threshold of the Church, but also along their catechumenal journey and even beyond baptism.

When the community "chooses those who will receive baptism," it turns again to "those who brought them."[6] These were probably the same people as the sponsors mentioned at the entry into the catechumenate. And if they were asked to witness to the way in which their catechumens lived during the period of formation, they were qualified to do so because they had shared the journey with them, and helped them and taught them to live according to the Gospel.

This is the role of "guide" that Theodore of Mopsuestia attributed to the sponsors: the candidate, who is a "stranger to the usages of the City [the Church]" needs "one of those who are attached to this city and who knows the customs to accompany him" in order to teach him "all that regards this city and the life in this place, in order that, without trouble and confusion, he becomes habituated to the customs of this grand city."

All evidence indicates that this accompaniment continued beyond the initiation. In fact, those whom John Chrysostom called the "spiritual fathers" were to show paternal tenderness in order to instruct their "sons" in spiritual matters and to urge them to virtue. The same applies, according to Pseudo-Dionysius, when a candidate chooses his sponsor; "he asks him to accept the responsibility of his admission and of all that concerns his future life."

We shall have occasion below to specify the role of the sponsors in the various liturgical celebrations. What we have already noted is sufficient to reveal the *meaning of their function*. In short, the sponsor is to be a witness-guarantor and a paternal guide. This double responsibility is assumed both in the name of the Church for the catechumen and in the name of the catechumen for the Church. The Christian becomes a sponsor to the degree that a prophetic role is exercised. He is witness to Christ before men of good will who are searching for God and primarily, in his daily life, for his neighbors for whom he reveals the evangelical message. And he continues to do this during the catechumenal formation and even beyond, for converts need to see the Gospel concretely lived by Christians like them. But he is also, before the Christian community, the witness who guarantees the seriousness of the conversion of the candidate at the various stages of the journey and especially for the entrance into the catechumenate and for access to baptism.

As guide, the Christian sponsor exercises the role of king— without, of course, any overtones of domination. He is responsible for introducing his protegé into the kingdom of Christ in order to show him the usages and the customs of the people he is joining. In exercising the role of guide, he assumes a true spiritual paternity, and he does this for the convert in the name of the Church. Reciprocally, one can also say that he is the guide charged with introducing the Church into the non-evangelized world to which the catechumen is humanly bound.

Prophet and king by virtue of his roles of witness and guide, the Christian sponsor, finally, exercises a certain priesthood via his own active participation in the liturgical celebrations. In our opinion, therefore, the function of sponsorship is an implementation of the sponsor's consecration to Christ as prophet, priest, and king that derives from baptism. And this explains why no

Christian need wait to be designated sponsor. Quite the contrary, every baptized person is a potential sponsor, but it is only when he/she begins to exercise this function that the Church recognizes sponsorship as such.

H. The Ministry of Sacramentalization

The sanctification of the converts, which is operative in the liturgical actions celebrated during the catechumenate, calls upon various ministries. Not only are clerics involved, the bishop, priests, deacons, exorcists, but also lay people, the catechists and sponsors.

The central place, obviously, is held by the *bishop,* the living image of the invisible God, like Jesus Christ in the midst of the Apostles.

St. Ignatius of Antioch often insisted "that no one do anything that concerns the Church apart from the bishop. . . . Where the bishop is, there is the community, even as where Christ Jesus is, there is the catholic church. It is not permitted, apart from the bishop, either to baptize or to celebrate agape."

If the author of the *Didascalia* demanded respect for the bishop, it was precisely because of his role as sanctifier:

> "By him, God gives you the Holy Spirit, by him you learn the Word, you know God, and you are known by him. By him you are signed, by him you become a son of the light. By him, in baptism, when he imposes his hands, the Lord witnesses to each of you and lets his holy voice be heard that says "You are my son, this day I have begotten you.'"

The bishop, as source of sanctification, is, however, not the only one to intervene in the baptismal initiation. This initiation is a true concelebration in which *the various clerics* play their proper roles.

In the *Apostolic Tradition,* we see priests anointing the catechumens with the oil of exorcism, baptizing (if the bishop allows them), and anointing the neophytes with the oil of thanksgiving. In all this, they are aided by the deacons.

The role of the deaconesses is specified by the *Didascalia,* which even assigns them a post-baptismal educational role.

They are not only directed to anoint the female catechumen, but "when she who is baptized leaves the water, the deaconess will receive her, will instruct her, and will nourish her in order that the infrangible seal be imprinted with purity and holiness."

St. Cyprian also speaks of prebaptismal exorcisms. The *Apostolic Tradition* reserves them to the bishop, but in the Church of Carthage, they were done by exorcists.

The liturgical role of the *sponsors* must be stressed in particular.

Hippolytus of Rome mentions their presence at the entry into the catechumenate and for the admission to baptism. They are the ones who have to witness to the fitness of their protegés at each of these stages.

Around the year 350, Theodore of Mopsuestia confirms this usage. He also indicates that the sponsor intervenes after the guarantees that follow the renunciation: "Your guarantor, standing behind you, lays the linen stole on your head, and raises you up."

A document from the fifth century shows that the sponsor also had the function of "receiving" the neophyte as he left the baptismal font.

This function can be extended still further: the celebrant often appealed not only to the sponsors themselves, but also to the entourage and the neighbors of the candidates, as Egeria describes for Jerusalem.

In all of this, we must not forget: it is ultimately the Church that begets, as it is the Church that witnesses and the Church that catechizes. The specialization of ministries makes concrete and renders more efficacious the triple function that belongs to the entire Christian community and that is always signified by the presence of this community.

CURRENT PASTORAL PERSPECTIVES

This rapid survey of ecclesial practice during the first centuries gives us a better understanding of the orientation proposed for us by the Rite of Christian Initiation of Adults. The Rite, which appeared on 6 January 1972, implements the conciliar perspectives we noted above.

We shall first present the orientations of this Rite and how they fit into the purest ecclesial tradition. Then, in the light of this, we shall suggest some of the efforts we shall have to make in order to live catechumenal initiation in a better manner.

A. The Orientations of the Rite

One of the features of the new Rite is the pastoral richness of its "Introduction." It is here that we find the authentic spirit of the restoration of the catechumenate.

The Entire Christian Community Is Responsible

This fundamental principle is recalled in the general introduction. It is the People of God, that is, the Church, that transmits and nourishes the faith received from the Apostles. It is for the People of God, in the first place, to prepare for baptism and to form Christians (Gl, No.7)

This principle is found again in the development of the ritual for adults. Two dimensions of this responsibility are emphasized in particular. All the baptized have a role to play with regard to the candidates: "the people of God, represented by the local church, should always understand and show that the initiation of adults is its concern and the business of all the baptized" (No. 41). The People of God have, first of all, a role in the first evangelization: "the community must always be ready to fulfill its apostolic vocation by giving help to those who need Christ." It also has a helping role "throughout their whole period of initiation," from the precatechumenate to the time of the mystagogia. And this role must be exercised on two levels: in the preparation for baptism (catechesis and education for life); in the liturgical celebration of the stages.

All the baptized must also *live with the catechumens*. This aspect, too rarely perceived, is expressed very clearly by the Rite: the community must not only aid the candidates, it must also journey with them and be converted with them (No. 4).

Indeed, the help given by the community will only be perceptible if all the baptized share the experience of continual conversion.

The Rite reaffirms the same principle with regard to Lent and the Paschal Season: the baptismal retreat that is Lent "renews the community of the faithful together with the catechumens" (No. 21). And during the time of mystagogia, "the community and the neophytes move forward together.... In this way they understand the paschal mystery more fully and bring it into their lives more and more" (No. 37).

All the members of the community are thus engaged in the Christian initiation of the converts, not only in helping themselves, but also in progressing with them in a life that continually becomes more Christian.

The *ministries and the more particular functions are*, nevertheless, foreseen by the Rite in order to assure the various aspects of catechumental education. They are of three kinds.

The *sacerdotal ministries* are assumed by the bishop assisted by his priests and deacons. It is the bishop who is primarily responsible for the initiation of adults (No. 12). In practice, it is for the priests and deacons to attend to the "pastoral and personal care of the catechumens" (Nos. 45, 46). This care extends from organization to celebration including the decision for admission. In all of this, however, they are always to act in collaboration "with the assistance of catechists or other qualified lay people" (Gl, No. 13).

The *ministers of catechesis* hold an important place in the formation of the catechumens since it is based on faith in the Word of God.

This function is not reserved to the bishops, priests, and deacons. The Rite grants it to "catechists" (No. 48) and to "other lay people."

It is exercised in the evangelization that calls unbelievers to conversion (No. 11), during the catechumenate (No. 19), and even after baptism during the time of mystagogia (No. 38).

The *ministries of sponsorship* are as important as those of catechesis, for the catechumenate is an initiation to the Christian life.

The Rite insists, first of all, on the role of those who "accompany" the converts at the admission to the catechumenate. As guarantors, they "witness to his morals, faith, and intention" (No. 42).

These presenters can then become the "sponsors." It is indispensable that each catechumen be accompanied by a sponsor "who is close to the candidate because of his example, character, and friendship . . . delegated by the local Christian community, and approved by the priest" (No. 43). The function of this sponsor, recognized officially during the liturgical ceremony of election, is threefold:

1. Liturgically, he "accompanies the candidate on the day of election, in the celebration of the sacraments, and during the period of postbaptismal catechesis" and then he "gives public testimony" for him.

2. Before baptism, "it is his responsibility to show the catechumen in a friendly way the place of the Gospel in his own life and in society, to help him in doubts and anxieties. . . ."

3. Finally, after baptism, he continues to watch over the newly baptized and helps him "to remain faithful to his baptismal promises."

In addition to these "canonical" sponsors, the entire group around the converts plays a sponsoring role. During the precatechesis, the Rite directs that the candidates should be helped in order to be able to "meet with the families and communities of Christians with greater ease" (No. 11). And during the catechumenate, the Rite states that the catechumens are to familiarize themselves with the practice of the Christiam life, "helped by the example and support of sponsors and godparents and the whole community of the faithful" (No. 19).

The *liturgical functions* belong primarily to the bishops, priests, and deacons, but the Rite notes that the laity participates in them in a real way:

1. by the presence of the community which is always required (Nos. 12,3; 70; 105; 138-139; 158; 182, etc.);
2. in exceptional cases of baptism of necessity (Gl, No. 17);

3. by simple episcopal delegation for the minor exorcism (Nos. 44; 48; and 66,5); by aiding the celebrant in the signing of the senses at the admission to the catechumenate (Nos. 84-85); by testifying as sponsors and as members of the community (Nos. 81, 136, and 143-146); by giving the blessings (Nos. 119-120); and by supporting their candidates during the scrutinies (Nos. 163; 170; 177), baptism (Nos. 220, 225-226), and confirmation (No. 231).

The office of discernment is also taken up collegially:

1. during the admission to the catechumenate: "With the help of the sponsors, catechists, and deacons, it is the responsibility of the pastors to judge the external indications of these dispositions" (No. 16).

2. during the election for baptism: "As a means to avoid an error in judgment, it would be wise to hold a deliberation on the suitability of the candidates before the liturgical rite is celebrated. This is done by those involved in training the catechumens—presbyters, deacons and catechists—and by the godparents and delegates of the local community. If circumstances permit, the assembly of catechumens may also take part" (No. 137).

The range of ministries and offices involved in catechumental initiation is thus to a large extent open-ended. The new Rite invites us to "actualize" the numerous possibilities it offers, while reminding us that the specialized ministries may neither diminish nor suppress the participation of all the members of the community in what is the task of the entire Church.

B. Some Suggestions

The two major themes that must guide our catechumental pastoral care are these.

1. No restoration of the catechumenate will be possible without a profound renewal of our communities. Indeed, the catechumenal initiation is a work of the Church that cannot be accomplished except within and by the community. Hence, the

community must endeavor to live according to the Gospel. It must have a manner of liturgical celebration that truly initiates the participants in a properly Christian manner of praying.

2. The effective participation of all the Christians in the initiation of catechumens presumes a complementary diversification of offices and ministries. This demands a creative effort and, at the same time, an openness of spirit.

The priest may no longer be the one who does everything. He must, from now on, in accordance with the principle of subsidiarity, share his functions to the degree they can be shared with the catechists and the sponsors.

The catechumenate may no longer be conceived solely as the work of three people—the priest, the catechist, and the sponsor—each doing his own work. For in each of these functions, the ministers will profit by being multiple, each providing the richness of their individual gifts. Thus, for example, the priest responsible will profit by reflecting and celebrating not only with the deacons, but also with other priests engaged in various ways in the journey of the catechumens; the catechist is not the only one to announce the Word. Others may do it for other catechumens, or under different forms for the same catechumens. It is therefore together that they must plan catechesis and search to multiply its forms, if such can favor Christian education. For example, some laymen could be specially delegated for the preparation of catechumens for marriage.

The canonical sponsor is not the only one to provide fraternal aid. There are many other ways of accomplishing sponsorship—groups, clubs, small communities—which will provide support for the catechumens. In Africa, for example, some aunts and some "older" brothers and sisters have specific roles to play.

Two things are required if one wants to progress in the directions stated above. *We have the duty to awaken our communities to the lived comprehension of the Church,* the People of God, as it has been explained by Vatican II. This awakening supposed continuous and concrete efforts, for to transform a mentality requires time and application. These efforts envisage particularly the bringing about of the understanding that every baptized person has an active role to play in the Church; that no one can assume his role without situating it in the whole in profound collaboration with the others; and that the Church must be lived and perceived as a fraternity and not as an organization.

This awakening will not be possible unless the leaders of the community accept the challenge not only to their pastoral customs, but also to their own theological vision including its personal spiritual dimensions.

The greatest number of Christians will participate in the cate-chumenal functions and ministries to the extent that we make an effort to form them. The good will of many Christians is not at stake. What often keeps them from acting is the impression that they have of being incompetent. This impression will disappear to the extent that we can help them: by personally attending to those who accept a responsibility, however minor it may be; by regularly providing them with formation that takes into account their personal faith as well as the pedagogy of their ministry.

The development of all these educative functions in the service of catechumens raises the question of the *recognition of the various ministries*. Without attempting to resolve it here, we will try to give a clear presentation of its different aspects.

The new Rite always uses two words, *"offices"* and *"ministries"* with regard to diverse roles. It thereby shows that everything does not fall into the same category. Certain roles are called *ministries* because they suppose a liturgical intervention of the Church: either an "ordination," as for the episcopacy, the priesthood, and the diaconate; or an "institution," as for the office of acolyte and lector, or any other function that the episcopal conference decides to institute.

The other roles are simply called *"offices."* They are indeed based on the reception of the sacraments of baptism and confirmation, but they are not the object of a particular ceremony. This does not mean that they do not have official recognition. This can occur under other forms. For example, one can say that the sponsors are publicly recognized in their function by the "liturgical" role that they play at the stage of election (No.

136). In certain dioceses, the catechists receive the mission to announce the Word of God from their bishop in a paraliturgy. Thus there is already a real recognition of the ministries and offices involved in catechumenal initiation.

What must be recognized? Certainly every function exercised for the benefit of the ecclesial Body. But this can occur simply by the fact of its being exercised, without the necessity of special intervention by the hierarchy. In this sense, there are those who think that the "mandates" must not be multiplied, for this would tend to devalue baptismal consecration, by contributing to the belief that one must wait for a special delegation to exercise any apostolic activity.

But without going so far, perhaps it is desirable that certain more particular functions—sponsorship catechizing—receive an induction, which would manifest simultaneously the importance that the Church attaches to the function assumed by the individual Christian, and the obligation that he officially takes on before the community.

When must such a ministry be recognized? At the beginning, or after a certain time?

To recognize it too early would be to risk having fragile commitment without follow-up. This would be the case, for example, if one "instituted" the sponsors at the entry into the catechumenate. This is what the Rite wanted to avoid by situating the recognition of the liturgical role of the sponsor only at the stage of election.

To wait too long in recognizing it would be to risk transforming the "institution" of the ministry into a "recognition for good and faithful services."

How to recognize each ministry? A wide range of ceremonies with considerable variation in solemnity can be envisaged.

It could be a true liturgical ceremony of institution like that recently promulgated for lectors (who actually receive the mission of catechist).

It could also be equally valid to have an explicit dialogue between the Church and the one charged with the mission (for example, the sponsor) during one of the liturgical stages of initiation.

It could also be, more simply, the clearly expressed acceptance by those responsible for the catechumenate.

In sum, before settling the matter definitely, searching and experimenting are necessary. And this is true not only for the recognition of the ministries, but also and primarily for their variety and application.

These ideas are pastoral orientations and not canonical decisions. The perspectives proposed by the Rite have, of course, a normative value, but these norms are themselves presented as guidelines. They are the signs indicating the direction which catechumenal pastoral care must explore. Far from closing the debate and fixing a detailed codification, they invite research.

Let us welcome these orientations and, letting ourselves be challenged, work effectively to assume, in a better way, the material mission that the Church invites us to perform for catechumens.

> "Grace was given to each of us according to the measure of Christ's gift.... And his gifts were that some should be apostles, some prophets, some evangelists, some pastors and teachers, for the equipment of the saints, for the work of ministry, for the building up of the body of Christ" (Eph. 4,7-13).

NOTES

1. Storm VII, 9, 52. On the excellence of the doctors according to Origen, see the beautiful texts cited by A. Vilela, La condition collégiale dos prètres au 3e siècle, Paris, 1971, pp. 128-29, The doctor "builds the Church of God," he is the "consoler," the "master and trainer of the faith," the "prophet of Christ."

2. On sponsorship of catechumens, see M. Dujarier, Le parrainage des adultes aux trois premiers siècles de l'Eglise, Paris, Cerf, 1963, 451 pp. "Le parrainage," in Concilium 22 (1967), pp. 53-56.

3. On the sponsorship of infants, see the studies of C. Brusselmans, *Sponsorship of children during the four first centuries of the Church*, The Catholic University of America, 1964. Some of the themes of this thesis are presented by the author herself in "Christian Parents and Infant Baptism," *Louvain Studies*, 1968-9, Nr. 2, pp. 29-39. M.-M. Van Molle, "Les fonctions de parrainage des enfants en Occident, de 550à 900," Diplôme de l'Année de Pastorale Liturgique, Saint-André-les-Burges, 1961. Cf. in *Paroisse et Liturgie*, 46 (1964), pp. 121-46.

4. Trad. Ap. 15 (SC 11 bis, p. 69).

5. Tes. Dom. II, 1, Cf. F. Nau, *La version syriaque de l'Octateuque de Clément,* revised by P. Ciprotti, Paris, Lethielleux, 1967, p. 57.

6. Trad. Ap. 20 (SC 11 bis, p. 79).

7. Didasc. XVI, XII, 2-3, (Nau, pp. 134-35).

Most Rev. Maurice J. Dingman

The Role of the Bishop in Christian Initiation

The bishop of the Diocese of Des Moines, Bishop Maurice J. Dingman can call upon an extraordinarily broad range of pastoral and academic experience. He is also the President of the National Catholic Rural Life Conference.

As I put the finishing touches on this paper it is the month of March. I am just beginning a series of Confirmations that will cover the months of March, April and May. These Confirmation ceremonies will take me into 43 parishes, some of them as far away as 170 miles. These ceremonies, as well as the travel to and from, will consume more than 200 hours of my time as well as 4,000 miles of travel. Could that time and that energy be spent more profitably in pastoral visitations and in promoting the catechumenate?

The present practice of confirming children is frustrating both for the bishop and for the parish, despite the fact that I like Confirmations. I think most pastors and their people would affirm that Confirmation is a hectic moment in the life of the parish. The occasion of Confirmation is an event that presently concerns eighth-graders who are approximately 13 years of age. The bishop's visit is a quick in-and-out affair. There is little time to share faith, to build visions, to dream dreams, to listen to hopes and expectations and to strategize for the building of the genuine Christian community. Why so much emphasis on Confirmation and so little on Baptism?

An attempt is being made at present to use Confirmation as the occasion of a real pastoral visitation. But it turns out less than satisfactory. After each Confirmation the parish holds a reception for the bishop. But the hour is late, the time is hurried, the ceremony has been long, everyone is weary, the bishop must be on his way. To attempt both the ceremony of Confirmation and a pastoral visitation on the same occasion proves to be a practical impossibility. That is my experience, I know an archbishop who almost never confirms. He delegates this task almost in its entirety to his two auxiliary bishops. I asked him about this and he confided to me that he found pastoral visitations much more effective for carrying out his role as shepherd of the flock.

RITE OF CHRISTIAN INITIATION OF ADULTS

I am convinced that the bishop could use his limited time and energies much more effectively than he does presently. Let us assume that the bishop is relieved of his responsibility for confirming children. What would happen if a bishop were to see a large part of his ministry in terms of involvement in the whole catechumenal process outlined in the RCIA? If evangelization is a priority, then the catechumenate is essential. Moreover, the rite has a meaning and a significance for those who are already Catholics. The catechumenate calls the entire faith community to accountability and consequently to a renewal and a deepening of its faith experience. It is in this context that the catechumenate could become an excellent opportunity for the faithful to "renew their own conversion" (RCIA, 4) and come to the full stature of Christ (Ephesians, 4:13).

I would characterize the Christian community in my diocese as a "slumbering giant." The people have benefited greatly from their participation in movements, e.g., Cursillo, Charismatic, Better World, Christian Life Communities, Marriage Encounter, Teens Encounter Christ, etc. New structures abound in the councils of priests and sisters as well as parish, regional and diocesan pastoral councils. New attitudes have been formed in accordance with Vatican II documents. But there is little aware-ness of the potentiality that resides in that faith community. Gifts of mind and heart abound. How can these charisms be tapped and put into operation for the good of the Church?

What is needed is an awakening of this "slumbering giant." I suggest that the RCIA is the explosive bomb than can alert the faith community to its potentiality for evangelization.

The document saw the light of day in 1972. Where has it been these past six years? When will it take on flesh and blood? When will it be translated into action? I am convinced that the RCIA might well be the most important document, along with the apostolic exhortation on evangelization, to come from Rome since the Vatican II documents themselves. These two documents need each other. They are complementary.

As a prelude to the practical discussion of episcopal pos-sibilities of involvement in the catechumenate, I would like to share the concepts and the principles which have guided my activities as shepherd of the flock which lives in southwest Io-wa, canonically the Diocese of Des Moines. In my quinquennial report to Rome in 1974, I listed sixteen principles by which I provided leadership to the diocese. These principles are eccle-siological. All of them are inspired by Vatican II. I will state four of them. Each of them benefit from an understanding of the *RCIA*.

FOUNDATION FOR RCIA IN CONCEPTS
AND PRINCIPLES OF VATICAN II

A. Community: The Principle of Interaction

Pope John XXIII stressed the dignity of the human person. The first chapter of his encyclical on peace is a classic enumer-ation of human rights as he speaks of the dignity and the nobil-ity of the human person. The thrust of the pontificate of Paul VI stressed the concept of community. These two concepts go to-gether: person and community. I say to my people: "I as a per-son can save my soul more easily if you as a community help me; you as a person can save your soul more easily if we as a community help you."

The sentence among all of the Vatican II documents that had the greatest impact on me is the one from the *Decree on Priests* (n. 6) which states, "The office of pastor is not confined to the care of the faithful as individuals, but is also properly extended to the formation of a genuine christian community." I had always envisoned my task as "saving souls." The balanced concept of "building christian community" was a new and compelling insight.

Pope Paul, in a general audience described community as "the focal point of Vatican II": "What is the focal point of Vatican II? . . . It is the Church. The Church is a Communion; a society bound together by bonds of its own; a great community of faith, hope and love."

The importance of "the community of the faithful" is strikingly illustrated in the RCIA. Very early the point is made that the initiation of catechumens takes place step by step in the midst of the community of the faithful. "The faithful, together with the catechumens, reflect upon the value of the paschal mystery, renew their own conversion, and, by their example, lead the catechumens to obey the Holy Spirit more generously" (n. 4). The community is deeply involved at every stage, in every period. The document frequently stresses the example and the support of sponsors and godparents and the whole community of the faithful. "The initiation of adults is (the) concern and the business of all the baptized" (n. 41).

B. Process: The Dynamic Principle

In the past we have been "event" conscious; today we are "process" oriented. Reference is made to this reality in the Vatican Council document on *The Church in the Modern World*. It says that, "Modern Man has substituted a dynamic and more evolutionary concept of nature for a static one; the result is an immense series of new problems calling for a new endeavor of analysis and synthesis" (n. 5). Our recent past has been very static. We are now encouraged to take on a mentality that is dynamic. Our categories of thinking have been typically Greek with little emphasis on time or history. Our thinking has been very conceptual, certainly not experiential. Today our thinking is much more Hebraic. We see the Church as a pilgrim people on a journey. We are Exodus people on our way to the promised land. Movement and process and development are highlighted.

The *Rite of Christian Initiation* provides an abundance of ideas that are dynamic. The document speaks about a "journey." It suggests a period for "maturing." It advocates "stages" in the celebration of sacraments. Sacrament is much more a process than a simple event. This is a challenge to the view that we have generally accepted. Sacrament is the celebrated event at the end of a process.

C. Experience: The Principle of Dialogue

If there was any one concept that characterizes the pontificate of Pope Paul VI, it was that of dialogue. His first encyclical used this as a theme. Again and again he has told us to be a listening Church. The bishop is cautioned to be in the midst of his people. The Directory for bishops emphasized his need to be in sincere and friendly dialogue with his pastors and people (n. 111). When Pope Paul spoke to the Laity Council in 1971, he asked for dialogue to reign and encouraged an ecclesial spirit.

To be a Church of dialogue the principle of equality must be recognized. We are not only a hierarchical Church (Second Vatican Council, *The Church*, 3); we are also People of God (*The Church*, 2). "We are all children of the Father who is in heaven, brothers in Christ, temples of the Holy Spirit, members of the Church. No lay person, then, can speak of the Church as an entity which is, so to speak, outside of him; you belong fully to the Church, you are the Church" (Pope Paul VI, Laity Council, March 20, 1971). All members share true quality in dignity and in the activity common to all the faithful for the building up of the body of Christ. (*The Church*, n. 32). All members share in the mission and ministry of the Church, and in the priesthood of Jesus Christ.

The greatest claim is not being a bishop, a priest, a sister, or a permanent deacon: the greatest claim is one's baptism. Again and again I say to my people, "Accept me by reason of my baptism"! Among the People of God we must stress community and basic equality. In that setting dialogue becomes possible and shared responsibility a reality.

Dialogue is strikingly portrayed in the catechumenal process. The whole RCIA document stresses relationships and interaction. Paragraph 298 speaks of the Christian community testifying to the suitability of catechumens on the occasion of their admission to the sacraments. Paragraph 135 states that the whole community must weigh carefully the decision about the maturiey of the catechumens at the time of the rite of election and the enrollment of names. Paragraph 137 tells us that it would be wise to hold a deliberation on the suitability of candidates before the liturgical rite is celebrated. Paragraphs 42 and 43 give the example of a person accompanying the candidate as a sponsor.

D. Balance: The Principle of Balanced Tension

In this period of transition in the Church we face the temptation to polarize. There are many positions we can take on the spectrum of opinion. We may never permit ourselves to be at either end of that spectrum. *In medio stat virtus.* We often are asked to make an either/or decision. Many are caught up in this syndrome. The kind of position we need today is both/and. It is easy to live at the extremes. It is difficult to live in balanced tension.

The American bishops of the United States in their collective pastoral of 1967, *The Church in Our Day*, spoke of this tendency to polarize and said that this "... has time and again led to excessive distinctions between the human and the divine in the Word made flesh, between the Christ of faith and the Jesus of history, between freedom and authority in religion, and, finally, between charism and institution" (p. 55). Pope Paul VI cautioned us in these words: "Let us keep our balance at the changes that are taking place around us" (Audience, July 5, 1972).

I suspect that the approach suggested by the *Rite of Christian Initiation* will not be easily accepted by some of our Catholic people. We must remember to keep our balance. We must not be afraid to implement the document in tension. The involvement of the community will seem needless and unnecessary to some. Attitudes associated with the individualistic approach, the old method of learning, the heavy emphasis on memorization, will test our patience. The balance called for is illustrated in paragraph 19 of the *Rite of Christian Initiation of Adults.* It speaks of four ways by which catechumens are brought to maturity. Knowledge of dogmas and precepts must be balanced with a familiarity with living the Christian way of life, celebrated in suitable liturgical rites and centered in a life that is apostolic and active in living the Gospel. Participation in the catechumenate serves to unite polarized groups within the Christian community. I define a bishop as one who gathers people together, and creates an atmosphere of hope and trust, within a dynamic of constant and patient dialogue.

PASTORAL PRIORITIES

Before addressing the key of catechumenal stages and the bishop's involvement in the RCIA, I will point out some current pastoral thrusts, particularly those on the National Conference of Catholic Bishops. These pastoral thrusts are in the areas of ministry, evangelization, catechesis and social justice. I believe personally that the RCIA has an unprecedented importance and a tremendous potential for the successful implementation of these key pastoral thrusts.

A. Ministry

One of the most exciting things happening in the Church today is the people's discovery of ministry. All members share in the mission and ministry of the Church and in the priesthood of Jesus Christ. Each person has been given special gifts by the

Holy Spirit. The reception of these gifts brings with it the right and the duty to use them for the service of one another and all the people.

When the Holy Father was addressing the cardinals of the Church, he drew their attention to the wonderful gifts and charisms which God has given to the people. He asked them how these gifts and charisms could be put to use for the welfare of the Church. As bishops we should call forth the gifts of the individuals for the service of the Church. We should call each Christian community to accountability for that same service to the Church.

At the November 1977 meeting of the National Conference of Catholic Bishops, Archbishop Jadot warned the bishops of an imminent problem—the shortage of priests. He expressed his worry that we will not be able to staff our parishes and institutions with priests as we have in the past. One of his solutions was to give greater ministerial responsibility to tha laity, both men and women.

There are many ministries involved in Christian initiation. The people are ready to respond. The document consistently says that the People of God should understand that the initiation of adults is its concern and its business (n. 41). The community is to minister to help the candidates and the catechumens throughout the whole period of initiation: the pre-catechumenate, the catechumenate, the illumination, and the period of post-baptismal catechesis.

B. Evangelization

On December 8, 1975 Pope Paul VI issued an *Apostolic Exhortation on Evangelization in the Modern World.* It was written at the request of the 1974 Synod of Bishops. In 1976 the Bishops of the United States specifically designated evangelization as a priority in the U.S. Church. In November of 1977 a national office of Evangelization was established. More that 100 dioceses have appointed liaison persons with this office.

Chapter V of the document speaks about the beneficiaries of evangelization. The first proclamation is to be addressed especially to those who have never heard the Good News of Jesus. As well as those people who have been baptized but who live quite outside christian life.

C. Catechesis

The 1977 World Synod of Bishops directed our attention to the RCIA. It said that more study should be given to the relationship between catechesis and the catechumenate. The potential of the document for the whole area of catechetics remains untested.

D. Justice

The 1971 World Synod of Bishops gave special attention to the subject of justice. The subject has taken on added importance since that date. The Vatican II Council set the direction in its document on the *Church in the Modern World*.

The RCIA presents four ways in which candidates are given pastoral formation and trained by suitable discipline (n. 19). The final way is the challenge to engage in the Church's apostolic life. The opportunity is offered for the catechumen to learn how to work actively with others, to spread the Gospel and build up the Church. They are told to do this by the testimony of their lives and the profession of their faith. Reference is made in a footnote to the Vatican Council's document on missionary activity which states that " ... the catechumenate ... is not a mere exposition of dogmatic truths and norms of morality, but a period of formation in the whole Christian life ..." (n. 14).

The call to real justice is changing the Church in the United States from *fortress* to *lighthouse*. Whereas in the past we have been concerned about the faith of an immigrant people, we are now reaching out to address the social problems of the world. The catechumenate prepares people for this challenge.

THE CATECHUMENATE: A BISHOP'S INVOLVEMENT

In my role as bishop I am constantly looking for processes and structures that integrate what I am doing as Ordinary of a diocese. Where can I find a canopy or an umbrella that will encompass what has been accomplished and give a rhythm to the days ahead? Where are there models that give balance, continuity and build faith community?

I have found a model in the restored catechumenate. I am ready to seize this historical tool for this historical moment. The catechumenal model might well be the approach that will integrate and bring greater order to my episcopal ministry.

My ultimate goal is to build an adult diocesan Christian faith community. But there are still many critical issues that remain partly resolved. I like the model that speaks of a journey, of a people who are on pilgrimage. My key question is: How do I operationalize the objective of an adult Christian faith community? I am more and more convinced that the model needed is the catechumenal model found in the RCIA. The heart of the model is in paragraph 19.

At this point I will suggest some practical things a bishop might do to promote the catechumenate.

The bishop should speak about the catechumenate in season and out of season. The catechumenal model can be constantly shared in pastoral letters and talks to priests, religious, and laity. Informal visits and conversations will be particularly effective. The bishop's preoccupation with the catechumenate can make all the people of the diocese aware of it as a model for integrating them into a faith community.

The pastors of the diocese are of paramount importance. Study days, the Annual Workshop, and other occasions can provide them opportunities for discussing the catechumenate. The Bishop's encouragement of the catechumenate is essential for their motivation.

The Dioceasan Pastoral Council could be the best group for promoting the catechumenate! They are an organization that coordinates all of the multifaceted activities of the diocese. It is the bishop's own advisory body. Their time can be well spent on consideration of the catechumenal model as the coordinating force in the diocese.

The establishment of a diocesan office of the catechumenate may be helpful. It might be called the "Catechumenal Commission" to act in conjunction with the liturgy commission and the office of religious education. The designation of an office or a commission would give tangible evidence of the bishop's concern for the catechumenate. Perhaps the catechumenate would more properly be attached to an office of evangelization. In any case I would suggest that it begin as an ad hoc committee, which could later be given more permanence as a commission, or as part of another office.

My rationale for such an ad hoc committee is the two World Synods of Bishops held since the RCIA document was issued in 1972. The 1974 Synod of Bishops considered the topic of evangelization; the 1977 topic was catechetics. It seems to me that both of these topics can be understood fully only in the context of the RCIA. Perhaps God in his providence has waited for this moment to give greater publicity and more acceptance to this foundational document. In a real sense it provides the heart for both evangelization and catechesis. Some authors are already using the terms evangelization and catechesis for the first and second periods of the RCIA. Pre-catechumenate is identified as a period for evangelization and the catechumenate as a period for catechesis. They are being seen as interrelated, components of the process of Christian initiation.

Another objective of a bishop is to share his insights with his fellow bishops. This can be done in conversations, as agenda for provincial, regional, and national meetings, and in discussion by the Bishop's Committees on Liturgy, Education, Canon Law.

The permanent diaconate program is making progress that can challenge the gifts and charisms of these men. The catechumenate offer them a challenge. They have much to offer since they are almost invariably married men. Their witness and leadership can be invaluable. Their participation can assure a successful catechumenate.

The catechumenate provides an excellent context for the Cursillo and similar movements to become part of the life of the parish. At the time of the Cursillo closing, the participants might be invited to give their time and energy to the "parish plan" of the catechumenate. Having just experienced the meaning of Christian community in a week-end of prayer and study, they will appreciate this invitation.

The catechumenate can serve a useful purpose in the diocese by giving a new meaning to parish, regional, and diocesan conciliar structures. Do we use them effectively? Many present structures are sterile because of a lack of challenge and incentive. The catechumenate could involve people and give impetus to their apostolate.

The catechumenate provides an excellent context for the Cursillo and similar movements to become part of the life of the parish. At the catechumenate program is a ready-made opportunity to help people to move into the main stream of parish life.

It would be well for bishops to gather statistics about the number of parishes in the diocese who are already involved in the catechumenate program. He could invite these pastors to a meeting and begin the dialogue. The opportunity for discussion would be provided and the right questions raised.

The bishop ought to begin immediately even on a small scale. My worship commission suggests that I begin in my participation at the cathedral. What better place to give witness to the rest of the diocese?

There are three occasions when the cathedral would serve as a gathering place for various stages of the catechumenate:

1. *The First Sunday of Advent.* During the Fall the parishes could be engaged in the pre-catechumenate stage of inviting prospective candidates. The beginning of Advent can be the occasion for enrollment into the catechumenate. The cathedral with the bishop presiding can be the ideal place for the catechumens to assemble publicly for the first time. Here, in the presence of the bishop and the whole diocesan faith community, the catechumen would make his intention known to the Church. "This celebration manifests their desire publicly and the Church expresses their reception and first consecration" (n. 14). Their names are written in the register of catechumens. From this moment they are "joined to the Church and are part of the household of Christ" (n. 18).

2. The First Sunday of Lent. The catechumens who have successfully pursued their catechumenate and have reached the plateau of making an "election" are invited to a celebration at the cathedral with the bishop presiding. The whole diocesan faith community gathered around the bishop "elects" the catechumens. Their names are now written in the "book of the elect" (n. 22). The decision of the bishop to receive their names takes place publicly in the presence of the faith community. This event should be celebrated with "great solemnity" since it is "the turning point in the whole catechumenate" (n. 23). The bishop enhances that solemnity by his presence.

3. The Easter Vigil. The sacraments of baptism, confirmation and the eucharist together constitute "... the final stage in which the elect come forward and, with their sins forgiven, are admitted into the People of God, receive the adoption of the sons of God and are led by the Holy Spirit into the promised fullness of time and, in the eucharistic sacrifice and meal, to the banquet of the Kingdom of God" (n. 27). All this should be done normally within the liturgy of the Easter Vigil (n. 208). The bishop should be an integral part of the liturgy of the Easter Vigil at the cathedral. Participation of other parishes of the diocese will come later. I see the possibility of the Easter Vigil taking place at some later date in some central building that could accommodate several thousands of people.

4. Pentecost Sunday. The final celebration in the cathedral can be on Pentecost Sunday. This would, in a sense, close the period of post-baptismal catechesis. Just as many nations were represented at the first Pentecost so in this celebration hopefully many parishes would be represented. Such a celebration would give added importance to the whole period of post-baptismal catechesis or mystagogia. Emphasis could be placed on ministry and the whole celebration could be mission oriented. The celebration would catapult the newly initiated into the apostolic life of the Church.

The bishop can have additional occasions for involvement in the catechumenate on the parish level. The occasion of his pastoral visitations can be occasions when, ". . . he meets the newly baptized and presides at a celebration of the Eucharist" (n. 239). The sponsors, godparents, etc. can join with the Bishop on that occasion. The pastoral visitations might be so arranged timewise that the Bishop could preside at some of the other stages of the catechumenate, e.g., the scrutinies (n. 25), the presentations (Profession of Faith, Creed, the Lord's Prayer, the Gospels).

ADDITIONAL COMMENTS

A. Confirmation

The current practice of Confirmation remains a question. The document is clear on the point that Confirmation should normally happen immediately after baptism and within the same liturgical event. Reference is made only to adult baptism (n. 34) but one is compelled to ask why this practice should not be applied also to infants and children, expecially if they are baptized at the Easter Vigil. If baptism can be celebrated shortly after birth, why not confirmation as well? If age is no serious obstacle to baptism, then theologically it should be no hurdle for confirmation.

The bishop has traditionally celebrated the sacrament of Confirmation. Opening this ministry of Confirmation to a priest should not create any problems for the bishop. First of all the bishop ought to see this as better pastoral practice and certainly theologically and liturgically more in keeping with the ancient practice. Far from constituting a restriction on the bishop it would seem to enhance his ministry. The bishop is now restricted to one segment of the whole process of Christian initiation, that of Confirmation. In the new approach he would be involved at every stage of the whole Christian initiation.

B. The Neo-Catechumenate

There are many adults who are already baptized but who need evangelization and catechesis. I see this as a further unfolding of the catechumenal model. The document refers primarily to those who are converts to the faith, but I see the process of the catechumenate as being a model for adult education. The same reasons apply. All are in need of further catechetical formation. This process adapted to the new circumstances can provide an excellent way for already baptized Catholics to grow and to come to maturity (n. 296).

C. Pastoral Visitations

I conclude with the basic premise of my paper. *Eliminate Confirmation from the bishop's routine of duties.* Substitute a new emphasis on pastoral visitations. This would be in keeping with the Roman Directory for bishops. A whole section, some six pages, is devoted to the subject of pastoral visitation (nn. 166-170).

The pastoral visitation responds to the admonition of the Second Vatican Council that the bishop should be in the midst of his people. In his person, the bishop can be a symbol of unity. In the process of the pastoral visit the bishop can celebrate Mass; preach the Word; visit with the priests, the religious and the people; to visit the sick; and help the poor. In this setting the bishop can address questions of ministry, education, moral problems, etc.

Preeminent among the concerns of the bishop should be the catechumenate with all of its ramifications.

The potential of the RCIA can only be measured by future experience. It deserves a hearing. It needs to be tried.

Tad Guzie

Theological Challenges

Tad Guzie has his PhD in historical theology from the University of Cambridge. The author of numerous books and articles on sacramental theology and catechesis, he is a frequent lecturer at workshops on religious education, liturgy, and sacraments throughout the U.S. and Canada.

I began work on this paper together with Bishop Dingman as he began work on his own paper—he as pastor, I as theologian. We talked about problems of the past and present, both pastoral and theological. Mostly we talked about the future, each of us from our own perspectives: we dreamed dreams and shared visions together. His paper contains some of the dreams and hopes of a pastor and church leader who is faced with the challenge of this massive project called "Christian initiation."

My own paper talks mostly about the theological dreams and visions which lie hidden in the *Rite of Christian Initiation of Adults*. It begins with some reflections on history, because I have found history a valuable way to relativize many assumptions about what is "traditional." But exploring the history of initiation during the early Christian centuries quickly became, for me, a springboard for extremely contemporary questions. So at various points in this paper I have summarized the theological challenges that are raised by the RCIA. They are challenges that affect our whole understanding of the church and its sacramental rites. The RCIA embodies very nearly the entire vision of church and sacrament which Vatican II articulated, and it will be interesting to see how ready we are to hear everything this official rite of the Roman Catholic Church is saying to us.

To put it bluntly, the RCIA blows the whistle on many theological presuppositions that have governed our Catholic religious lives for over a thousand years. It is to this problem of mentality and attitude and presuppositions from the past that my "theological challenges" are directed.

A bishop today might well possess the qualities of the *episkopos* called for in the famous passage from the third chapter of 1 Timothy. But the writer was talking about the presiding elder of a small charismatic community. If we take the church structure which this writer knew, and if we translate into today's terms the job he was thinking about, we would have to say that he gives us an ideal description of someone like the chairperson of a parish council.

Today we place eucharistic leadership at the center of the bishop's role in the church. But liturgy does not appear as an organizing hierarchical principle until Ignatius of Antioch in the second century. Saint Paul does not mention liturgical leadership in *any* of his lists of offices or gifts that build the community. The first signs of liturgy or eucharistic presidency as a principle of hierarchical organization appear more than half a century after the death of Jesus. We simply do not know how liturgy or eucharist were organized during the first few generations of the church's existence.

These two examples are reminders that, in a time of renewal when we are drawn back to the sources which help us to reflect on our origins and traditions, it is important not to misunderstand the purpose of reflection on history. It is tempting to look in the pages of the New Testament for some model which we can reconstruct and imitate. But which model will that be? We have learned that if there is little resemblance between the structures of the NT churches and the structures we possess today, there is also no single model in the NT churches. Every serious scholar of the early church warns us that we have to be extremely careful when we look at any of our present church structures and say "Christ instituted this" or "That role is divinely inspired."

Christians should always be charismatic people. But Christianity will never again be a tiny charismatic sect, believing in an obscure condemned criminal and waiting for his imminent return, perhaps next week.

Christians should always have an impact on history. But civilization will never again be identified with a church which crowned emperors and gave its rulers a divine sanction.

These are various ways of saying, "You can't go home again"—a profound little sentence which encapsulates the historical consciousness of the late twentieth century.[1]

The documents of the patristic church have been a precious source of ideas for our current liturgical renewal. Until Vatican II, Catholic liturgy had embodied mostly the experience and tradition of the medieval church. Since Vatican II, we have been learning that the Catholic tradition is larger than the tradition of the Middle Ages and broader than the Council of Trent. But we also hear Catholics today asking, "Why do we have to do it the way the early church did it?"

The RCIA draws upon many ideas and models that were tested by the patristic church. That is, we have looked to the experience of the early church and have found there many forms for interpreting and expressing *our own* experience of Christian faith. The danger is that some might see this rite simply as a return to a past age's way of going about things. Anyone who has compared the letter of the rite with the letter of the patristic sources knows that this is not so. And this brings us to theological challenge:

> **1.** *The RCIA offers us a sacramental process, not just a ritual. On every page we are told to adapt, adapt, adapt.*

I shall spell out some of the dimensions of this challenge later in this paper. First I think it would be good to talk about the role of the bishop (pastor) in the initiation of catechumens, as that role had taken shape by the fourth and fifth centuries.[2]

Again, "you can't go home again." But there are still some lessons to be learned from the past, and some models that might be fruitful for the future.

First, the patristic bishop was in charge of the *catechesis* of candidates for baptism. He saw to the appointment of catechists, and he himself took an active part in the catechesis, especially during Lent (the period of election). Secondly, he presided *liturgically* over the final ceremonies of initiation, above all the Easter Vigil. His catechetical function then continued throughout the Easter season, as he explained to the neophytes the experience of the bath, the meaning of the anointings, the white garment, the blessings, the table fellowship. Thirdly, throughout the whole process there was a *judicial* function. That is, the bishop had much to do with setting criteria for membership in the Christian community.

These three functions suggest that a bishop in the patristic church saw the initiation of catechumens as a very real priority. Of course, a bishop in those days was more like a pastor of a large parish than the administrator-bishop we have come to know. Still, the patristic model is interesting, because it looks as though the average pastor today is far less involved in the initiation process than were their progenitors in the patristic church.

The breakdown of the bishop's (pastor's) involvement in the initiation process was a result of something more than a sheer increase in the number of Christians (parishioners). As Christianity gradually became the preferred religion of the state, baptism came to serve another purpose quite different from entrance into the paschal mystery. It became a kind of credit card that one needed in order to get anywhere in Christendom.

This affected all three of the areas mentioned above. In the area of *catechesis*, theologians would continue to talk about the spiritual and ecclesial effects of the sacraments of initiation. But the fact of the matter was that baptism came to serve social as well as ecclesial purposes. Baptism became a kind of birth certificate. As baptism became a birth certificate, the catechumenate, with its emphasis on gradual entry into a total human and spiritual process, was bound to disappear. A birth certificate does not call for a process.

As for *liturgy*, during the early centuries the meaning of Christian initiation was so tied up with the paschal mystery that it was not considered fitting to celebrate initiation except at the season when the whole community was solemnly celebrating the death and resurrection of Jesus. As baptism came to serve other societal purposes, this link with the paschal season was lost. The celebration of baptism came to depend on when a child was born, not on the time when the faith community celebrates the Easter mystery. Eventually the assembly of the faithful disappeared quite thoroughly from the whole process of initiation, and baptism came to be a private ceremony.

Almost every pastor inherits this situation. An unknown couple comes to him and asks him to baptize their baby. He wants to say to them, "I don't know who you are, you have no relationship to this faith community that I am aware of, and everything inside me tells me to say *no* to this baptism." His feelings are entirely correct, and they have to do with the relation between baptism and the community. I shall come back to this question later.

By the time we reach the Middle Ages, the bishop (pastor) had abandoned his involvement in both the catechetical and liturgical dimensions of initiation, partially because of an increase in the numbers of Christians. The desire of bishops in central Italy to "confirm" the initiation of the newly baptized, by reserving the second anointing after baptism for a later ceremony, attests to the decreasing involvement of the bishop. But in addition to the problem of sheer numbers (which is no different today, when a bishop has to arrange his schedule around confirmation instead of baptism), the *judicial* role of the bishop had also shifted. As Christendom developed, bishops (pastors) spent increasing portions of their time doing the work of civil magistrates. For example, we hear Augustine complaining about the amount of time he had to set aside for civil duties in fifth-century Hippo. Any pastor today will attest to similar non-pastoral demands on his time, be it only fixing a burst water pipe in the school building.

The expansion of the bishop's role into civil matters—or, one might suggest, the expansion of the pastor's role into building maintenance—was accompanied by increasing abandonment of any judicial role in establishing criteria for membership in the Christian community. Theologians would continue to talk about the importance of the link between baptism and the faith of the church. But that link was no longer very visible in the way baptism came to be celebrated. Nor was it observable in pastoral insistence on conscious commitment, or on active faith on the part of a baby's parents.

The theological motive for baptism also shifted. For many centuries, baptism along with its accompanying rituals ("confirmation") and admission to the eucharistic table, celebrated a final stage in the process of beginning a new life in Christ. From the very beginning, Christians understood that sacramental initiation placed them in a condition of hope over against slavery to the sin of the world. But this conception of a new standing in the face of the "sin of the world" should not be identified with what we have come to know as "forgiveness of original sin."

Saint Augustine, early in the fifth century, was the first to state that *individual persons* are guilty of the sin of the world, and blameworthy for it *before* any acts of personal sin. This teaching was destined to shift the pastoral motives for baptism.

The doctrine that we know as "original sin" developed only gradually, and it had much to do with the practice of infant baptism. Augustine reasoned that infant baptism must "do" something, effect something for the baby, even apart from conscious awareness—because, as he understood it, the church has "always" baptized infants. It did not occur to Augustine to call the practice into question; he simply accepted it. He also looked at the question from the viewpoint of what sacraments do for the *individual* instead of the community; I shall return to this point later. Augustine also worked with a faulty translation of Romans 5:12 and was pressed to explain how all of us had sinned "in" Adam's sin. In any case, Augustine concluded that baptism removes personal guilt which is inherited from Adam and transmitted through the male semen.[3]

Again, it is important to distinguish Christian awareness of the mystery of evil, the "sin of the world," from the idea of individual blameworthiness prior to any personal sin. The idea that baptism "forgives original sin" is unknown to the church of the first few centuries. Someone like Tertullian, who was hardly a libertine, felt that the semen of the sexual union transmitted holiness, not sin.[4] And Saint Paul argued that a non-Christian spouse is made holy through union with a Christian spouse, on the grounds that the children of a Christian parent are holy, not unclean (1 Cor 7:14). Like Tertullian, Paul presupposes that the gift of God's love precedes the mystery of evil, even apart from baptism.

Augustine looked at a current practice, that of infant baptism, and from it he argued to a theological theory. It is not until the ninth century that we find a writer reversing the argument, stating that there *is* original and individual guilt for the sin of the world, and *therefore* one must be baptized.[5] Perhaps the reversal is already implicit in Augustine. But Augustine would have insisted that none of this makes any sense apart from the faith of the church, and such factors as the conscious commitment of a baby's parents. The subsequent tradition did not so insist.

The doctrine of original sin developed only gradually. No one can deny the truth about the reality of evil that it affirms. We are certainly born into an ambiguous world, where the invitation to ego-centeredness is as strong as the invitation to explore the depths of one's self, and so to abandon the ego and find God. But we also have to be attentive to what the doctrine of original sin has left unsaid. Let's call this theological challenge:

> **2.** *The Lord loves all of us from the first moment of our conception.*

To put this in catechetical language, it is not baptism that makes us members of God's family. We belong to God's family from the first moment of our existence. Christian faith and baptism are a response to a call to belong *in a particular way* to the family of God. Through baptism we are initiated into the family of *Jesus*, into a community which is called to become *aware* of how the love of God has been made manifest in Jesus. To be baptized is not to enter the world of grace, because the grace and love of God is already there, it is freely given, it surrounds our existence, and we are all in contact with it from the first moment of our conception. But to be initiated into the family of *Jesus* is a different matter, a matter of entering into a conscious process in which the business of dying and rising becomes the pattern for one's life-style.

We are all born, at one and the same time, into the mystery of love and into the mystery of evil. For over a thousand years, following the school that developed out of Augustine's dispute with the Pelagians, the western church has given a curious priority to the mystery of evil. And so we come to theological challenge:

> **3.** *Our pastoral approach to baptism has implied that we are first born into the mystery of evil, and only in baptism do we securely contact the mystery of love. The RCIA gives first priority to the mystery of God's love for us, and it nowhere suggests that we need to be absolved from an original evil.*

This amounts to asking whether Catholics are willing to return to a theology which begins with the reality of God's love rather than the reality of sin and evil. Vatican II's *Dogmatic Constitution of the Church* (#16) made a dramatic move away from the perspective of the Augustinian school of thought, when it affirmed in so many words that God loves everyone who is born into this world, prior to baptism and apart from baptism. The RCIA spells out the same thing in the liturgical and sacramental realm.

Still, the idea that "baptism is necessary for salvation" is deeply engrained in Catholic consciousness, perhaps western Christian consciousness. Early enough, the Christian tradition felt uncomfortable with this idea and came up with the escape clause of "baptism of desire." It is strange how concepts can get in our way, once we have put the cart before the horse or posed the wrong question. What the concept of baptism of desire says, in an involuted but nonetheless formal way, is that it is faith in God and *not* baptism which is necessary for salvation.

The history that I have been tracing brings us to theological challenge:

> **4.** *The most traditional priority of the Christian Church lies with the conscious commitment of candidates for baptism, or of a baby's parents, not with the Rite of Baptism itself.*

We have been using baptism as the beginning of the salvation process, largely because of the theological (superstitious?) support provided by the doctrine of original sin. If this trend is to be reversed, and if we are to become truly comfortable in understanding the rite of baptism as a "final stage" of a growth process (RCIA #27), we have to revise the sacramental presuppositions of the last thousand years.

The tendency of any tradition which is so rich in ritual as the Roman church will always be to sacramentalize before there has been sufficient evangelization or lived faith experience. This tendency or temptation applies to any of our sacraments. The temptation is doubly strong in the area of initiation because of a long-standing fear, backed up by a single tradition which began in North Africa, that one is not really "safe" until the water is poured.

Again, one should not overlook the social climate in which the doctrine of original sin developed. I doubt that the rite of water baptism would have taken priority over the faith of the community, and the catechumenal process of entering into the life of that community, if baptism had not become a ticket into society as well as admission into the church. These historical circumstances were preserved in the American Catholic immigrant church, insofar as baptism gave an infant a requisite identity with its parents' culture. In any case, apart from such circumstances as these, baptism could have remained a "final stage" in a total process of initiation, and not have become a rushed first step. If the theology of original sin took root in a climate where membership in the church and in society became indistinct, perhaps society's discarding of baptism as a birth certificate will help the Christian church to return to richer motives for baptism.

Still another development in sacramental theology took place as Christian faith became Christendom. As the church became identified with society or indistinct from it, the faith assembly lost its distinctive ecclesial identity. This may be one reason why there was a shift from an ecclesial understanding of the sacraments to an individualistic understanding. For the early church *sacraments happen to the whole community*, and this was the starting point for understanding what happens to individuals. As the sense of being church waned, *sacraments now happened to individuals*, and the individual became the starting point for understanding the effect of the sacraments.

The question which Augustine addressed, and which eventually gave us original sin as the chief motive for baptism, was essentially an individualistic question: "What happens to the unconscious baby who is baptized?" Other church fathers—and Augustine himself, I think, in other contexts—would have put the question this way: "What are we doing, and what happens to *all of us* when we celebrate baptism around and with this child?"

> **5.** *Sacraments happen to the community, not just the individual. The individual person is not the starting point for understanding the effects of the sacraments.* [6]

To use again the example of infant baptism, the element of conscious commitment is not something that is provided only years later, when the child begins to respond consciously to baptism. It is already present—and the *Rite of Infant Baptism* insists that it *must* be present—in the faith of the parents and those who will surround the child with the atmosphere of Christian faith. One can raise many questions about the practice of infant baptism; but it is a *theological* problem only if we think of the sacrament as something that is *done to the baby* rather than as something *we do* as a community of faith.

I keep referring to infant baptism because that, after all, has been 99% of our experience of baptism. The RCIA, in describing the ministries and offices associated with initiation, first describes at great length the ministry of the *community*, since initiation "is the business of all the baptized" (#41). Only then are the individual ministries of sponsor, godparents, and clergy (in that order!) described. But are we yet in a position to *hear* this? Can we appreciate what the RCIA says about the experience of the catechumenate and the function of the faith community in the adult experience, until we look very frankly at the *absence* of the community from the whole experience of infant baptism? "If they do these things in the green wood, what will happen in the dry?"

Let me give two examples of this problem of the community's involvement in baptism. Many Catholics have been exposed to baptisms at Sunday Mass, and this has raised much consciousness about the ecclesial meaning of baptism. But many people are also walking into that monthly baptismal Mass and saying, "Oh darn, I've caught the baptism Mass." The reaction is quite correct, because most parishioners have had no more involvement with the person being baptized than they had before. Ritual can go only so far in involving the community, if there is not a community experience which backs up the ritual.

A second example: The Bishops' Committee on the Liturgy has issued regulations that baptisms should take place not in a private home but in the parish church building. This is based on the sound ecclesial principle, articulated in the church's official rites, that baptism is not a private family event but one which involves the whole local church. But this presupposes that some portion of the local church is involved enough with candidates for baptism to warrant insistence on baptism in the church building as a symbol of that involvement. A good many Catholics have been mystified by the insistence that the baptism of their child be celebrated in the church building, when in fact the assisting community turns out to be the same family group that would have been present in their living room.

This illustrates the Catholic temptation to address a problem through sacramental legislation, and to assume that legislation will make a vision happen. I thoroughly endorse what the revision of our rites has done for the church, even the pain and discomfort it has cost. But we are now at the point where a new legalism could be as damaging as the old. Many young Catholic families have rediscovered baptism as a time for the *family* to celebrate its own Christian commitment. But the link between this genuinely sacramental moment for the *family* and the larger *parish* community might not yet have been experienced.

One can readily say that the American bishops are visionary in insisting that baptisms be celebrated in the parish building rather than in a family's living room. One can also suggest that the bishops are bypassing a needed step in the whole process of building community, namely, a family's coming to its own realization that this family is truly "church."

The above examples illustrate the extent of the challenge issued by the RCIA when it talks about the primacy of the community's ministry in the initiation process. It will take a long time to involve our existing parishes, even small portions of them, in the adult catechumenate. If our people have not been practically and realistically involved in the initiation of *infants*, how can we expect them to get interested in taking responsibility for the initiation of *adults*? I am convinced that in the American Catholic church, there is no better starting point for interesting our people in the catechumenate than in getting them involved in the baptism of infants—beginning with little more than simple hospitality toward young parents, and gestures which would integrate them into the parish community.

Our present parish structures make it difficult to address this task because so many of American Catholics' expectations of the parish presuppose a school model. Even if there is no longer a school, we still tend to work out of the school model. According to this model, young people drop out of close parish involvement when they leave grade school. The parish then picks them up again after they are married, when their own children are ready to begin school. This leaves a period of some ten or fifteen years when the parish is little present to people's lives.

One of the experiences of the adult catechumenate is a period in which candidates are integrated ever more fully into the life of the community (RCIA #19). But let us not overlook the baptized. What does the average parish have to offer to people between the ages of, say 15 and 30? Is there in fact, in most of our parishes, any kind of "community" into which these people can be comfortably integrated?

The average parish is not a community, and it is unrealistic to assume that it can ever become "a" community. Rather, a parish is an *assembly* of *many communities*. Those communities include active and dedicated groups, which may have formed as a result of experiences like CFM, Cursillo, Marriage Encounter, etc. There is also the "Community of the Five Rear Pews," which hopefully can be touched and called to conversion by other communities. I would suggest that in addressing the question of the community's ministry in the initiation process, we need to call forth ministry for *communities*, i.e. committed groups already existing within the parish, rather than think in terms of the whole parish *assembly*. This model of the parish as an assembly of many communities may help us to get a handle on the problem of the many ministries involved in initiation.

Let us return to a point mentioned earlier and make it theological challenge:

> **6.** *If ritual sacraments are the final stage of a total experience, not the first step, we must ask how much lived experience needs to be brought to the celebration of a sacrament.*

The RCIA articulates a view of sacrament which is quite new to our experience, because we have been using sacraments as the beginning of the process rather than as a final stage. The new *Rite of Penance* has raised the same problem. In that rite, sacramental absolution is described as a "completion" of a process of conversion (#6), an idea which is perfectly parallel to baptism-comfirmation-eucharist as the "final stage" of initiation.

But this conception is quite foreign to us. For many centuries we have been saying, "Go to confession and get forgiveness." The new rite says, "Experience the Lord's forgiveness, then go to confession and celebrate it." The rite quite bluntly gives a view of sacramental forgiveness which is the reverse of the way we have used confession. I would suggest that the new penance rite will have been implemented when we can say that this sentence from the rite has come true: "Faithful Christians, as they experience and proclaim the mercy of God in their lives, celebrate with the priest the liturgy by which the church continually renews itself" (#11). The problem is the same for communal penance as for individual confession. If the ceremony has not been prepared for by a whole community process of conversion and renewal, general absolution will become just another case of the cart before the horse, sacramentalization before evangelization.

It is difficult for us really to believe in the parable of the Prodigal Father. The father had never stopped loving his son and welcomed him instantly; he wasn't even interested in the boy's "confession." This is not the way human justice works, and it is not generally the way we have viewed the sacrament of penance. Catholics have tended to see confession with the mindset of the elder son: You are not forgiven until you have made your speech, recited your list of sins, given some guarantees, and proven yourself worthy to join the rest of us who haven't strayed.

One is reminded again of challenge No. 3: Do we begin with the mystery of God's love, or are we to remain fixated with sin and evil? God's continual and faithful love for us is *the* "good news." We are never *not* forgiven. The problem is our *acceptance* of the forgiveness that is always there for us.

All of this is parallel to the vision contained in the RCIA. The question is not one of becoming okay with God, but rather of receiving and celebrating the love that surrounds us from the first moment of our existence. The sacraments do not confer a grace that was absent. Sacraments proclaim and enable us to own a love that is already present to us. A sacrament celebrates the Lord's giving, certainly. But his giving is not confined to the sacrament. What we need to focus on, within the sacrament, is our taking the love of God home with us, with a fresh awareness of that love. And that new awareness is the substantial part of the "grace of the sacrament."

This is heady stuff, and it will be interesting to see if we as a church can hear it, receive it, and live on it. When we talk about the sacraments in the way our new rites do, placing so much emphasis on experience and awareness, we are running counter to a thousand-year-old tradition, in which experience and awareness were not the important sacramental questions.

The medievals liked to speak of how "fitting" it is that there be seven sacraments, since seven is a symbol of wholeness. It is fitting, then, that I conclude with a seventh challenge:

> **7.** *The central question for the Catholic Church and its leadership is whether we can turn ourselves around and begin with the lived experience of faith, rather than sacramental services, as the definition of what our church is about.*

NOTES

1. R. Wilken, *The Myth of Christian Beginnings* (Doubleday, 1971), chap. 7.

2. For historical studies, see Hugh Riley, *Christian Initiation* (Studies in Christian Antiquity, vol. 17; Catholic University Press, 1974); *Made Not Born* (Murphy Center for Liturgical Research; Notre Dame Press, 1976); and Daniel Stevick's excellent essay in *Holy Baptism* (Supplement to Prayer Book Studies no. 26; Church Hymnal Corporation, 800 2nd Ave., New York 10017).

3. For a study of Augustine's difficulties, see Gary Marvin, "Augustine's Theology and Infant Baptism"; and John Kremer, "Objective Efficacy"; in *Resonance* (1968, no. 6; St. Meinrad School of Theology), pp. 48-83. For another critique of the theory of original sin, see A. Ganoczy, *Becoming Christian* (Paulist, 1976), pp. 25-68.

4. Tertullian, *De baptismo* 18.27.

5. Walafrid Strabo; see texts in *Monumenta Christiana selecta*, vol. 8 (Paris: Desclee, 1959), ed. J. C. Didier, pp. 208-09, 239-41.

6. J. Murphy-O'Connor develops the idea that the individuality of Christians is not that of independent agents. See "Eucharist and Community in First Corinthians," *Worship*, 50 (1976) 370-85.

Edward K. Braxton

Adult Initiation and Infant Baptism

A priest of the Archdiocese of Chicago, Edward K. Braxton is currently theological consultant for Archdiocese of Washington, DC. He earned his doctorate in theology from the Catholic University of Louvain, Belgium.

Until a decade ago, Jesus' self-identification with bread and wine in the Eucharist had certain unchanging associations. Some of these were a unique building designated as sacred space, sacred golden vessels, communion railings, a kneeling posture for reception on the tongue of bread that was unlike any bread experienced in ordinary life. Only the priest could touch the host. The ceremony was marked by stately ritual, incense, richly ornate vestments, flickering candles, stained glass windows, Gregorian chant, awesome organ music, and profound silence.

Today, however, the celebration of the Eucharist is likely to be much more informal and interpersonal with many of the above-mentioned symbols either absent or considerably de-emphasized. It may have been thought that changing the "offering of Mass" to "celebration of the Eucharist" was only an external change in the expressions, signs, symbols, and rituals that would leave the internal experience of the "real presence" unaffected. This was not the case. It never is when a people's symbol system is altered. For many, the Eucharist is no longer *experienced* as the "real presence" in the manner it once was.

299

While official Catholic theology has always been concerned to preserve such theoretical ideas and expressions as "transubstantiation," the depth structures of religious meaning and experience has always been mediated by sign, symbol, ritual act, and myth.

Ostensibly the radical changes in the signs, symbols, rituals and narratives that constituted the sacrament of Baptism were intended only to put the ancient meaning of these rites into clearer focus and better relief, but in fact these reforms raised a host of far-reaching theoretical and practical questions that were not foreseen. One of the most important of these questions is this: Is Adult Initiation now to be considered the normative mode of initiation into the Catholic Church? If so, what does this say about the ancient and much defended practice of infant Baptism? Or to put it another way: do the stages of the New Rite of Christian Initiation offer norms and challenges to the indiscriminate practice of infant Baptism and call for other alternatives?

In this paper I shall explore the historical and dogmatic issues involved with the question of infant Baptism, examine the General Instructions of the New Rites for adult initiation and infant baptism, examine representative arguments of liturgical theologians, and offer some concluding remarks on human experience, presence, and conversion.

HISTORY AND DOCTRINE

In Jewish history we find antecedents to New Testament Baptism. There are purification baths (Ex. 19:10-14; Lv. 15:5-13), proselyte baptisms, rites of circumcision, and Essenian baptism. Infant initiation seems clear in proselyte baptism and circumcision, but it is not found in any other rites.[1]

The New Testament Church does not manifest any special concern over the question of infant Baptism. Considering the structure of family life it is likely that sacramental baptism did include infants, but there is no specific mention of it. In Acts we read that Lydia "and the people of her house" were baptized, (Acts 16:15, cf. also 33; 18:8; 1 Cor 1:16). There is no consensus among theologians such as Barth, Jeremias, Cullmann and Aland on the existence of infant Baptism in the early church but it is difficult to exclude the positive probability that infants were baptized.

In the writings of Polycarp and funeral epitaphs, specific evidence for the practice of infant Baptism can be found in the 2nd and 3rd centuries. In the 4th century many prominent Christians postponed Baptism until later in life, Basil, Ambrose, Chrysostom, Jerome, and Augustine among them. However, at that time Baptism was viewed more as the sacrament of pardon than as the sacrament of incorporation into the Body of Christ.

It was not until the time of Augustine that Baptism was considered as the sacrament for the forgiveness of original sin. Before that, it signaled the forgiveness of actual sins. In the case of infants, there can be no question of actual sin but Chrysostom justified infant Baptism saying that, though they have not sinned, justice, sonship, and inheritance is given them as well as the grace to be brothers, members of Christ, and dwellings of the Holy Spirit. He does not speak of original sin.

It was during Augustine's controversy with the Pelagians that Baptism began to be associated with original sin. But it was the very practice of infant baptism that confirmed the reality of original sin for Augustine. Some have thought that the affirmation of original sin was the earliest reason for infant Baptism but this seems not to be the case. It was not until the 9th century, when Wilafrid Strabo reversed Augustine's argument by saying that *because* of original sin infants *must* be baptized, that the presently accepted connection between the two realities was established.

In his defense of infant Baptism Augustine suggests three ways in which an infant can be said to receive and profess the faith of the Church. First of all there is the faith of the child himself manifest in the faith of those presenting him for Baptism, the *offerentes*. This ritual act grants faith to the child though psychologically he is unchanged. Second, there is the particular faith of the child's parents. In adults conversion and faith precede sacramental signs but in the infant the signs precede the exercise of the life of faith. However, post-baptismal Christian education is seen as an integral part of the sign. Third, there is the faith of the Church. Augustine is aware that in some cases the faith of parents may be defective or even non-existent. For this reason Augustine stresses that it is not the parents or *offerentes* alone who present the newborn to God. It is rather an act of faith on the part of the whole Church.[2]

During the 10th, 11th, 12th, and 13th centuries the Neo-Manicheans objected to the practice of infant Baptism arguing that infants were not capable of faith or belief. They took Mk. 16:16 literally. "Whoever believes and is baptized shall be saved; and whoever does not believe shall be condemned." But since infants cannot possibly make a conscious and responsible expression or act of faith, they cannot validly receive the sacrament. To meet these objections Augustine's position on the supplying faith of the Church was repeated and augmented by Lombard's distinction between the habit and the act of faith. The Council of Vienne (1311-12) declared that this position was probable (DB, 904). Aquinas and Bonaventure also held to this view. The faith of the Church supplies for the infant and the sacrament itself communicates to the infant the theological virtues of faith, hope, and charity. In subsequent centuries the role of the faith of the Church and its full implications regarding the responsibility of the local Christian community to nurture the faith of the infant seems to have been overlooked as the emphasis was placed upon faith infused *ex opere operato.* But since an infant does not perform discursive operations this infused faith must be something other than the intellectual affirmation of religious propositions. This question seems to have gone unaddressed.

The Councils of Florence and Trent formalized this developing tradition. In 1438-45 the Council of Florence declared that "The effect of this sacrament [i.e., Baptism] is the remission of original and actual sin, and also of the punishment due to sin. No satisfaction, therefore, is to be enjoined on the baptized for their past sins; and those who die before they commit any sin immediately obtain the kingdom of heaven and the vision of God" (DB, 693).[3] The Council of Trent 1545-63 declared:

If anyone says that because infants do not make an act of faith, they are not to be numbered among the faithful after they receive baptism and, moreover, that they are to be rebaptized when they come to the use of reason; or if anyone says that it is better to omit baptism of infants rather than to baptize merely in the faith of the Church, those who do not believe by an act of their own: let him be anathema. (DB 869) If anyone says that when these baptized infants grow up they are to be asked whether they wish to ratify what their sponsors promised in their name at baptism; and if they answer in the negative, they are to be left their own judgment, and that until they come to their senses, they are not to be forced to a Christian life by any punishment except that of being kept away from the Eucharist and the reception of other sacraments: let him be anathema. (DB, 870)[4]

Trent goes on to say of Original Sin:

If anyone denies that newly born infants are to be baptized, even though they may have been born of baptized parents, or says that they are indeed baptized for the remission of sins but that they do not contract from Adam any original sin that must be expiated in the bath of regeneration to obtain eternal life; and, consequently, that for them the form of baptism—for the remission of sins—is to be understood, not in a true, but in a false sense: let them be anathema. Because the words of the Apostle: "As through one man sin entered into the world and through sin death, and thus death has passed into all men because all have sinned" (See Rom. 5:12), cannot be understood in any other way than as the Catholic Church everywhere has always understood them. Because of this rule of faith, in accordance with apostolic tradition even infants, who have not yet committed any personal sins, are baptized for the remission of sin in a very true sense, that they may be cleansed by regeneration of what they have contracted by generation. For "unless a man be born again of water and the Holy Spirit, he cannot enter into the kingdom of God" (John 3:5) (DB, 791).[5]

As recently as June 1968, Pope Paul VI reaffirmed the general line of these teachings in his "Credo of the People of God":

We believe that in Adam all have sinned, which means that the original offense committed by him caused human nature, common to all men, to fall to a state in which it bears the consequences of that offense, and which is not the state in which it was at first in our first parents, established as they were in holiness and justice, and in which men knew neither evil nor death. It is human nature so fallen, stripped of the grace that clothed it, injured in its own natural powers and subjected to the dominion of death, that is transmitted to all men, and it is in this sense that every man is born in sin. We therefore hold, with the Council of Trent, that original sin is transmitted with human nature, not by imitation but by propagation, and that it is thus proper to everyone.[6]

There is very little doubt that most ordinary Catholic lay people are of the persuasion that all infants should be baptized and that the central reason for this is to free the infant from the constraints of original sin. Indeed, anyone in pastoral ministry knows that the death of unbaptized infant brings not only great sorrow but also affirmations of limbo as the final state of this soul lacking in sanctifying grace. Americans can all recall the celebrated case in the United States in which a Jesuit priest dramatically baptized the infant of a woman who was outspoken in her support of abortion. The local pastor had refused to baptize the child on the grounds that the woman had separated herself from the community of the Church. The Jesuit's motive seems to have been that whatever one thinks of the mother's position the infant should not be deprived of the sacrament.

More personally, I recall the conflict caused in the family of a priest friend of mine when he refused to baptize his sister's infant since neither his sister nor her husband had even a minimal association with the Christian community. He told them that if they believed that spiritual benefit would come to their infant by means of the rite alone, independent of a minimum of care on their part, then either of them could perform it. No priest was needed. But he reminded them that the sacraments were symbols and not magic. His parents and relatives were appalled at his "unpriestly" conduct!

The connection between the Adamic narrative, original sin, and the urgency of infant Baptism is made somewhat problematic in the light of contemporary biblical scholarship, which seriously questions the literal and historical validity of the account of the "fall." These hermeneutic developments have not rejected the significance of the Adamic myth, but they have raised serious questions about the nature of "Original Sin" and baptism. In this regard Paul Ricoeur has written:

The harm that has been done to souls during the centuries of Christianity, first by the literal interpretation of the story of Adam, and then the confusion of this myth, treated as history, with later speculations, principally Augustinian, about original sin, will never be adequately told. In asking the faithful to confess belief in this mythico-speculative mass and to accept it as a self-sufficient explanation, the theologians have unduly required a *sacrificium intellectus* where what was needed was to awaken believers to a symbolic superintelligence of their actual condition.[7]

When the narrative of Adam is thought of more as a universal parable than as documented history, the theology of man's sinful condition shifts its focus from biological generation to the sinful condition of the world into which all people are born. In this context Baptism becomes somewhat less a rite of purification and more a rite of incorporation into the Christian community that struggles to reject sin with the help of the Spirit. As a rite of Christian initiation it is a call to transformation. The faith that is celebrated in Baptism becomes less a set of propositions to which intellectual assent is given and more a response to a call—a life long process of religious development symbolized and stimulated by the sacrament. Clearly if this is the nature of the sacrament, it is intended essentially for adults and only by way of analogy and extension for infants. These developments present us with two key problems. First of all, they set up a theological discontinuity with the tradition under examination. Second, while these may be the conclusions of many biblical scholars, liturgists, and theologians, they are not all shared by the people in the pews or by the magisterium as is indicated by the Pontifical Credo cited above. This brings up the problem of theological elitism.

THE GENERAL INSTRUCTION OF THE NEW RITES OF INITIATION

Like the revision of the sacrament of reconciliation the revised rites of Christian Initiation do not come at the beginning of liturgical reform but rather after the Church has been involved in more than a decade and a half of liturgical renewal. For this reason the documents manifest a greater appreciation of the far-reaching nature of liturgical reform as well as reveal the benefit of a renewed pastoral orientation, various consultations, and experiments. In the case of initiation a clear distinction has been made between the "Initiation" of adults and "Baptism" of children. There are now two separate rites with separate general instructions. In the adult rite, Baptism is the climactic moment in the larger initiation process. An examination of these instructions clearly indicates, on the one hand, that the Church firmly intends to maintain both adult and infant Baptism and, on the other hand, that the document's own account of the intrinsic nature of adult initiation raises some question about the long standing practice of infant Baptism.

The very arrangement of the rite for adults before that of children suggests that it is the primary instance of initiation. The instruction begins by acknowledging that the spiritual journey of adults is very diverse and marked by discernable stages. There is the point of initial conversion in which a person expresses his or her desire to become a Christian and is accepted as a catechumen. This is followed by the more profound preparation for the sacraments, when the catechumen's faith has grown to maturity. Finally, there is the actual reception of the three sacraments of initiation, Baptism, Confirmation, and Eucharist. In all, there are four periods: the precatechumenate, a time for hearing the first preaching of the gospel; the catechumenate, set aside for complete catechesis; the period of purification and enlightenment or illumination (Lent) for a more profound spiritual preparation; and the post-baptismal catechesis or mystagogia (Easter Season), marked with a new experience of the sacraments and of the Christian community (see Nos. 5-8).

The seriousness and progressive nature of each stage are underscored. After the educational and formational elements of the catechumenate are underway, worthy catechumens are "elected" to take part in the coming sacrament. To signal this election by God and the Church the names of the candidates are inscribed in the book of the elect. This solemn election is the turning point of the entire catechumenate. The elect are further prepared for the sacraments by scrutinies that reveal what is weak or defective in a candidate and support what is strong and upright (see Nos. 21-25).

In the final stage the elect are admitted into the people of God, adopted as sons and daughters of God, filled with the Spirit, and nurtured at the table of the Lord. It is important to note that the instruction states that *prior* to the celebrations of the sacraments of Baptism, Confirmation and Eucharist, the candidates come forward *"with their sins forgiven"* (see No. 27). Does this mean to suggest that the forgiveness of sin is accomplished along the way and before the actual Baptism? And what sin is being referred to? The actual sin of the catechumen or original sin or both, and why is this not clearly specified in the light of the import ascribed to it in earlier Church pronouncements?

The instruction stresses the personal, active, mature, and adult involvement that is expected of all of those who are initiated.

> Adults are not saved unless they come forward of their own accord and are willing to accept the gift of God by faith. Baptism is the sacrament of faith, not only the faith of the Church but also the candidates' own faith, and it is expected that it will be an active faith in them. When they are baptized, they should not receive such a sacrament passively, for of their own will they enter into a covenant with Christ, rejecting their errors and adhering to the true God (No. 30).

The stage structure of the new adult initiation is marked by a strong but non-explicit awareness of the developmental dynamic of human growth, maturity, and commitment as uncovered by the pioneering research of Jean Piaget, Lawrence Kohlberg, and Erik Erickson. In the United States, James Fowler has translated the implications of Kohlberg's stages of moral development into a model of faith development that supports the stage structure of the new ritual.[8] If this instruction is taken seriously, the restoration of the catechumenate will take high priority in the Church's life. The indiscriminate baptism of *adults* will have to be examined. If adults are given a fuller appreciation of Christian initiation, there will be definite benefits to the sacrament of Christian marriage. Perhaps those who are not mature in their Christian self-understanding would be discouraged from a sacramental union they are incapable of grasping.

We turn now to the instruction for the baptism of children. The text begins by stressing the ancient tradition and the importance of baptizing infants even though they are not sufficiently mature to profess personal faith. Following the mandate of John 3:5, which declares that "unless a man is reborn of water and the Holy Spirit, he cannot enter the kingdom of God," the instruction reaffirms the tradition that children are to be baptized into the faith of the Church and should not be deprived of this communion. The instruction is quick to note, however, that if the true meaning of the sacrament is to be fulfilled, children must be formed, as they grow to maturity, in the faith in which they have been baptized. So even in the case of infants, strong emphasis is placed on the subsequent education, formation, and personal appropriation of the life of faith (see Nos. 1-3).

The instruction stresses the natural and central responsibility of parents who should be suitably knowledgable of the Christian faith and the meaning of the sacrament. The responsibility of the parents extends beyond preparation for, and active celebration of, the sacrament to the continued nurturing of the faith of their child and, with the help of the parish priest, to present the child for the sacraments of Confirmation and Eucharist. There is no mention of Baptism, Confirmation, and Eucharist as triadic components of one initiation rite as it is in the case of adults (see Nos. 5 and 19). Surprisingly, the instruction does not refer to the question of original sin but it does state that infants should be baptized within the first weeks after birth and in danger of death they should be baptized without delay. This caution could be referring implicitly to the traditional concern about the fate of deceased infants who are still marked by original sin or it could refer only to the *Quam primum* of John 3:5 (see No. 8).

Part V of the instruction allows for various adaptations by individual conferences of bishops. The main paragraph under the heading has vital implications whose impact will only be known as time passes and practices develop. The text reads:

> In many countries parents are sometimes not ready for the celebration of Baptism or they ask for their children to be baptized, although the latter will not afterwards receive a Christian Education and will even lose the faith. Since it is not enough to instruct the parents and to inquire about their faith in the course of the rite itself, conferences of bishops may issue pastoral directives, for the guidance of parish priests, to determine a longer interval between birth and baptism (No. 25).

This statement clearly separates itself from any possible mechanical understanding of the faith of the Church or from the *ex opere operato* effectiveness of the sacraments. Mere baptism in a ritualistic sense is not the goal of the instruction. The active and enthusiastic cultivation of a lively faith is what it seeks. Therefore if parents are clearly not willing or able to meet their responsibilities then the sacrament may be delayed for an unspecified period of time. Could the delay at least hypothetically extend to the point when the child could make a responsible personal choice? This is probably not a valid interpretation. Again there is no mention of the urgent need for infant Baptism at the earliest possible moment in order to be rid of original sin. Pertinent here also is the silence of the document on the baptism of miscarried fetal life, though mention is made of hospital Baptisms in emergencies.

The general instruction for both adult initiation and infant Baptism are positive in tone. While it is clearly a purification ritual, the emphasis is placed not upon the remission of original or even actual sin but upon incorporation into a community of faith, which of course announces its rejection of sin. Because a lively, active, informed, and mature faith is sought the importance of catechesis is fully elaborated, spelling out the particular responsibilities of bishop, priest, deacon, parish community, parents, godparents, the adult catechumen, catechists, relatives, and friends. This aspect of the document is as refreshing as it is challenging. It is refreshing because it separates itself from any magical or automatic "functioning" of the sacraments apart from the supportive, sustaining faith of a particular family in a particular community in communication with the faith of the whole Church. Faith is characterized as an ongoing and developmental reality and the paradigm for Christian faith is clearly the adult and not the child.

Perhaps the most striking contrast between the two rites is the separation of Baptism, Confirmation, and Eucharist in the case of children. For adults these three sacraments constitute one moment that is the high point of their initiation. The reason for their separation in the case of children is not given. If it is argued that a child cannot grasp the meaning of Confirmation and Eucharist, hence the delay, the same can be said of Baptism for which the faith of the Church is said to be sufficient.

THE ARGUMENTS OF LITURGICAL THEOLOGIANS

It is clear from the two general instructions that the official theology of the Church concerning Baptism has developed and changed a great deal since the time prior to the Council. That change has clearly been much influenced by contemporary theological ferment and ecumenical dialogue. Notably the rites of Christian initiation are described in dynamic and developmental terms. There is a dramatic move away from a static model of the sacrament to a deeper appreciation of an ongoing process. Hence the various key moments of the human journey are rightly sacramentalized by liturgical journeys. But the sacraments are not "mere symbols" in an extrinsic sense; they are "true symbols" in an intrinsic sense, that is they have the potential to bring about what they symbolize.

The real question that emerges is this: At what point in one's life journey is it appropriate to symbolize and sacramentalize the life long conversion-reconciliation process? Should it be at the very beginning when an infant has no reflective awareness of this journey but when the universal Church as well as the local church and family pledge themselves to bring forth this awareness? This position stresses the divine self-giving to one who has no reflexive awareness of this event. Or should the sacrament-symbol be celebrated as a young adult when one has attained a degree of awareness of the journey, has a conscious sense of divine self-giving and is striving to appropriate the identity of the "New Being"? This position stresses the aptness of the sacrament to mark and sustain the beginning of the *conscious* process of interiorizing the Christian life. Or would it be better to celebrate this process in mid-life when one has lived out the Christian adventure with fuller intensity, when one has played out the role of prodigal daughter or son again and again only to find the Father's forgiveness ever more solicitous? This position stresses the aptness of the sacrament as the radical support for the Christian on his or her life journey.

Finally, would it be more fitting to celebrate the sacrament symbol towards the end of a truly Christian life when the evidence of transformation is apparent? This position stresses the importance of the sacrament as the authentication of a Christian life well-lived. In the light of the traditional theology of the baptism of desire and Karl Rahner's theology of the anonymous Christian—which acknowledges the encounter with God in other religions as well as the fact that Christianity may be seen as the "extraordinary means" of salvation since most of the world people have not been, are not, and quite likely will not become Christians—there does not appear to be any special "danger" involved in delaying the celebration of the sacrament indefinitely. Is this not precisely what happens in the case of adult converts who enter the Church at maturity or in their old age?

However, there remains the question of emphasis. For the sacrament is not only a sign of a process. It is a catalyst to the process itself. Further, other sacraments such as Eucharist and reconciliation are available along the way. For the most part the theological debate seems to be over the continuation of the baptism of infants.

There can be little question that on the level of pastoral practice in many churches in America, infant Baptism is a rather routine Sunday afternoon activity that is not particularly inspiring, challenging, or meaningful to priest, parents, godparents, or the infant. Aidan Kavanagh's criticism of the passive quasi-magical approach to this ritual is unfortunately not completely a caricature. He writes:

"...baptism-confirmation does not initiate the *faith* of an individual, [it] does not *confect* faith on the spot out of nothing, to inject it like an unheard of miracle drug or a disembodied heart muscle into the vacant veins or chest cavity of a passive receiver. This surgical-pharmaceutical view of faith, and its correspondingly clinical view of Christian initiation, should be called what it is: it is theological heresy because God calls one to faith as he pleases; it is psychological rubbish; it is pastoral myopia; it is ritual magic. It is a symptom of an administrative mind's passion for neatness having laid waste the rich and raunchy complexness of man's existence— a complexness that is the only soil, out of which mystery, fascination, symbol, awe, exhilaration, and a sense of the holy can emerge."

He continues:

"To reduce baptism-confirmation for neatness' sake to a quasi-magical confection of faith on the one hand or a quasi-surgical excision of the great wart known as original sin on the other, and to attempt to make even this somehow compelling in fifteen minute ceremonies done privately in corners with teacups of water and a smear or two of grease is unacceptable. It reaches tragic proportions when this perfunctoriness is made to bear the additional weight of attempting to reflect, actualize, and predict what a Christian truly is in a compelling way."[9]

But even accepting all of this as instructive and challenging to every pastor and every parent is no reason to argue that children should not be baptized. Christopher Kiesling avers that suggestions to abandon the practice of infant baptism place too much emphasis upon the meaningfulness of the ceremony and the conscious participation of the subject:

... the idea of postponing baptism until a child is old enough to make up his own mind is an idea which overemphasizes the ceremonial aspect of baptism at the expense of the more important gift of God's grace which is already at work in the gift of upbringing by Christian parents and the Christian community and which the ceremony of baptism celebrates. Postponement of baptism is an idea which overstresses the individualness of salvation by not recognizing sufficiently the intimacy of human relations, especially between a child and his family and community, through which God grants his grace. It is an idea, finally, which threatens to cut off from a child a critical grace from God—the pledge of Christian parents and the community to rear a child so that he is oriented to God in the likeness of Christ in the depths of his personality.[10]

Kavanagh, however, argues that, if we are to be consistent with the implications of adult initiation which is the prime analogate, some changes in the indiscriminate baptism of infants are inevitable. These changes would include a restored and intelligible initiation sequence in which the anomalies of the present pastoral practice can slowly be absorbed. He writes:

> Such a restored sequence may well involve as normal: a) enrolling infants as catachumens at an early age; b) guiding them through the catechumenate in a careful progression until an age of free acceptance of Christ and his Church is determined by catechist, family, pastor and congregation; c) full initiation through Lenten observance, baptism-confirmation-eucharist on Holy Saturday-Easter, and post-baptismal catachesis through that Eastertide. This is largely what we do now, except that we baptize infants at a) reconcile them through penance and education and communicate them at b) and confirm them at c) with some more education.[11]

In Kavanagh's view such a restructuring would not be arbitrary. It would rather clarify some of the ambiguities in the present sequence. For the present practice of making confirmation a kind of adult initiation implicitly states that infant baptism is in fact functioning as an "enrollment" in a catechetical process.

In December 1973, seventy-five liturgists gathered at the Franciscan Renewal Center in Scottsdale, Arizona, on the tenth anniversary of the promulgation of the Constitution of the Sacred Liturgy. This representative cross section of America liturgists developed six points concerning initiation:

1. The rite of Christian initiation should normally consist of the unified sacramental event in which the three now separated moments (Baptism, Confirmation, Eucharist) are integrated. The *full rite* is to be used at *any age* when a person is initiated (emphasis added). As an act of the Church, the rite of initiation is most properly celebrated in the midst of the congregation.

2. Within the economy of the sacraments, adult initiation should be the practical norm. The Church's understanding of Baptism is most fully demonstrated when an adult is baptized.

3. Infant baptism derives from the adult form. It places specific responsibilities upon the adult community. When parents and the congregation accept these responsibilities, the celebration of infant Baptism proclaims the initiative of God's love.

4. The entire Easter season from Lent to Pentecost is derived from the public practice of adult Baptism. The meaning of Baptism is best demonstrated when it is celebrated within the context of the Church's dramatic shaping of time, whose climax is in the Easter Season.

5. For children of responsible Christian parents, two different patterns of initiation might well coexist: the celebration of the full rite of initiation (Baptism, Confirmation, Eucharist) shortly after birth, to be followed by catechesis appropriate to succeeding stages of development; or enrollment of the infant as a catechumen, with initiation to be celebrated at a later age after catechesis.

6. Catechumenate. The development of viable and visible catechumenate structures on a parish, inter-parish, or diocesan basis is essential to the renewal of the sacrament of initiation. We urge that everywhere this thoroughly restored and fully celebrated rite be implemented and adapted and that the simpler forms of the new ritual be reserved for extreme exceptions.[12]

□ □ □

Two points are to be made:

1. Unlike the instructions themselves Kavanagh and Gallen both urge that if infants are to be baptized they should enter the whole initiation process (Baptism, Confirmation, Eucharist) remaining faithful to the normative practice of adult initiation. The progression should be from the ritual bath to the ritual meal. The separation is the result of an historical accident and

a basic misunderstanding. The historical accident is the fourth century development of Church congregations so large that all could not get to the annual Easter vigil and hence the bishops journeyed out to confirm at a later time. The misunderstanding has to do with the view that confirmation is something like a puberty rite that can only be celebrated when the candidate is sufficiently mature. But when liturgical documents refer to maturity in confirmation the referent is the maturity of the sacrament and not of the candidate.

2. The second point is that, again unlike the instructions themselves, the positions of Kavanagh and Gallen like those of many liturgists in America and in Europe clearly foresee the possible abandonment of the practice of baptizing infants. Instead of baptism, there would be a rite of welcoming that would be distinct from initiation followed by some form of enrollment and catechesis. Number 25 of the instruction allows for delay, not as a normal practice but at the discretion of a local hierarchy.

There seems to be no convincing theological argument against the maintaining of the unity of the initiation event (Baptism, Confirmation, Eucharist) whether it is celebrated for children or adults. Perhaps time, pastoral practice, and further discernment will result in greater harmony between the position of liturgists and the official Vatican Instruction. The thornier question remains that of putting off the baptism of infants until they are old enough to be catechized. The question has two distinct aspects, the one practical, the other theoretical.

If it were judged desirable to discontinue the indiscriminate practice of infant Baptism the practical problem would center around the conflict that would immediately arise with the almost instinctive and certainly church cultivated sense on the part of many parents that their child simply "must" be baptized as soon as possible after birth. Scripture scholars, systematic theologians, and liturgists may have radically re-interpreted the theology of original sin. The general instruction itself may have all but omitted any references to washing away of original sin, but in the United States at least, the vast majority of Catholic parents have been so well indoctrinated about the "onus" of original sin and limbo as the fate of infants who die without Baptism, that many would consider any suggestion that their child's Baptism be delayed as depriving them of something to which they have a right and putting their child in great peril.

Besides this, not a few parents approach the Baptism of their children as essentially a social ritual or a response to what may be termed "natural religion" with little or no thought of a genuinely ecclesial commitment. For this reason parents may seek baptism for various reasons: 1) a superstitious and magical view of religion that sees Baptism as a protection of the infant against physical or spiritual evils; 2) a need for societal identification, which concerns not the Church community but the sociological group into which the child is born, e.g., certain ethnic groups whose ethnic identity is dramatically associated with being "Catholic"; 3) an opportunity for a festive celebration of the family's joy and happiness at the birth of a child; 4) a desire for a kind of spiritual "insurance policy" that will protect the newborn from damnation when they die; 5) a vague sense of "the sacred," the "holy" or a renewed sense of gratitude before the mystery of life and death (mother and child have survived in good health).[13]

It is commonly recognized that many of the sacraments coincide with peak experiences or key moments of "passage" in the human experience. Therefore it is not surprising that many of the effects and attitudes associated with infant baptism are non-discursive "gut feelings" that have little explicit connection with Christianity. Obviously the Church can either build on the best of these "foundations," stressing symbol and mystery, or it can implicitly sustain superstition and magic. To say that many of the unthematized feelings which a number of Catholic parents bring to the rite of their child's Baptism are not particularly Christian or even compatible with the Christian world view is not to say that they are not powerful and important parts of the way people have made the world manageable and tamed the unknown.

Change, if it is desirable, will not be brought about easily. In practice, such a change would certainly require major cateche-

316

sis or even evangelization of many adults on a scale that has never been undertaken before. Hence, we must always distinguish what may be theologically desirable in a theoretical sense and appropriate pastoral practice in the concrete.

It is important to keep these remarks about parents in perspective. We should not lose sight of the new vitality that exists among the laity in many places. More and more we see signs of adults who have benefited from adult education and Christian formation programs. They have an articulate understanding of the Christian faith. In some cases they may even have a better grasp of the pastoral and social implications of Vatican II than some of the priests who serve them. Some of these couples would fully appreciate suggestions to delay the baptism of a child. Or, animated by the Spirit, their reasons for insisting upon their child's baptism may be precisely those of mature and committed Christians wishing to share the gift of life with their children.

The theoretical question deals with what I will term two different anthropologies that seem to underlie the two general instructions. They account at least in part for why these documents felt no compelling need to speak of adult initiation as the normative practice or to suggest only a catechetical enrollment for infants. The different anthropologies are psychological and ontological. The instruction on adult initiation is essentially, though not exclusively, operating with a psychological anthropology that takes seriously the philosophical developments since Kant's critique of earlier scholastic thought.

This post-Kantian view suggests that personhood is constituted by being a conscious subject. The real, the true, the known, and the experienced are all measured by the self-assembling structures of our dynamic subjectivity.[14] For this reason the adult initiation rite stresses the conscious, aggressive, and developmental involvement of the adult Christian in stages of growth as he or she advances from initial interest to responsible and vital membership in the Christian community. This instruction does not deny ontological anthropology. It may even tacitly be building upon it. But it does not elaborate the rite with reference to it.

Avoiding the rationalism that made the work of authors such as Christian Wolff so vulnerable to the Kantian critique, this instruction looks at the infant not in his or her particularity as a potential existential subject but in his or her particularity as a unique being, loved by God, and possessing a spiritual soul that can in some manner be really and truly affected by the loving self-donation and self-presencing of God. This presence of God's love intimately within the individual infant's soul is not real, true, known, or experienced in the sense that is essential in the psychological anthropology. It is not available empirical data in the individual's self-consciousness. What is being suggested by the documents is that in the case of infants the sacrament symbolized and in "some way" effects the unmediated immediacy of God's presence as gift to all of his creation. This can be "real" and "true" whether or not the child has reflexive, conscious, or thematized awareness of it. And the later life of the child will be the better because of the effects of this prior but unknown divine immediacy. Here, if you will, the sacrament is more for the "soul" than it is for the "subject." Its referent is essentially, though perhaps not exclusively, ontological rather than psychological.

As the two instructions unfold, the one for adult initiation makes no mention of ontological changes, sacramental character, or the infusion of sanctifying or actual grace, which are all clasically formulated with the receptive spiritual soul as the referent and not the existential subject. To be sure, there is no denial of any of these factors, either. In the case of infants where the existential subject has only a flickering self-awareness the instruction speaks in more classical and static terms suggesting that grace is given in the sacramental act and then enriched and developed in the "graceful" interaction of the young child with the familial and subsequent ecclesial communities. Clearly those who would ban infant Baptism altogether are favoring the psychological anthropology exclusively. Whereas those who argue that infant Baptism is defensible as long as it is not regarded as the normative procedure, and the general instruction, which all but gives the two rites equal footing, are holding the psychological anthropology and the ontological anthropology in a tension, now favoring one, now favoring the other. Since each of the approaches has native limitations and strengths, their ideal relationship is that of complementing each other. In the history of philosophy as well as of theology, however, we see that one is often favored to the rejection of the other.

A corollary issue that must be at least mentioned here is the question of the fate of the dead. There seems to be less and less consensus among Catholics about the meaning of biblical language concerning the resurrection of the body and the subsequent more philosophical language concerning the immortality of the spiritual soul. In what sense is personal, self-conscious survival after death essential to Christianity? It is not surprising that some of those who favor the psychological anthropology are willing to leave the question of "afterlife" open, while those who favor the ontological anthropology hold firmly that with death, life is not ended but merely changed. Is baptism the principal way of incorporation into the People of God here and now? Or is it more importantly the attainment of certain spiritual resources needed for a life to come?

HUMAN EXPERIENCE, PRESENCE, AND CONVERSION

If we hold the psychological model and the ontological model in tension, we find that the human condition is a complex network of "patterns of experience." These patterns may at times be experienced as the mediation of the mystery of God present as gift and at other times as the eruption of evil, alienation, emptiness, wretchedness, and sin.

The key patterns of human experience are the biological pattern in which we encounter the vast potential and painful limits of our enfleshed condition; the psychological pattern in which we encounter a great range of affects, feelings, moods, passions, images, symbols, dreams and fantasies that constitute a complex internal communication system; the aesthetic pattern in which we encounter form, tone and color, as we are caught up in the elemental sweep of wonder in the face of beauty in the natural world or in the arts; the social pattern in which we encounter the other now as "it" to be used, now as "you" to be acknowledged, and now as "thou" to be cherished as the beloved in Martin Buber's sense. The experience of self-transcending love and intimacy in family life, marriage, and friendships paradoxically fills up one's "soul-space" and at the same time makes one more aware of an existential void.

The dramatic pattern of experience is our encounter with "stories" that sometimes illuminate our individual and collective lives as meaningful and of value and at other times underscores them as so much sound and fury signifying nothing. The mystical pattern is that in which we have occasional experiences of "ecstasy," the glimpse of a hidden wholeness which is ordinarily not seen or seen only "through a glass darkly." The intellectual pattern is that in which we encounter the eros of our minds to know everything about everything and the paradox that no matter how great a knowledge we amass, the horizon of the unknown seems undiminished. To be sure many of us do not advert to or reflect upon the meaning of this network of experiences.

But whether we do or not, they have the potential to involve each one of us in moments that heighten our awareness of the ever-present grace and favor of God summoning us to be our best selves and more. They (or at least our misdirected responses to them) also have the potential to ensnare us in dehumanizing, self-destructive attitudes, feelings, and actions that are so denaturing of ourselves and others that they can only be termed sin. These over-arching patterns are both intersubjective (or psychological) insofar as they are adverted to or effect our conscious subjectivity, and ontological insofar as they effect our subconscious and more, our radical and essential state or mode of being in the world.

Because of these interlocking patterns, parents, family, church, and the larger community mediate the presence of sin and grace to children in both an ontological and a psychological manner. Before the infant is even conceived there is an ongoing relationship between his parents. This relationship is marked at times by deep love and intimacy and at other times by alienation and estrangement. The news of the child's conception may well significantly alter the relationship between the parents. In one case, love and intimacy are intensified while in another alienation and estrangement may be exacerbated.

The psychological, economic, and social state of the couple and their immediate family and closest friends during the pregnancy and early weeks of life are also important. In one family, these days may be marked by quiet joy. The expectant mother may cultivate certain personal modes of reflection and prayer as she carries the new life. Husband and wife may even make special efforts to renew their Christian faith and enrich their interior world with shared prayer and reflection. Perhaps the Eucharist is celebrated more often in the home and the parents themselves and their children create various para-liturgies all anticipating the birth of the child as well as the Baptism.

In another home there may be no thought of the Baptism until someone else mentions it or it may have been thought of but in only a routine manner. Now it is obvious that the newborn child has no conscious knowledge of these many realities either prior to his birth or in the weeks before his Baptism but our ever increasing knowledge of developmental psychology constrains us not to say that their impact is negligible or that later in life he will not be affected by the sin and grace of the family situation into which he was born. It is these complex structures of human relationship that must be attended to and investigated if we are to come to a contemporary appreciation of the wisdom that may be contained in the ontological anthropology and its defense of both the value and the significance of early Baptism for the infant and the family. We are here reminded of the argument that grace builds upon nature.

The reform of the rites of initiation have been issued at a juncture of unprecedented change and development in the Catholic Church. All about us we see the decline of common meaning. Basic religious discourse about God, Jesus, Church, ministry, sacraments, faith, hope, love, and the Christian life no longer evokes the same understanding from the people in pews, the parish priests, the university theologians, and the bishops. The Church's self-understanding has been radically enmeshed in a classical cultural matrix, but a modern non-normative empirical notion of culture is emerging. The process of disengaging what is obsolete in classical culture and engaging what is apt in modern culture is risky as well as painful. It has unleashed a sweeping pluralism in the Catholic Church ranging from orthodox, to liberal, to neo-orthodox, to radical, to revisionist theological stances.[15]

In the face of so much upheaval it is understandable that the desire for direction and some irreducible starting point can lead to either scriptural, dogmatic, or liturgical fundamentalism. Such a fundamentalism takes its stand on a particular interpretation of a central passage of Scripture, a literal and non-historically contextualized view of a pivotal magisterial pronouncement, the details of rubric and ritual, or an unbending interpretation of a particular liturgical action such as Christian initiation. This is inevitable because these are important expressions that mediate the religious meaning disclosed by an originating religious experience. Prudence will win the day. But it will not be the prudence that follows the safest course, but that which follows the best one.

In an epoch of such unprecedented ferment, it is helpful to disentangle what I take to be the central overlapping and complementary modes of conversion that constitute the human adventure as a journey to Christian maturity and that are sacramentalized in Initiation and Baptism. It is helpful to distinguish conversion as religious, theistic, Christian, ecclesial, moral, and intellectual. By conversion I mean a transformation of horizon. It is not the result of argument alone because it is self-involving and to a degree self-authenticating. Briefly, by religious conversion I mean a radical response to life's mystery as gracious and meaningful.

Theistic conversion is the affirmation that the foundational ground of this graciousness and meaning is what is implied by the often terribly abused word, God.

Christian conversion affirms that in the person of Jesus exalted as the Christ we have the paradigmatic disclosure of how God would be if he were other than God.

The turn to community is ecclesial conversion. It is a sense of peoplehood, history, and tradition. It is not as much faith

322

"in" the Church as it is assembling "as" the Church to proclaim faith in the mystery of God in Jesus Christ.

Moral conversion is the struggle for self-consistency between the values one affirms and the deeds one incarnates. This is the never ending quest for authenticity in one's public and private world.

Intellectual conversion recognizes that truth is one. Hence there is a willingness to let issues mature and avoid rash judgments. It is the recognition that the conflicts that may obtain in religion, and theology may in fact be complementary from a higher viewpoint. And this is necessarily the case because of the limits of language, of the historicity of the human race, and of the permanence of mystery.

These modes of conversion constitute the Christian journey. The rite of Christian initiation as the *Sacramentum Fidei* anoints, nurtures, and urges onward those who set out on this pilgrimage to God. Clearly no two people integrate them in the same manner or with the same emphasis. They are not a neat sequence but a convoluting process. One person's religious conversion is theocentric, another's is christocentric. One takes his stand on generic faith, another embraces the details of beliefs and their systematic elaboration. Or again one considers religious language to constitute an amalgam of metaphysical facts while another considers it to be a non-factual symbol system composed of metaphor and image.

By its very nature, then, those who embark on the journey of conversion have as their final goal not the affirmation of propositions or the obeying of rules but the deep and abiding transformation of their person. The ritual actions of adult initiation and infant Baptism signal this transformation process. The implementation of the full implications of these new rites shall be, I suspect, a long and piecemeal procedure marked by excesses and misinterpretations of all kinds. The catechetical and pastoral responsibilities involved in such an implementation are challenging indeed. Clearly no such catechumenate of the sort envisioned in the document presently exists in most local parishes. The success of the new rites may hinge in great part upon its establishment.

Those who fear of scriptural, theological, and liturgical discontinuity are not without cause.

In my judgment, the arrangement that adult initiation is the normative paradigm is a sound one. Again I must emphasize, however, that this judgment does not imply that we should discontinue infant baptism as a pastoral adaptation of that norm. Yet *indiscriminate* infant baptism must be seriously questioned, and appropriate rites of infant enrollment must be developed.

Finally, we must frankly acknowledge that a number of theological and pastoral questions lurk behind this discussion. Among them are: in the light of the present ecumenical and world religion sensitivities, what *must* one "do," "be," "believe," or "think" to "be saved"? What is the specific meaning of being saved? Is it generically communion with God and specifically (in our tradition) participation in the Passover of Jesus? What is the relationship of these rites to the growing diversity of beliefs on the part of the Catholic people concerning the fate of the dead? Is discontinuity always to be viewed as undesirable in Catholic theological development? Does the fear of discontinuity produce theological contortions such as the declaration "as the Church has always taught"? Are there ways of recognizing and discerning growth and maturity in the Christian life? How do we enable those engaged in pastoral ministry to become competent practitioners of what can only be termed "the pastoral art" so that they may understand the multiple factors present in their concrete situation and be able to discern what will and what will not sustain and nurture the Christian Adventure?

NOTES

1. For this brief historical overview I am following the unpublished lecture notes of John Melloh, S.M., University of Notre Dame, Notre Dame, Indiana.

2. cf. Christiane Bursselmans, "Christian Parents and Infant Baptism," *Louvain Studies*, Spring 1968, pp. 32-34.

3. cf. *The Church Teaches: Documents of the Church in English Translation.* St Louis: Herder Books Co., 1955, p. 274.

4. Ibid., pp. 271-272.

5. Ibid, pp. 159-60.

6. cf. *The Pope Speaks*, Vol. 13, No. 3 (1968), p. 278.

7. Paul Recoeur, *The Symbolism of Evil.* Boston: Beacon Press, 1967, p. 239.

8. cf. James Fowler, "Stages in Faith: The Structural-Developmental Approach," A Chapter in *A Symposium on Moral Development and Moral Education.* Thomas Hennessy, S. J., editor.

9. cf. Aidan Kavanagh, "Imitation: Baptism and Confirmation," *Worship.* Vol. 46, No. 5. May, 1972, pp. 263-64.

10. cf. Christopher Kiesling, "Infant Baptism," *Worship*, Vol. 42, No. 10, p. 626.

11. cf. Aidan Kavanagh, *Simple Gifts*, Vol. II, The Liturgical Conference of America, Washington, D. C.

12. cf. John Gallen, "American Liturgy: A Theological Locus," *Theological Studies*, Vol. 35, No. 2, June, 1974, pp. 307-08.

13. cf. Brusselmans, *op. cit.*, pp. 29-30.

14. cf. Bernard Lonergan, "The Subject," *A Second Collection*, Edited by William F. J. Ryan and Bernard Tyrrel, London: Darton, Longman, and Todd, 1974. pp. 69-86.

15. cf. David Tracy, *Blessed Rage for Order: The New Pluralism in Theology.* New York: The Seabury Press, 1975.

Joseph Gelineau, S.J.

The Symbols of Christian Initiation

Joseph Gelineau, S.J., needs no introduction to the American Church. He is currently teaching at the Institut Catholique in Paris and is a member of the Centre national de pastorale liturgique of France.

Editor's note: The following pages are a transcription of an oral presentation by Father Gelineau, translated, rewritten, and edited by Tad Guzie, Kevin Hart and Jane C. Redmont.

"Catechumenate" and "initiation" are two ecclesial practices which are inextricably intertwined and whose interrelationship may be understood in several ways. And so, I would like to begin by specifying exactly what I mean by these two terms, as well as the assumptions underlying the title I have chosen.

First of all, if we understand "initiation" as the entire process of being incorporated into the life of the Church and of penetrating more deeply into that life, then one can define "catechumenate" as a moment within that process of initiation. In this narrow (and more modern) sense, the catechumenate is simply the period of time between conversion and baptism. It would include neither the period of evangelical preparation before enrollment in the catechumenate, nor the ongoing conversion and education following the sacraments of initiation.

Initiation can also be understood as a total process. In this (more traditional) sense, the catechumenate is seen as the total formation for Christian life involving a doctrinal aspect, a moral aspect, and a sacramental aspect. It is in this sacramental aspect of Christian formation that the initiatory dimension is found. Traditionally, the word "initiation" refers directly to the sacraments of initiation. To use the phrase "Christian initiation" to mean the entire process of becoming a Christian is a recent development. There is nothing "wrong" with this modern redefinition of initiation. However, it is necessary to remember that, according to long Christian tradition, what is specific in the process of becoming a Christian is the initiatory aspects of the sacraments. The sacraments belong to the initiatory mode of handing-on, or transmitting, elements of the Christian life.

To understand clearly what I mean by this "initiatory" mode of transmission, let me point out that in most societies, we can distinguish three modes of transmitting the elements of life important to that society. The first mode is the transmission of knowledge—what we would call "teaching." The key verb in this mode is "to know." The second mode is that of "apprenticeship," involving the learning of skills. Here, "to know how" is the key phrase. The third mode of handing-on elements of the life of a society, and the one upon which I will focus, can be called "initiation." It is a purely symbolic mode, whose goal is neither the teaching of knowledge, nor the learning of skills, but penetrating into life itself. Here the key phrase is "learning how to live."

The most important thing for any human being—and all the more for a Christian—is to love. None of us can really learn how to love, but we all need to know how to love well: to love, not by possessing an object of love, but by freely recognizing and accepting the other person. Initiation processes situate individuals in relation to one another. They involve what I will call the "education of desire." They structure society through the existence of such major symbols as the relationship between man and woman, father and son, mother and daughter, husband and wife.

This has been discussed at length in the works of contemporary anthropologists. If the essence of Christianity is—as I would suggest—that we relate to God as God's children and to each other as brothers and sisters, we must have been educated into these relationships, and that process is the "education of desire." The function of the sacramental and symbolic is to facilitate this education of desire.

Western society and the Church since the Renaissance have had as their privileged mode of transmission, the first mode I mentioned—knowledge. Thus, our culture has given a privileged place to the university and the school. Likewise, the Catholic Church has stressed the paramount importance of the catechism, and, particularly in the United States, of the Catholic schools. Privilege and power resided in knowledge. Of utmost importance in the Church was to have correct doctrine—orthodoxy. Just how important correct doctrine was for the Church is reflected in the power held by the Holy Office during much of the Church's history.

Ever since the transition to contemporary industrialized society, it is the second mode, apprenticeship, which has predominated. One can well understand why in our Western world, whose social structures are undergoing radical transformation, we are trying to discover every possible means to exercise control over ourselves, nature and society. Our age has given preeminence to what can be called in the broad sense the "political"—that, which is concerned with power and organization, with the control of people, groups and structures.

This development has not been without consequence in the Church. After the Second Vatican Council, we were reminded that there could be no evangelization without action on behalf of justice. Christians were called to change the structures of society. The Church undertook the task of changing itself as an institution. This began at the Council, spread to religious orders, and soon reached diocesan and parish levels. We are still investing a great deal of energy in this "political" effort—one might even call it a "technological" effort—of changing the institution.

It is clear that these first two modes of knowing have borne their fruit: Many Christian individuals are very enlightened people—they have knowledge. Many are very committed to changing cultural and ecclesial structures—they have know-how. But what about the third mode—initiation—which teaches us how to live? Here, we seem to have failed. People do not seem to feel free. Their knowledge has produced no inner liberation, nor are they at ease in the structures they have changed. They have not been able to rebuild their inner, emotional, affective self within their primary human community or within the Church. I would like to suggest a few reasons for the lack of effectiveness of the third mode of transmitting the elements of life—initiation—in our contemporary Church.

The first reason is rather well known by now: it is the shattering of the symbol systems which previously structured our society. This breakdown is what most differentiates contemporary Western society from traditional cultures, where symbols played—and still play—an all-encompassing role, affecting an being affected by social and matrimonial relations, customs and moral behavior. The liturgies of all religions in traditional culture exist in a symbiotic relationship to the surrounding culture.

The clearest sign of this shattering of symbol systems in our culture is the disappearance of the Roman liturgy. The Roman liturgy no longer exists, if we understand "liturgy" as an expression of faith within a given culture. When I went to Solemn High Mass as a child, I was celebrating the Roman liturgy. Since the Council, however, the Roman liturgy exists only as a museum piece which gets its daily dusting thanks to Archbishop Lefèvre. Our liturgy since Vatican II is no longer the Roman liturgy. Rather it is up to us to recreate the liturgy of the Church. And this has yet to be done.

The problem is that true symbolic structures always function in a way which is not known consciously. When, for example, we speak our native language, we do not really notice its structures until we begin to learn another one. Nor are we conscious of the customs and courtesies which structure our society until we go abroad. It was only when I was in America that I began to realize that the French shake hands each time they say "hello," even to people they have known for years. Knowledge and tech-

330

nology are conscious processes; ritual and symbolic structures are not.

The second reason for the ineffectiveness of the initiatory mode of knowing is the most difficult and the most important for our purposes here. What paralyzes us in our attempt to re-create the liturgy and renew the Church is a false conception of what symbols and symbolic action are. In trying to situate liturgical or symbolic expression relative to human experience, it is customary to use the following (mis)conception: an individual human subject has an experience and subsequently tries to express this experience through some rite or symbol. The individual already *knows* the meaning of the experience, and so it is simply a question of trying to match up his or her experience with the right symbol to express that predetermined meaning. I know of no more dangerous image or conception of liturgy and symbol than this.

For in reality—and this is supported by contemporary research in the fields of anthropology and psychology—the process is precisely the opposite. What comes first is the rite, the symbol, the symbolic structure. This is what is primary. It is through the existence of a rite or a symbol that the subject comes to discover or perceive a meaning for an experience. The meaning is not understood before the symbolic expression, so expressive symbols cannot simply be programmed in advance. It is in taking part in a symbolic structure which is already given that I find the meaning!

This correct understanding of how ritual functions helps us to explain one of the fundamentals of Christian theology: Baptism is not first of all the expression of my faith in Jesus Christ; rather, Baptism is what makes me a Christian. And it is this symbolic ritual which will help me to *discover* a meaning for my experience of faith.

The rite *situates* the individual. We need to give serious attention to this reality and to its consequences. Ritual produces individual events, beginning from existing symbolic structures. In contrast, our contemporary mode of thinking, acting, encountering life which I previously referred to as the political mode, tries to establish social structures—including symbolic structures—beginning from individual instances. It tries to establish social structures which can be controlled through technological means.

Now both of these modes of knowing are necessary and coexist in our society. But I have noticed that we tend to view liturgy exclusively according to the political mode of defining symbols to meet the standards of already preconceived meanings for human and faith experiences. When this happens, ritual is always reduced, either to gnosis—esoteric knowledge—or to social manipulation.

Thus because the meaning is (supposedly) already perceived even before the ritual begins, our liturgies today are largely catechetical, involving lengthy explanations during the liturgy. Often, what is most visible in today's liturgies is not the symbolic act, but what is being said during the liturgy. I am not opposing word to ritual, because to me word *is* ritual. Neither am I saying that words should not communicate concepts and notions. What I am emphasizing is that words cannot take the place of nonverbal experience in liturgy, and yet that is precisely what we often try to do. For example, if a friend were to write a poem, would we not find it absurd if she were to say, "I have just written a beautiful poem, but before I read it to you, let me explain exactly what I'm trying to say"? Or likewise, if a musician were to compose a symphony and before its debut, try to explain exactly what he wanted to express through the music, who would want to listen? And yet that is what we try to do with our liturgies.

That is why in none of the Easter Vigils I have celebrated have I ever given any explanation whatsoever of what was going on. Either rites and symbols speak for themselves—and in that case, why bother to explain? Or they do not speak, in which case any attempt to explain them in words only makes things all the more obscure.

It is no accident that the mystagogical catechesis in the early Church occurred after the rites of initiation. The true reason for this was not preoccupation with the secrecy of the mysteries. The true reason was pedagogical: one can only understand what has already been situated symbolically. Symbolic ritual enables us to discover for ourselves what would otherwise remain "hidden."

Let me share an experience which has taught me a great deal about how people can discover meaning through symbol. At a recent celebration of the Easter Vigil, we began with the liturgy of the Word in the middle of the nave. The Vigil was understood as a going up toward the light and the proclamation of the Lord's resurrection. Now, our church is not a parish church and has no baptismal font. Although we were not celebrating any baptisms that evening, I did not want to lose the baptismal symbolism of the Vigil. So at the end of the Liturgy of the Word, the paschal candle was brought into the nave in total silence. (When you want to make a liturgical gesture which really means something, you cannot say a word. Before or after the gesture, yes. But never while you are making that gesture.) In our church there is a long room which runs parallel to the nave. At the end of the alleluia, without any preliminary explanation, we began to sing the litany of the saints. Two people began to walk from the nave into this parallel room. Others followed and the procession continued with the singing of the litany of the saints.

The room next to the nave had been left in total darkness, except for a spotlight in the ceiling directly over a large bowl of water. As they entered the room, the two leaders stopped singing. The singing began again only when people emerged from the room. The passage through the dark room with the bowl of water was completely silent.

When people entered the room, they looked at the water; some made the sign of the cross, some drank, some sprinkled themselves or splashed water over their heads; some did nothing. After the Easter Vigil I got a lot of reactions. But the one which always came first was, "I was overwhelmed when I passed through the room with the water." Why? Precisely because there was no explanation, no pre-established meaning given to the bowl of water. Everyone had to find a meaning in this event, to situate themselves in relation to it, to take a stand. And these are the two functions of symbol: to invite us to find meaning in them, and to call us to take a stand. That is why a symbol is creative; that is why symbols liberate; that is why symbols, and not verbal explanations, structure our lives.

Perhaps one reason why we fill our liturgies with so much verbiage is that they become very safe, very predictable, and so *everyone* can *understand* them. But to shift the emphasis from word to symbol—that becomes risky! Someone might miss what they are supposed to catch!

Imagine that you want to pass a precious object to another person—a Ming vase for example. There are two ways of doing this. You can give it to someone, saying, "Please carry this over to so-and-so, and be careful! It's worth millions!" So your intermediary takes it with great care and caution and hands it over with even greater caution, paralyzed with the fear of dropping the vase. But there is another way. You can throw the precious object directly to someone, as you would a ball. This is far more risky, but in doing this you have given the person the opportunity to catch it on his or her own. Perhaps it won't work; perhaps you (or the catcher) are going to miss. But if we don't run this sort of risk, nothing new will ever happen.

Liturgy and ritual involve "throwing balls" to people. Sometimes, a few of the people catch one of the balls. Sometimes. It depends upon their desire. It depends on a lot of things.

Instead of letting liturgy help people discover meaning for themselves, it is widely used by pastors as an instrument for social manipulation—as a way to get people involved, and as an instrument of moral teaching. All this is not necessarily bad, but it is not the essence of liturgy. Symbol and rite are essentially the place for new creation. And according to the popular misconception of liturgy mentioned above, there is no room for anything new: I begin with something that is already past—an experience or understanding—and I express it in a ritual. I already know the meaning of an event, and I symbolize it. But by definition, ritual is exactly the opposite.

What occurs in ritual is that one experiences desire. Ritual creates a distance between the subject—the individual human agent—and the object of desire—for example, God or Jesus. And in this distance I find meaning, I take a stand, I situate myself as a free agent. In and of itself symbol or ritual mean nothing. What it does, however, is to situate the individual by creating an "empty place" between this person and the object of desire so that something can happen: namely, that the individual motivated by desire for the object, be "forced" to try to discover—or better yet, to create—a meaning.

A third reason for the lack of effectiveness of the initiatory mode of knowing today has already been mentioned in this symposium several times: symbolic poverty. It cannot be denied that some very ancient and traditional symbols no longer enable people to discover meaning. I find it rather frightening to realize that the fundamental baptismal symbol of immersion—immersion into the death of Christ and rising with the Risen Christ—is simply not functioning in the experience of many Christians today. Rather, the few drops of water sprinkled on the head are understood almost exclusively as the washing away of original sin. Thus, when it comes to baptizing infants, because the connection between immersion in water and entrance into the paschal mystery has been lost, parents often ask whether a few drops of water sprinkled on their child's head is really "necessary."

It seems to me that we should highlight the significance of the baptismal rite—whether for children or adults—by emphasizing some of the other symbolic actions as well. The oils could be strongly perfumed, and a new set of festive clothes could be given to the baptized.

The poverty of baptismal symbols is also due in part to the separation of this sacrament from the other two initiating sacraments. Take baptism apart from confirmation and eucharist, and the full significance of entrance into the Church and participation in the fullness of the paschal mystery becomes diminished.

Part of the problem with baptismal symbolism is due also to the fact that the rite is often understood as a sacralization of birth. We will not be able to restore full and specific significance to baptismal symbolism (in the case of infant baptism) until we also develop an additional ritual, distinct from baptism, which would celebrate the *birth* of the child as a gift from God. Whatever it is, infant baptism is not a ritual sanctification of birth.

A fourth reason for the lack of initiatory effectiveness is the fact that sacraments have been cheapened, their value undercut in two ways. First of all, there is a tendency to celebrate the sacraments—the Eucharist in particular—too often. Sacraments reveal meaning only to the extent that they create an empty space—to the extent that they are different from everyday experience. If the festive Sunday Eucharist is celebrated every day, what results is a devaluation of the Eucharist—too much of a good thing. A second reason for the devaluation of the sacraments is that their relation to human desire is not sufficiently taken into account. Personally, I regret the disappearance of the Eucharistic fast. And I have seen real benefits in the lives of certain Christians who fast even from the Eucharist.

It is because these two important dimensions have been disregarded that the sacraments have become part of our consumer society. Because they are so readily, so frequently, and so ordinarily available, they are incapable of engendering that essential element of desire which we need if we are to be motivated to search for, discover, or create meaning through symbols.

A fifth reason for initiatory ineffectiveness has also been discussed at length in our meetings: the absence of real community. There is no possibility for symbolization unless it happens within a community of interpretation. That is what we call the faith of the Church. If all we have is a group of juxtaposed individuals, anything can signify anything.

The problem which confronts us today is that given the fact that modern times have shattered our symbol systems, we cannot borrow from society symbols capable of supporting the weight of meaning which liturgy must bear. We cannot borrow them from society because they are no longer there. I am not speaking of cultures which still have symbolic structures—cultures where folklore has not yet died or become objectified. I am speaking of industrialized Europe and North America. Since we cannot borrow symbols from the society, and since nobody can really create symbols, let alone symbolic structures, how are we going to invest the Church of today with its indispensable symbolic apparatus? Only by revitalizing universal symbols, all of which have to do with the human body: top and bottom, front and back, inside and outside. And there is eating, drinking, sharing. When symbols are built around these fundamental, universal, relational, and life-giving dimensions of human life, they can once more create meaning through authentic individual experience.

But can this be done? Is it possible to revitalize symbols in a culture so impoverished as ours? I have only one answer: try it, and you will be surprised. It has happened to me, and it continues to happen all the time. If all we do is *talk* to people about symbol, rituals, and liturgical ceremonies, we will accomplish nothing at all. But if we gather around the Word of God to pray together, then something happens.

Look what happens when the liturgy is celebrated in someone's home. The first time the atmosphere is often one of almost total deritualization: a bare kitchen table, a glass from the sink, an ordinary table wine, a slice of ordinary bread, no vestments for the celebrant. But after a few times, the hostess adds a beautiful flower to the table. Soon, it's the most beautiful glass in the house. Slowly—so very slowly—you realize that something is happening, something is being built.

But we can also make mistakes. We must have the right, the permission, and the opportunity to make mistakes. At any rate, we have to try. The reason why liturgy at this time is not going anywhere is because we are not trying to make it go anywhere. We're too busy trying to explain it! We must call in the musicians, the poets, the dancers. And then? Well . . . we'll see.

Epilogue

Six days of discussion on these papers led to a host of reflections. It was not our intention to produce a formal statement of consensus at the end of the week. But throughout the week, certain realizations kept coming back and certain conclusions kept emerging. The members of the symposium entrusted an editorial staff with the task of putting together this epilogue, which contains a few of the emphases and important points of convergence that came out of our discussions.

Many terms had to be clarified as we went along. "Catechumenate," for example, has two meanings, both of them reflected in the foregoing papers. The first meaning is a restricted and technical one: in this sense, the catechumenate is the particular period of development between enrollment as a catechumen and the rite of election that begins the final preparation for the sacraments of initiation. In a larger sense, "catechumenate" was taken to comprise the whole process that begins with a candidate's earliest evangelization and continues, after the sacraments of initiation have been celebrated, into the stage of post-baptismal catechesis, when the newly baptized are integrated still more fully into the community. More properly, this larger sense is termed "Christian initiation." It is part of the Church's work of building the Body of Christ.

Implementation of the *Rite of Christian Initiation of Adults* is not a simple matter of new programs or new diocesan offices. The basic themes that came back again and again throughout our week together concerned the total faith community, the continual conversion of that community, and the meaning of integration into that community.

The English translation of the RCIA is subtitled "A Provisional Text." But a key distinction needs to be made. The *texts of the ritual* are provisional—and indeed many participants noted that few efforts have been made to adapt the ritual to the American cultural scene. The language of the prayers needs much work. For example, the ritual has to be adjusted carefully to the American catechumen who has already been baptized—more catechized, less catechized, uncatechized—and who is now seeking admission into the Catholic community. The texts, even after they are definitely translated, must remain a resource and not become a fixed and hardened rite.

But still, for all the questions of textual adaptation, the introduction to the RCIA contains a vision of Christian life and the meaning of life in the Church that is in no sense transitory or provisional. The introduction gives us not only a theology of initiation, but also an ecclesiology. This introduction, and not the ritual details, is the starting point for all of us.

The RCIA is revolutionary in the way that it makes explicit what is only implicit in our other revised rites. All of our new rites lay emphasis on the continual conversion and response in faith that are prerequisites for any sacrament. But the RCIA spells out in detail how conversion, which is so central to the message of Jesus, is not an enthusiastic moment but a *journey*.

The journey of the catechumen cannot be conceived apart from the journey of the whole Christian community. The conversion of catechumens will be individualistic and elitist unless these men and women can be integrated into a community that sees conversion as a *continual* journey constituting the life and mission of the Church. Programs for the Christian initiation of adults will become just another "movement" alongside many others if we forget that conversion is constitutive of the entire Christian journey.

The catechumens, as catechumens, can exercise a very special ministry for the baptized. By their very presence, they remind the faithful of their own need for conversion and their need for rediscovering the common journey that is shared by all, the baptized and the unbaptized.

Much has already begun in North America. If there are challenges and problems, there has also been progress. Those who have worked pastorally with the RCIA have discovered that it can, of itself, be an excellent vehicle for renewal.

The Rites of Christian Initiation enrich our perception and practice of the sacraments; Baptism, Confirmation, and Eucharist are distinctive moments in one single process of initiation. Moreover, by outlining a whole host of ritual actions, they help us see how the sacraments can be celebrated as an unfolding that expresses and sustains gradual growth in conversion. During the Symposium, we were heartened by the reports from the various cultural communities on how they were creatively adapting the model of Christian initiation to their own cultures. Particularly fertile contributions are being made, on the American scene, by the Hispanic and Black communities.

The programs associated with the RCIA cannot be independent, however. It is particularly important that the restored catechumenate be integrated with the ministries of evangelization and parish renewal, which have recently become a major pastoral concern of the American bishops. The RCIA calls on all of our resources, on the ministries that exist and those that are yet to be developed. The concept of Christian Initiation affects religious education at every level: children, teens, adults, the elderly. The reason for this is that the RCIA provides a sound learning model. The journey it outlines contains all the elements of the total process by which people experience, reflect, learn, and own what they have learned. In this sense, the model of Christian Initiation is a model for all religious education.

Up to the present, our religious education models have generally been models for the education of children. While the problem of initiating children into the Church was not taken up formally as a separate topic, it was evident that the theology contained in the RCIA raises serious questions about indiscriminate infant Baptism, about Confirmation as a separate sacrament, and about confession as a sacrament of initiation. The Church has always adapted its sacramental and pastoral practice to the concrete situation of the faithful. The RCIA has created a new situation with regard to the initiation of children, and sacramental and catechetical programs for children will have to pay critical attention to the model reflected in the RCIA.